Collector's Library — *How many have you read?*

Collector's Library

ON SOCRATES

ON SOCRATES

PLATO
Charmides, Lysis, Laches,
Symposium, Apology, Crito, Phaedo

ARISTOPHANES
The Clouds

XENOPHON
Symposium

Collector's Library

This edition published in 2004 in the
Collector's Library of Essential Thinkers
an imprint of CRW Publishing Limited
69 Gloucester Crescent, London NW1 7EG
Re-issued in the Collector's Library Series in 2009

ISBN 978 1 905716 72 2

1 3 5 7 9 10 8 6 4 2

Typeset in Great Britain by Antony Gray
Printed and bound in China by Imago

Contents

Introduction

A. SOCRATES AS A PERSON: HIS LIFE

The life of Socrates presents us with the same kind of problems as the life of Jesus Christ. We have few biographical details, and those we do have must be treated with caution because they nearly all come from his greatest admirer, Plato. We have to remind ourselves that Socrates was condemned to death by the majority verdict of a jury of five hundred Athenians. It is clear that their picture of him was a good deal less flattering than ours. What follows here is our (that is to say, Plato's) picture, because that is almost the only picture we have. In its favor we can say that Plato knew Socrates a great deal better than did the people who condemned him to death.

Socrates was born at Alopeke, a village near Athens, in the year 469BCE. His father Sophroniscus was a sculptor or stonemason; his mother was Phaenarete, a midwife. At some point Socrates married a woman called Xanthippe. This must have been fairly late in his life, since his three sons were still children when he died at the age of seventy. According to Xenophon and others, she henpecked him, and if this is true, there will be those who find it hard to blame her. Socrates did little in the way of earning a living, and though he often talks about the education of children, Plato makes no mention of his showing much interest in his own.

7

We know Socrates served in the army in two campaigns in Northern Greece: at Potidaea, between 432 and 429BCE, and at Amphipolis, in 422BCE. And he certainly fought in the battle of Delium (424 BCE), because Alcibiades (in Plato's *Symposium*) describes his courage in the retreat from Delium, after the Athenians had been defeated by the Thebans. Alcibiades, as a wealthy aristocrat, served in the cavalry. Socrates was in the infantry, but so intimidating was his appearance, according to Alcibiades, that the Thebans left him alone, and went after easier targets.

Socrates lived his entire life in Athens. Apart from military campaigns, he claimed never to have left Athens in his life. As a young man he seems to have studied astronomy and natural science, and this is how Aristophanes caricatures him in his play *The Clouds*. His Socrates runs a school with pupils (the thinking-house), and spends his time hanging in a basket in order to get a closer view of the heavenly bodies. On this view, Socrates is one of the sophists (see below). In fact, Socrates had no school, and (at least formally) no pupils. He professed an interest in the beauty of boys and young men, but it was their characters and minds, not their bodies, which engaged him.

Socrates took no part in political life, apart from those duties which came his way in the normal course of democratic procedure. He claimed to have a divine voice (his *daimonion*) which never told him what to do, but from time to time did tell him what not to do. This voice, he said, told him to keep out of politics. And when events did require him to play a part, the wisdom of his divine voice was apparent. Selected by lot to be president of the committee preparing business for the assembly of the people, he was laughably ignorant of the procedure for putting a matter to the vote. When Athens was a democracy, he made himself unpopular with the people by objecting to the (illegal) trial of the generals who failed, in stormy conditions, to pick up the Athenian survivors after the naval victory at Arginusae. And when Athens was defeated by Sparta, and democracy was replaced by the oligarchic regime of the Thirty Tyrants, he made himself unpopular with them too by refusing to have anything to do with their campaign of murder and intimidation. So he had something of a gift for making enemies. The surprise, perhaps, is that he survived as long as he did.

Socrates' death

In 399BCE Socrates was accused (by Anytus, Meletus and Lycon, politicians in the newly restored democracy) of 'not believing in the gods the city believes in, and corrupting the young.' The first part of the charge was somewhat absurd, since practically nobody in Athens believed in the gods the city believed in, and Socrates clearly did believe, very devoutly, in a good god of some kind. The second part of the charge had more substance. Indeed, if corrupting the young meant teaching them not to accept the irrational views of their elders without question, then without doubt Socrates was guilty.

The procedure at an Athenian trial was very different from that at a modern trial. Trials took place during a single day. To make bribery of jurors more difficult, juries were very large (for Socrates' trial the jury numbered five hundred), and chosen by lot from those citizens who presented themselves as available for jury service. There were no professional lawyers, and no public prosecutor, so prosecutions were brought by individuals. Speeches were timed by a waterclock, which was stopped while evidence from witnesses was heard.

The prosecution spoke first, followed by the defendant (making his own speech). After these two speeches, the jury voted the accused innocent or guilty. If innocent, he was released. If guilty, the jury next voted on the sentence. The procedure here was for the prosecution and defense each to suggest a penalty, and for the jury to decide between the two. No compromise was allowed. In practice the prosecution very often suggested the death penalty, largely as a way of concentrating the defendant's mind. If you have already been found guilty, and you know the sentence will be either death or what you yourself suggest, the chances are you will suggest something realistic.

It is unlikely that many people in Athens wanted to put Socrates to death. What they possibly did want, more than anything else, was an apology (in the modern sense of the word). Among those who had been his keenest supporters were Alcibiades, who betrayed Athens and for a time advised the city's enemies, the Spartans, and several of the aristocrats who made up, or supported, the Thirty Tyrants. Socrates had no time for tyranny, but he was also fairly scathing about democracy, and it was not absurd, when his admirers overthrew the democracy, to see his influence at work. So a humble apology, perhaps combined with a promise to behave differently in future, might have been enough to get him off with a fine.

If an apology was what the jurors wanted, they certainly did not get one. Socrates at his trial remained unrepentant. He said they were lucky to have had him acting as their conscience for so long. When found guilty (by the comparatively narrow margin of 280 votes to 220), he refused to suggest a realistic alternative to the death penalty. He was put to death (humanely, with hemlock) about a month later.

Plato

Plato (c. 427–347BCE) was born in Athens (or possibly Aegina, near Athens) and lived most of his life in Athens. As a young man he listened to Socrates, and was profoundly influenced both by his teachings and by the manner of his life. He developed a wide-ranging system of philosophy, of which the core is a rationalistic ethics, but which extends also to logic, metaphysics and theory of knowledge.

In all his writings, Plato makes Socrates the mouthpiece for the views he is putting forward. There has been much discussion of the question: Did Socrates really hold these views? To which there is no entirely satisfactory answer. There is some agreement, however, that the Socrates of the early dialogues is true to life, whereas the Socrates of the later dialogues comes out with views which are not those of the historical Socrates, but of Plato himself. There is less agreement on the middle dialogues.

Of the dialogues selected for this volume, none are late. *Charmides*, *Laches*, *Apology* and *Crito* are generally regarded as being early, *Symposium* and *Phaedo* as being from the middle period. *Lysis* may be early or middle.

B. SOCRATES' CONTRIBUTION TO PHILOSOPHY

Athenian education and the sophists

The age in which Socrates lived was a time of rapid educational change. Boys were sent to school until they were about about sixteen years old (girls, to all intents and purposes, were not educated at all in Athens; one of the things about Sparta which impressed Socrates and Plato was the fact that girls and boys received a very similar education). The education the boys received was predominantly literary, based in particular on Homer, who was to the Greeks what the Bible used to be to us. But in the early fifth century BCE, for a boy leaving school there were no universities in Athens, and no further education of any kind.

In the second half of the 5th century, the need for higher education was filled, at any rate for the rich, by the sophists. Sophists were (often itinerant) teachers who specialized in subjects such as grammar, etymology, science, astronomy and rhetoric. Of these rhetoric was by far the most important, for two reasons. First, in a society where all political decisions were taken by an assembly of the citizens, a career in politics depended on the ability to persuade the assembly. And second, the nature of the Athenian law courts was such that inability to speak could put you at some considerable risk. Litigation was common, rules of evidence were nonexistent, appeals to popular prejudice were the norm, and there were no professional lawyers. If you were accused, you had to make your own defense, and your life and property might depend on how well you made it.

Socrates' teachings

Socrates was not a sophist, according to Plato. He had no school and no pupils, and took no money from anybody for teaching them anything. Not long after Socrates' death Plato was to set up the Academy, and a generation after that Aristotle founded the Lyceum, to offer what we would call further education, but Socrates never did more than engage people in conversation. It is clear, however, that even without a school and formal pupils, he was a teacher.

In which case, what did he teach? Essentially, three things: two ethical, the third methodological. Socrates was the first person to say that we should never knowingly do harm to anyone, whereas conventional morality required you to do good to your friends and harm to your enemies. And he combined this with the belief that all goodness can, in the final analysis, be reduced to knowledge. This is why so much attention is paid, in Socratic dialogues, to the difference between knowledge (which must be true) and belief or opinion (which may be false). In Socrates' view, all wrong behavior is the result of some kind of failure to understand. Cowardice, for example, is the result of the wrong belief that death is something to be feared.

His methodological innovation is the idea that for any progress to be made in a discussion or argument, there must be agreement between the people holding the discussion at each step in the argument. The traditional method of argument, consisting of assertion and counter-assertion, at increasing volumes, makes no progress at all, as we see every day of the week in modern politics.

Socratic method

What happens in a typical Socratic dialogue (in the *Charmides*, *Lysis*, or *Laches*, for example) is that Socrates finds himself in a conversation with somebody who has some pretension to knowledge, and cross-examines him on this supposed knowledge. In the *Laches*, for example, he converts a discussion of fighting in heavy armor into a question more to his liking: 'Tell me, if you can, what is courage?' Laches gives the soldier's answer: 'he is a man of courage who does not run away, but remains at his post and fights against the enemy.' Socrates finds fault with this definition; it is amended; Socrates finds fault with the amendment; and so on. There are a number of things to be said about this technique. First, it is extremely annoying for the cross-examinee. Second, the outcome is inconclusive: at the end of the discussion, Socrates and Laches are still unsure what courage is. Third, despite the inconclusiveness, each succeeding definition of courage is a clear improvement on the one before. And fourth, for all his claims to know nothing, Socrates does have an end in view, and is throughout the discussion gently nudging his victim in the direction of saying that courage is knowledge.

C. THE SELECTIONS IN THIS VOLUME

Charmides, Lysis, Laches

Charmides, Lysis, and *Laches* are typical 'what is?' dialogues, trying to define things which are agreed to be good. In Charmides, 'what is *sophrosune* (temperance), the virtue that is shown in self-command and dutiful behavior?' It seems that this virtue can be identified with the self-knowledge that Socrates, along with many other Greeks, valued so highly. *Lysis* is an enquiry into friendship, where self-forgetting devotion most displays itself. *Laches* is concerned with courage, the soldier's virtue.

Plato's Symposium

The *Symposium* is the most accessible of all Plato's dialogues. Set in the year 416BCE, it describes a party given by the poet Agathon to celebrate his winning the first prize at the Lenaea, an Athenian festival of tragic drama. The guests decide that they will each in turn make a speech in praise of love. This set speech format prevents Socrates using his customary technique of question-and-answer; it allows him to put forward the theory that sexual love is the first step on a ladder which leads to the contemplation, by the mind alone, of pure goodness; and it allows Alcibiades, the best-looking and most charismatic young Athenian of the day, to pay tribute to Socrates by describing his own unsuccessful attempts to seduce him.

Apology

The word *apologia*, in Greek, means a defense, not an apology. It is worth pointing this out because if there is one word Socrates conspicuously does not use anywhere in the *Apology*, it is the word 'sorry.' The *Apology* is the speech Socrates made (or maybe the speech Plato thought he ought to have made) at the trial which led to his condemnation and execution. The intention of his prosecutors, in all probability, was to humiliate him, make him accept some responsibility for the anti-democratic behavior of his protégés, and maybe extract some promise of better behavior in future.

Socrates refused to have anything to with this scenario. He made an unconciliatory speech, and on being found guilty refused to suggest a realistic alternative to the death penalty. He said he regarded himself as a public benefactor: if he were to be treated as he deserved, he should be given free meals at public expense for the remainder of his life. The jury, not surprisingly, voted for the death penalty – for very little gain, as Socrates pointed out in his final speech. At seventy years of age, he was not going to live much longer anyway, so all they would have achieved was to win themselves a reputation for putting wise people to death. 'They will call me wise, even though I am not wise.'

Crito

In Athens, if you were condemned to death, the sentence was usually carried out promptly. No messing about with appeals, or death-row delays. However, Socrates' trial was held on the day after the garlanding of the ship which the Athenians traditionally sent, once a year, to Delos. This was a very ancient custom, and its purpose was to thank Apollo for the help he gave Theseus when Theseus delivered the Athenians from their subjection to Crete, and the payment of annual human tribute to King Minos and the Minotaur. While the ship was away, no executions could be carried out, and in this particular year its return was delayed by contrary winds. So Socrates remained in prison for some little time after his conviction.

During this time his friend Crito arranged for him to escape (something which many people in Athens might have been quite glad to see happen). Crito had friends in Thessaly, who would be happy to see Socrates, and offer him hospitality. Socrates refused to escape. Having spent most of his life urging people to act justly, he argued, he would make himself a laughing-stock if he now himself acted unjustly. He had chosen to live in Athens, and be governed by her laws. He could not now disobey those laws simply because their outcome, in one situation, was not to his liking.

Phaedo

The *Phaedo* presents Socrates' arguments, on the day of his death, for the immortality of the soul. One thing that can be said for certain about these arguments is that they will not persuade anyone who does not already believe in the immortality of the soul, any more than arguments for the existence of God have ever persuaded those who did not already believe in God. However, that is not really the point. What is so impressive and moving in the *Phaedo* is the calmness and courage shown by Socrates in the face of death, and the affection felt for him not only by his friends, but even by the jailer and executioner whose job it was to administer the hemlock.

Xenophon's Symposium

Xenophon was a contemporary of Plato. Like Plato, he sat at the feet of Socrates as a young man (though unlike Plato, he may most of the time have missed the point of what Socrates was saying). Politically, Xenophon's sympathies were with Sparta and the oligarchic faction in Athens, and when democracy was re-established in Athens in 401, he chose to go abroad, where he spent most of the rest of his life.

His *Symposium*, which records a conversation and entertainment at a dinner given by Callias for the young Autolycus, is very different from Plato's. He is less interested in philosophy than in personal anecdote and dinner-party talk, and his Socrates is barely recognizable as the person who dominates the Platonic dialogues. It has been said of Xenophon that he misunderstood Socrates as profoundly as he admired him, and his *Symposium* supports that view.

Aristophanes' The Clouds

Aristophanes portrays Socrates as an out-and-out sophist. He does have a school, he does take pupils, he does charge them money, and though he does not exactly teach rhetoric, his school does offer a Better Logic and a Worse Logic, the Worse Logic being the one which allows its exponents to speak unjustly and win arguments. Moreover, he denies the conventional gods, instead worshipping the Clouds (who are the play's chorus). This picture contains all the elements which Socrates describes in the *Apology* as contributing to the popular prejudice against him, so it is interesting that Plato, in the *Symposium*, nonetheless portrays Socrates and Aristophanes as good friends.

D. CONCLUSION

So, what are we to believe? Was Socrates the saint and martyr depicted by Plato? Or the bumbling figure presented by Aristophanes and Xenophon? On balance, we have to go with Plato. Aristophanes was a satirical playwright. Like any satirist, he had good reason to misrepresent the object of his satire. And Xenophon was a down-to-earth, practical military man, who may not have fully grasped the importance of Socrates' innovations in ethics and techniques of argument.

The argument for believing Plato is that the Socrates he shows us makes the three great contributions to the creation of philosophy which I have described above: the view that goodness consists not in helping your friends and harming your enemies, but in never harming anybody at all; the view that goodness and knowledge are the same thing; and the view that for progress to be made in discussion or argument, there must be step-by-step agreement between the people involved. It is not easy to see why Plato would give the credit for these to Socrates, rather than claim it for himself, unless Socrates really did hold those views, and really did lead an inspiring life of the kind Plato describes.

TOM GRIFFITH

Further Reading

Aristotle, *Nicomachean Ethics*

H. Carpenter, *Jesus*

L. Fischer, *The Life of Mahatma Gandhi*

Lao Tzu, *Tao te ching*

M. Meredith, *Nelson Mandela*

N. Niwano, *Shakyamuni Buddha: a Narrative Biography*

Plato, *Republic*

William Tyndale, *The New Testament* (especially the four gospels)

PLATO
CHARMIDES

CHARMIDES
or Temperance

Persons of the dialogue
SOCRATES, *who is the narrator*
CHARMIDES
CHAEREPHON
CRITIAS

SCENE: *The palaestra of Taureas, which is
near the temple of Basile.*

Yesterday evening we returned from the army at
Potidaea, and having been a good while away, I
thought that I should like to go and look at my old
haunts. So I went into the palaestra of Taureas, which
is over against the temple of Basile, and there I found
a number of persons, most of whom I knew, but not
all. My visit was unexpected, and no sooner did they
see me entering than they saluted me from afar on all
sides; and Chaerephon, who always behaves like a
madman, started up from among them and ran to me,
seizing my hand, and saying, How did you escape
from the battle, Socrates? (An engagement had taken
place at Potidaea not long before we came away, of
which the news had only just reached Athens.)

Just as you see me now, I replied.

There was a report, he said, that the engagement
was very severe, and that many of our acquaintance
had fallen.

That, I replied, was not far from the truth.

I suppose, he said, that you were present.

I was.

Then sit down here, and tell us the whole story, which as yet we have only heard imperfectly.

So saying he led me to a place by the side of Critias the son of Callaeschrus, and when I had sat down and saluted him and the rest of the company, I told them the news from the army, and answered their several inquiries.

Then, when there had been enough of this, I, in my turn, began to make inquiries about matters at home – about the present state of philosophy, and about the youth. I asked whether any of them were remarkable for wisdom or beauty, or both. Critias glanced at the door and saw some youths coming in, and disputing noisily with one another, followed by a crowd. Of the beauties, Socrates, he said, I fancy that you will soon be able to form a judgment. For those who are just entering are the advance guard and lovers of the great beauty of the day, as he is thought to be, and he is likely to be not far off himself.

Who is he, I said; and who is his father?

Charmides, he replied, is his name; he is my cousin, and the son of my uncle Glaucon: I rather think that you know him too, although he was not grown up at the time of your departure.

Certainly, I know him, I said, for he was remarkable even then when he was still a child, and I should imagine that by this time he must be almost a young man.

You will see, he said, in a moment what age he has reached and what he is like. He had scarcely said the word, when Charmides entered.

Now you know, my friend, that I am not good at measuring, and in the presence of the beautiful I am like a measuring line without marks; for almost all young persons appear to be beautiful in my eyes. But at that moment, when I saw him, I confess that I was quite astonished at his beauty and stature; all the company seemed to be enamoured of him; amazement and confusion reigned when he entered; and a second troop of lovers followed behind him. That grown-up men like ourselves should have been affected in this way was not surprising, but I observed the boys and saw that all of them, down to the very smallest, turned and looked at him, as if he had been a statue.

Chaerephon called me and said: What do you think of the young man, Socrates? Has he not a beautiful face?

Most beautiful, I said.

But you would think nothing of his face, he replied, if you could see his naked form: he is absolutely perfect.

And to this they all agreed.

Ye gods, I said, what a paragon, if he has only one other slight addition!

What is that? said Critias.

If he has a noble soul; and being of your house, Critias, he may be expected to have this.

He is as fair and good within, as he is without, replied Critias.

Then, before we see his body, should we not ask him to strip and show us his soul? He is surely just of an age at which he will like to talk.

That he will, said Critias, and I can tell you that he is indeed a philosopher already, and also a considerable poet, not in his own opinion only, but in that of others.

That, my dear Critias, I replied, is a distinction which has long been in your family, and is inherited by you from Solon. But why do you not call him, and show him to me? For even if he were younger than he is, there could be no impropriety in his talking to us before you, his guardian and cousin.

Very well, he said; then I will call him; and turning to the attendant, he said: Call Charmides, and tell him that I want him to come and see a physician about the illness of which he spoke to me the day before yesterday. Then again addressing me, he added: He has been complaining lately of having a headache when he rises in the morning: now why should you not make him believe that you know a cure for the headache?

Why not, I said, if only he will come.

He will be sure to come, he replied.

So he came as he was bidden. Great amusement was occasioned by everyone making room and pushing with might and main at his neighbour in order to sit next to him, until at the two ends of the row one had to get up and the other was rolled over sideways. And he came and sat down between Critias and me. But I, my friend, was beginning to feel awkward; my former bold belief in my powers of conversing naturally with him had vanished. And when Critias told him that I was the person who had the cure, he looked at me in an indescribable manner, and made as though to ask me a question. And all the people in the palaestra crowded about us, and at that moment, my good friend, I caught a sight of the inwards of his garment, and took the flame. Then I could no longer contain myself. I thought how well Cydias understood the nature of love, when, in speaking of a fair youth, he warns someone 'not to bring the fawn in the sight of the lion to be devoured by him', for I felt that I had been overcome by a sort of wild-beast appetite. But still when he asked me if I knew the cure for the headache, I answered, though with an effort, that I did know.

And what is it? he said.

I replied that it was a kind of leaf, which required to be accompanied by a charm, and if a person would repeat the charm at the same time that he used the cure, he would be made whole; but that without the charm the leaf would be of no avail.

Then I will write out the charm from your dictation, he said.

With my consent? I said, or without my consent?

With your consent, Socrates, he said, laughing.

Very good, I said; so you know my name, do you?

I ought to know you, he replied, for there is a great deal said about you among my companions; and I remember when I was a child seeing you in company with Critias here.

I am glad to find that you remember me, I said; for I shall now be more at home with you and shall be better able to explain the nature of the charm, about which I felt a difficulty before. For the charm will do more, Charmides, than only cure the headache. I dare say that you have heard eminent physicians say to a patient who comes to them with bad eyes, that they cannot undertake to cure his eyes by themselves, but that if his eyes are to be cured, his head must be treated too; and then again they say that to think of curing the head alone, and not the rest of the body also, is the height of folly. And arguing in this way they apply their régime to the whole body, and try to treat and heal the whole and the part together. Did you ever observe that this is what they say?

Yes, he said.

And they are right, and you would agree with them?

Yes, he said, certainly I should.

His approving answers reassured me, and I began by degrees to regain confidence, and my natural heat returned to me. Such, Charmides, I said, is the nature of the charm, which I learned when serving with the army from one of the physicians of the Thracian king Zamolxis, who are said to be able even to give immortality. This Thracian told me that in these notions of theirs, which I was just now mentioning, the Greek physicians are quite right as far as they go; but Zamolxis, he added, our king, who is also a god, says further, that 'as you ought not to attempt to cure the eyes without the head, or the head without the body, so neither ought you to attempt to cure the body without the soul; and this,' he said, 'is the reason why the cure of many diseases is unknown to the physicians of Hellas, because they disregard the whole, which ought to be studied also; for the part can never be well unless the whole is well.' For all good and evil, whether in the body or in the whole man, originates, as he declared, in the soul, and overflows from thence, as if from the head into the eyes. And therefore if the head and body are to be well, you must begin by curing the soul; that is the first and essential thing. And the cure of the soul, my dear youth, has to be effected by the use of certain charms, and these charms are fair words; and by them temperance is implanted in the soul, and where temperance comes and stays, there health is speedily imparted, not only to the head, but to the whole body. And when he taught me the cure and the charm he added: 'Let no one persuade you to cure his head, until he has first given you his soul to be cured by the charm. For this', he said, 'is the great error of our day in the treatment of human beings, that men try to be physicians of health and temperance separately. And he strictly enjoined me not to let anyone, however rich or noble or fair, persuade me to give him the cure, without the charm.' Now I have sworn, and I must keep my oath, and therefore if you will allow me to apply the Thracian charm first to your soul, as the stranger directed, I will afterwards proceed to apply the cure to your head. But if not, I do not know what I am to do with you, my dear Charmides.

Critias, when he heard this, said: The headache will be a blessing to my young cousin, if the pain in his head compels him to improve his mind: yet I can tell you, Socrates, that Charmides is not only pre-eminent in beauty among his equals, but also in that quality for which you say you have the charm, temperance, is it not?

Yes, I said.

Then let me tell you that he is the most temperate of the young men of today, and for his age inferior to none in any quality.

Indeed, Charmides, I said, I think that you ought to excel others in all good qualities; for if I am not mistaken there is no one present who could easily point out two Athenian houses, whose union would be likely to produce a better or nobler scion than the two from which you are sprung. There is your father's house, which is descended from Critias the son of Dropidas, whose family has been commemorated in the panegyrics of Anacreon, Solon, and many other poets, as famous for beauty and virtue and all other high fortune: and your mother's house is equally distinguished; for your maternal uncle, Pyrilampes, is reputed never to have found his superior for stature and beauty in Persia at the court of the great king, or anywhere on the continent of Asia in all the places to which he went as ambassador; that whole family is not a whit inferior to the other. Having such ancestors you ought to be first in all things, and, sweet son of Glaucon, your outward form is no dishonour to any of them. If to beauty you add temperance, and if in other respects you are what Critias declares you to be, then, dear Charmides, blessed is the son your mother bore. And here lies the point; for if, as he declares, you have this gift of temperance already, and are temperate enough, in that case you have no need of any charms, whether of Zamolxis or of Abaris the Hyperborean, and I may as well let you have the cure of the head at once; but if you have not yet acquired this quality, I must use the charm before I give you the medicine. Please, therefore, to inform me whether you admit the truth of what Critias has been saying – have you or have you not this quality of temperance?

Charmides blushed, and the blush heightened his beauty, for modesty is becoming in youth; he then made the graceful reply that he really could not at once answer, either yes or no, to the question which I had asked: For, said he, if I affirm that I am not temperate, that would be a strange thing for me to say against myself, and also I should give the lie to Critias, and to many others who (according to him) think that I am temperate: but, on the other hand, if I say that I am, I shall have to praise myself, which would be ill manners; and therefore I do not know how to answer you.

I said to him: That is a natural reply, Charmides, and I think that you and I ought together to inquire whether you have this quality about which I am asking or not; and then you will not be compelled to say what you do not like, neither shall I rashly have recourse to medicine: therefore, if you please, I will share the inquiry with you, but I will not press you if you would rather not.

There is nothing which I should like better, he said; and as far as I am concerned you may proceed in the way which you think best.

I think, I said, that it would be best to approach the question in this way. If temperance abides in you, you must have an opinion about her; she must give some intimation of her nature and qualities, which may enable you to form a notion of her. Is not that true?

Yes, he said, that I think is true.

You know your native language, I said, and therefore you must be able also to express your opinion.

Perhaps, he said.

In order, then, that we may form a conjecture whether you have temperance abiding in you or not, tell me, I said, what, in your opinion, is temperance?

At first he hesitated, and was not very willing to answer: then he said that he thought temperance was doing all things orderly and quietly, for example walking in the streets, and talking, and indeed doing everything in that way. In a word, he said, I should answer that, in my opinion, temperance is a kind of quietness.

Are you right, Charmides? I said. No doubt some would affirm that the quiet are temperate; but let us see whether there is anything in this view; and first tell me whether you would not acknowledge temperance to be of the class of the noble and good?

Yes.

But which is best when you are at the writing-master's, to write the same letters quickly or quietly?

Quickly.

And to read quickly or slowly?

Quickly again.

And in playing the lyre, or wrestling, quickness or sharpness are far better than quietness and slowness?

Yes.

And the same holds in boxing and in the pancratium?

Certainly.

And in leaping and running and in bodily exercises generally, actions done quickly and with agility are good and noble, those done slowly and quietly are bad and unsightly?

It seems so.

Then, I said, in all bodily actions, not quietness, but the greatest agility and quickness, is noblest and best?

Yes, certainly.

And is temperance a good?

Yes.

Then, in reference to the body, not quietness, but quickness will be the more temperate, if temperance is a good?

Apparently, he said.

Again, I said, which is better – facility in learning, or difficulty in learning?

Facility.

Yes, I said; and facility in learning is learning quickly, and difficulty in learning is learning quietly and slowly?

True.

And is it not better to teach another quickly and energetically, rather than quietly and slowly?

Yes.

Once more, which is better, to call to mind and to remember quickly and readily, or quietly and slowly?

The former.

And is not cleverness a quickness of the soul, and not a quietness?

True.

Is it not then best to understand what is said, whether at the writing-master's or the music-master's or anywhere else, not as quietly as possible, but as quickly as possible?

Yes.

And further, in the searchings or deliberations of the soul, not the quietest, as I imagine, and he who with difficulty deliberates and discovers, is thought worthy of praise, but he who does so most easily and quickly?

Quite true, he said.

Well then, in all that concerns either body or soul, swiftness and activity are clearly better than slowness and quietness?

Probably.

Then temperance is not quietness, nor is the temperate life quiet – certainly not upon this view; for the life which is temperate is admitted to be the good. And of two things one is true – either never, or very seldom, do the quiet actions in life appear to be better than the quick and energetic ones; or supposing at the best that of the nobler actions there are as many quiet as quick and vehement; still, even if we grant this, temperance will not be acting quietly any more than acting quickly and energetically, either in walking or talking or in anything else; nor will the quiet life be more temperate than the unquiet, seeing that temperance was placed by us among the good and noble things, and the quick have been shown to be as good as the quiet.

I think that you are right, Socrates, he said.

Then once more, Charmides, I said, fix your attention more closely and look within you; consider the effect which temperance has upon yourself, and the nature of that which should have this effect. Think over all this, and tell me truly and courageously – what is temperance?

After a moment's pause, in which he made a real manly effort to think, he said: My opinion is, Socrates, that temperance makes a man ashamed or modest, and that temperance is the same as modesty.

Very good, I said; and did not you admit, just now, that temperance is noble?

Yes, certainly, he said.

And therefore that temperate men are good men?

Yes.

And can that be good which does not make men good?

Certainly not.

And you would infer that temperance is not only noble, but also good?

That is my opinion.

Well, I said; but surely you would agree with Homer when he says, 'Modesty is not good for a needy man'?

Yes, he said; I agree.

Then I suppose that modesty is and is not good?

Apparently.

But temperance, whose presence makes men only good, and not bad, is always good?

That appears to me to be as you say.

And the inference is that temperance cannot be modesty – if temperance is good, and if modesty is as much an evil as a good?

All that, Socrates, appears to me to be true; but I should like to know what you think about another definition of temperance, which I have just remembered that I heard from someone, 'Temperance is doing our own business.' Please consider whether he was right who affirmed that.

You wicked boy! I said; this is what Critias, or some other philosopher has told you.

Someone else then, said Critias; for certainly I have not.

But what matter, said Charmides, from whom I heard this?

No matter at all, I replied; for the point is not who said the words, but whether they are true or not.

There you are in the right, Socrates, he replied.

To be sure, I said; yet I should be surprised if we are able to discover their truth or falsehood; for they are a kind of riddle.

What makes you think so? he said.

Because, I said, he who uttered them seems to me to have meant one thing, and said another. Is the schoolmaster, for example, to be regarded as doing nothing when he reads or writes?

I should rather think that he was doing something.

And does the schoolmaster write or read, or teach you boys to write or read, his own name only, or did you write your enemies' names as well as your own and your friends'?

As much one as the other.

And was there anything meddling or intemperate in this?

Certainly not.

And yet you were doing what was not your own business if reading and writing are a form of doing.

35

But they certainly are.

And the healing art, my friend, and building, and weaving, and doing anything whatever which is done by art – these all clearly come under the head of doing?

Certainly.

And do you think that a state would be well ordered by a law which compelled every man to weave and wash his own coat, and make his own shoes, and his own flask and strigil, and other implements, on this principle of everyone doing and performing his own, and abstaining from what is not his own?

I think not, he said.

But, I said, a temperate state will be a well-ordered state.

Of course, he replied.

Then temperance, I said, will not be doing one's own business; not at least in this way, or doing things of this sort?

It seems not.

Then, as I was just now saying, he who declared that temperance is a man doing his own business had a hidden meaning; for I do not think that he could have been such a fool as to mean this. Was he a fool who told you, Charmides?

Nay, he replied, I certainly thought him a very wise man.

Then I am quite certain that he put forth his definition as a riddle, thinking that no one would easily discover the meaning of the words 'doing his own business'.

I dare say, he replied.

And what is the meaning of a man doing his own business? Can you tell me?

Indeed, I cannot; and I should not wonder if the

man himself who used this phrase did not understand what he meant. Whereupon he laughed slyly, and looked at Critias.

Critias had long been showing uneasiness, for he felt that he had a reputation to maintain with Charmides and the rest of the company. He had, however, hitherto managed to restrain himself; but now he could no longer forbear, and I am convinced of the truth of the suspicion which I entertained at the time, that it was from Critias that Charmides had heard this answer about temperance. And Charmides, who did not want to defend it himself, but to make Critias defend it, tried to stir him up. He went on pointing out that he had been refuted, at which Critias grew angry, and appeared, as I thought, inclined to quarrel with him; just as a poet might quarrel with an actor who spoiled his poems in reciting them; so he looked hard at him and said –

Do you imagine, Charmides, because you do not understand the meaning of this definition of temperance that its author likewise did not understand the meaning of his own words?

Why, at his age, I said, most excellent Critias, he can hardly be expected to understand; but you, who are older, and have studied, may well be assumed to know the meaning of them; and therefore, if you agree, and accept his definition of temperance, I would much rather argue with you than with him about the truth or falsehood of the definition.

I entirely agree, said Critias, and accept the definition.

Very good, I said; and now let me repeat my question – Do you admit, as I was just now saying, that all craftsmen make or do something?

I do.

And do they make or do their own business only, or that of others also?

That of others also.

And are they temperate, seeing that they do not make or do their own business only?

Why not? he said.

No objection on my part, I said, but there may be a difficulty on his who proposes as a definition of temperance, 'doing one's own business', and then says that there is no reason why those who do the business of others should not be temperate.

Nay, said he; did I ever acknowledge that those who do the business of others are temperate? I said, those who make, not those who do.

What! I asked; do you mean to say that doing and making are not the same?

No more, he replied, than making and working are the same; thus much I have learned from Hesiod, who says that 'work is no disgrace'. Now do you imagine that if he had meant by working and doing such things as you were describing, he would have said that there was no disgrace in them – for example, in the manufacture of shoes, or in selling dried fish, or sitting for hire in a house of ill fame? That, Socrates, is not to be supposed: but I conceive him to have distinguished making from doing and work; and, while admitting that the making anything might sometimes become a disgrace, when the employment was not honourable, to have thought that work was never any disgrace at all. For things nobly and usefully made he called works; and such makings he called workings, and doings; and he must be supposed to have deemed only such things to be man's proper business, and all that is hurtful, not to be his business: and in that sense Hesiod, and any other wise man, may be reasonably supposed to call him wise who does his own work.

O Critias, I said, no sooner had you opened your mouth than I pretty well knew that you would call that which is proper to a man, and that which is his own, good; and that the makings of the good you would call doings, for I am no stranger to the endless distinctions which Prodicus draws about names. Now I have no objection to your giving names any signification which you please, if you will only tell me to what you apply them. Please then to begin again, and be a little plainer. Do you mean that this doing or making, or whatever is the word which you would use, of good things, is temperance?

I do, he said.

Then not he who does evil, but he who does good, is temperate?

Yes, he said; and you, friend, would agree.

No matter whether I should or not; just now, not what I think, but what you are saying, is the point at issue.

Well, he answered; I mean to say that he who does evil, and not good, is not temperate; and that he is temperate who does good, and not evil: for temperance I define in plain words to be the doing of good actions.

And you may be very likely right in what you are saying; but I am surprised that you think temperate men to be ignorant of their own temperance?

I do not think so, he said.

And yet were you not saying, just now, that craftsmen might be temperate in doing another's work, as well as in doing their own?

I was, he replied; but what is your drift?

I have no particular drift, but I wish that you would tell me whether a physician who cures a patient may do good to himself and good to his patient also?

I think that he may.

And he who does so does his duty?

Yes.

And does not he who does his duty act temperately or wisely?

Yes, he acts wisely.

But must the physician necessarily know when his treatment is likely to prove beneficial, and when not? And must every worker necessarily know when he is likely to be benefited, and when not to be benefited, by the work which he is doing?

I suppose not.

Then, I said, the physician may sometimes do good or harm, without knowing which he has done, and yet in doing good, as you say, he has done temperately or wisely. Was not that your statement?

Yes.

Then, as would seem, in doing good he may act wisely or temperately, and be wise or temperate, but not know his own wisdom or temperance?

But that, Socrates, he said, is impossible; and therefore if this is, as you imply, the necessary consequence of any of my previous admissions, I will withdraw them and will not be ashamed to acknowledge that I made a mistake, rather than admit that a man can be temperate or wise who does not know himself. For I would almost say that self-knowledge is the very essence of temperance, and in this I agree with him who dedicated the inscription, 'Know thyself!' at Delphi. That inscription, if I am not mistaken, is put there as a sort of salutation which the god addresses to those who enter the temple; as much as to say that the ordinary salutation of 'Hail!' is not right, and that the exhortation 'Be temperate!' is far better. If I rightly understand the meaning of the inscription, the god speaks to those who enter his temple, not as men speak; but whenever a worshipper enters, the first word which he hears is 'Be temperate!' This, however, like a prophet he expresses in a sort of riddle, for 'Know thyself!' and 'Be temperate!' are the same, as I maintain, and as the words imply, and yet they may be thought to be different; and succeeding sages who added 'Never too much', or, 'Give a pledge, and evil is nigh at hand', would appear to have so distinguished them; for they imagined that 'Know thyself!' was a piece of advice which the god gave, and not his salutation of the worshippers at their first coming in; and they dedicated their own inscriptions under the idea that they too would give equally useful pieces of advice. Shall I tell you, Socrates, why I say all this? My object is to leave the previous discussion (in which I know not whether you or I are more right, but, at any rate, no clear result was attained), and to raise a new one in which I will attempt to prove, if you deny it, that temperance is self-knowledge.*

Yes, I said, Critias; but you come to me as though I professed to know about the questions which I ask, and as though I could, if I only would, agree with you. Whereas the fact is that I am inquiring with you into the truth of that which is advanced from time to time, just because I do not know; and when I have inquired, I will say whether I agree with you or not. Please then to allow me time to reflect.

Reflect, he said.

I am reflecting, I replied, and discover that temperance or wisdom, if it is a species of knowledge, must be a science, and a science of something.

Yes, he said; the science of a man's self.

Is not medicine the science of health?

True.

And suppose that I were asked by you what is the use or effect of medicine, which is this science of health, I should answer that medicine is of very great use in producing health, which, as you will admit, is an excellent effect.

Granted.

And if you were to ask me what is the result or effect of architecture, which is the science of building, I should say houses, and so of other arts, which all have their different results. Now I want you, Critias, to answer a similar question about temperance or wisdom, which, according to you, is the science of a man's self. Admitting this view, I ask of you, what good work, worthy of the name wise, does temperance or wisdom, which is the science of a man's self, effect? Answer me.

That is not the true way of pursuing the inquiry, Socrates, he said; for wisdom is not like the other sciences, any more than they are like one another: but you proceed as if they were alike. For tell me, he said, what result is there of computation or geometry, in the same sense as a house is the result of building, or a garment of weaving, or any other work of any of the many other arts? Can you show me any such result of them? You cannot.

That is true, I said; but still I can show you that each of these sciences has a subject which is different from the science. The art of computation, for instance, has to do with odd and even numbers in their numerical relations to themselves and to each other. Is not that true?

Yes.

And the odd and even numbers are not the same with the art of computation?

They are not.

The art of weighing, again, has to do with lighter and heavier; but the art of weighing is one thing, and the heavy and the light is another. Do you admit that?

Yes.

Now, I want to know, what is that which is not wisdom, and of which wisdom is the science?

You are just falling into the old error, Socrates, he said. You come asking wherein wisdom or temperance differs from the other sciences, and then you try to discover some respect in which it is like them; but it is not, for all the other sciences are of something else, and not of themselves; wisdom alone is a science of other sciences and of itself. And of this, as I believe, you are very well aware: and you are only doing what you denied that you were doing just now, trying to refute me, instead of pursuing the argument.

And what if I am? How can you think that I have any other motive in refuting you but what I should have in examining into myself? Which motive would be just a fear of my unconsciously fancying that I knew something of which I was ignorant. And at this moment, I assure you, I pursue the argument chiefly for my own sake, and perhaps in some degree also for the sake of my other friends. For would you not say that the discovery of things as they truly are is a good common to all mankind?

Yes, certainly, Socrates, he said.

Then, I said, be cheerful, sweet sir, and give your opinion in answer to the question which I asked, never minding whether Critias or Socrates is the person refuted; attend only to the argument, and see what will come of the refutation.

I think that is reasonable, he replied; and I will do as you say.

Tell me, then, I said, what you mean to affirm about wisdom.

I mean to say that wisdom is the only science which is the science of itself as well as of the other sciences.

But the science of science, I said, will also be the science of the absence of science.

Very true, he said.

Then the wise or temperate man, and he only, will know himself, and be able to examine what he knows or does not know, and to see what others know and think that they know and do really know; and what they do not know, and fancy that they know when they do not. No other person will be able to do this. And this is wisdom and temperance and self-knowledge – for a man to know what he knows, and what he does not know. That is your meaning?

Yes, he said.

Now then, I said, since the third time brings luck, let us begin again, and ask, in the first place, whether it is or is not possible for a person to know that he knows what he knows, and that he does not know what he does not know; and in the second place, whether, if perfectly possible, such knowledge is of any use.

That is what we have to consider, he said.

Well then, Critias, I said, see if you are in a better position than I am. I am in a difficulty. Shall I tell you the nature of the difficulty?

By all means.

Does not what you have been saying, if true, amount to this: that there must be a single science which is wholly a science of itself and of other sciences, and that the same is also the science of the absence of science?

Yes.

But consider how monstrous this proposition is, my friend: in any parallel case, the impossibility will be obvious to you.

How is that? And in what cases do you mean?

In such cases as this: suppose that there is a kind of vision which is not like the ordinary vision, but a vision of itself and of other sorts of vision, and of the defect of them, which in seeing sees no colour, but only itself and other sorts of vision: do you think that there is such a kind of vision?

Certainly not.

Or is there a kind of hearing which hears no sound at all, but only itself and other sorts of hearing, or the defects of them?

There is not.

Or take all the senses together: can you imagine that there is any sense which is a sense of itself and of other senses, but is incapable of perceiving the objects of the senses?

I think not.

Could there be any desire which is not the desire of any pleasure, but of itself and of all other desires?

Certainly not.

Or can you imagine a wish which wishes for no good, but only for itself and all other wishes?

I should answer, No.

Or would you say that there is a love which is not the love of beauty, but of itself and of other loves?

I should not.

Or did you ever know of a fear which fears itself or other fears, but none of the objects of fear?

I never did, he said.

Or of an opinion which is an opinion of itself and of other opinions, and which has no opinion on the subjects of opinion in general?

Certainly not.

But, it seems, we are assuming a science of this kind, which, having no subject-matter, is a science of itself and of the other sciences?

Yes, that is what is affirmed.

It is certainly a curiosity if it really exists: we must not however as yet absolutely deny the possibility of such a science, but continue to inquire whether it exists.

You are quite right.

Well then, this science of which we are speaking is a science of something, and is of a nature to be a science of something?

Yes.

Just as that which is greater is of a nature to be greater than something else?

Yes.

And this something else is less, if the other is conceived to be greater?

To be sure.

And if we could find something which is at once greater than itself and greater than other great things, but not greater than those things in comparison of which the others are greater, then that thing would have the property of being greater and also less than itself?

That, Socrates, he said, is the inevitable inference.

Or if there be a double which is double of itself and of other doubles, both they and itself will be halves; for the double is relative to the half?

That is true.

And that which is more than itself will also be less, and that which is heavier will also be lighter, and that which is older will also be younger: and the same of other things; that which has a nature relative to self will retain also the nature of its object: I mean to say, for example, that hearing is, as we say, of sound or voice. Is that true?

Yes.

Then if hearing hears itself, it must hear a voice; for there is no other way of hearing.

Certainly.

And sight also, my excellent friend, if it sees itself must have a colour, for sight cannot see that which has no colour.

No.

Do you remark, Critias, that in several of the examples which have been recited the notion of a relation to self is altogether inadmissible, and in other cases hardly credible – inadmissible, for example, in the case of magnitudes, numbers, and the like?

Very true.

But in the case of hearing and sight, or in the power of self-motion, and the power of heat to burn, and so on, this relation to self will be regarded as incredible by some, but perhaps not by others. And some great man, my friend, is wanted, who will satisfactorily determine for us whether there is nothing which has an inherent property of relation to self rather than to something else, or some things only and not others; and whether in this class of self-related things, if there be such a class, that science which is called wisdom or temperance is included. I altogether distrust my own power of determining these matters: I am not certain whether such a science of science can possibly exist; and even if it does undoubtedly exist, I should not acknowledge it to be wisdom or temperance, until I can also see whether such a science would or would not do us any good; for I have an impression that temperance is a benefit and a good. And therefore, O son of Callaeschrus, as you maintain that temperance or wisdom is a science of science, and also of the absence of science, I will request you to show in the first place, as I was saying before, the possibility, and in the second place, the advantage, of such a science; and then perhaps you may satisfy me that you are right in your view of temperance.

Critias heard me say this, and saw that I was in a difficulty; and as one person when another yawns in his presence catches the infection of yawning from him, so did he seem to be driven into a difficulty by my difficulty. But as he had a reputation to maintain, he was ashamed to admit before the company that he could not answer my challenge or determine the question at issue; and he made an unintelligible attempt to hide his perplexity. In order that the argument might proceed, I said to him, Well then, Critias, if you like, let us assume that this science of science is possible; whether the assumption is right or wrong may hereafter be investigated. Admitting its complete possibility, will you tell me how such a science enables us to distinguish what we know or do not know, which, as we were saying, is self-knowledge or wisdom? Was not that it?

Yes, Socrates, he said; and the rest I think follows: for

he who has this science or knowledge which knows itself will become like the knowledge which he has, in the same way that he who has swiftness will be swift, and he who has beauty will be beautiful, and he who has knowledge will know. In the same way he who has that knowledge which is self-knowing, will know himself.

I do not doubt, I said, that a man will know himself, when he possesses that which has self-knowledge: but what necessity is there that, having this, he should know what he knows and what he does not know?

Because, Socrates, they are the same.

Very likely, I said; but I fear I remain as stupid as ever; for still I fail to comprehend how this knowing what you know and do not know is the same as the knowledge of self.

What do you mean? he said.

This is what I mean, I replied: I will admit that there is a science of science; can this do more than determine that of two things one is and the other is not science or knowledge?

No, just that.

Is it then the same thing as knowledge or want of knowledge of health, or the same as knowledge or want of knowledge of justice?

Certainly not.

The one is medicine, and the other is politics; whereas that of which we are speaking is knowledge pure and simple.

Very true.

And if a man has only knowledge of knowledge, without any further knowledge of health and justice, the probability is that he will only know that he knows something, and has a certain knowledge, both in his own case and in that of others.

49

True.

Then how will this knowledge or science teach him to know what he knows? For he knows health not through wisdom or temperance but through the art of medicine, and he has learned harmony from the art of music and building from the art of building, but in neither case from wisdom or temperance: and the same of other things.

It seems so.

How will wisdom, regarded only as a knowledge of knowledge or science of science, ever teach him that he knows health, or that he knows building?

It is impossible.

Then he who is ignorant of these things will only know that he knows, but not what he knows?

True.

Then wisdom or being wise appears to be not the knowledge of the things which we do or do not know, but only the knowledge that we know or do not know?

That is the inference.

Then he who has this knowledge will not be able to establish whether a claimant knows or does not know that which he says that he knows: he will only know that he has a knowledge of some kind; but wisdom will not show him of what the knowledge is?

It seems not.

Neither will he be able to distinguish the pretender in medicine from the true physician, nor between any other true and false professor of knowledge. Let us consider the matter in this way: if the wise man or any other man wants to distinguish the true physician from the false, how will he proceed? He will not talk to him about the science of medicine; for as we were saying, the physician understands nothing but health and disease.

True.

But the physician knows nothing about science, for this has been assumed to be the province of wisdom alone.

True.

And further, since medicine is science, we must infer that he does not know anything about medicine.

Exactly.

Then the wise man may indeed know that the physician has some kind of science or knowledge; but when he wants to discover the nature of this he will ask, What is the subject-matter? For the several sciences are distinguished not by the mere fact that they are sciences, but by the nature of their subjects. Is not that true?

Quite true.

And medicine is distinguished from other sciences as having the subject-matter of health and disease?

Yes.

And he who would inquire into the nature of medicine must test it in health and disease, which are the sphere of medicine, and not in what is extraneous and is not its sphere?

True.

And he who wishes to make a fair test of the physician as a physician will test him in what relates to these?

He will.

He will consider whether what he says is true, and whether what he does is right, in relation to health and disease?

He will.

But can anyone pursue the inquiry into either unless he have a knowledge of medicine?

He cannot.

No one at all, it would seem, except the physician can have this knowledge; and therefore not the wise man; he would have to be a physician as well as a wise man.

Very true.

Then, assuredly, wisdom or temperance, if it is no more than a science of science and of the absence of science or knowledge, will not be able to distinguish the physician who knows what concerns his profession from one who does not know but pretends or thinks that he knows, or any other professor of anything at all; like any other artist, the wise or temperate man will only know the man of his own trade, and no one else.

That is evident, he said.

But then what profit, Critias, I said, is there any longer in wisdom or temperance which yet remains, if this is wisdom? If, indeed, as we were supposing at first, the wise man were able to distinguish what he knew and did not know, and that he knew the one and did not know the other, and to recognize a similar faculty of discernment in others, there would certainly be a great advantage in being wise; for then we should never make a mistake, but should pass through life the unerring guides of ourselves and of those who are under us. We should not attempt to do what we did not know, but we should find out those who know, and hand the business over to them and trust in them; nor should we allow those who were under us to do anything which they were not likely to do well, and they would be likely to do well just that of which they had knowledge; and the house or state which was ordered or administered under the guidance of wisdom, and everything else of which wisdom was the lord, would be sure to be well ordered; for with truth guiding and error eliminated, in all their doings men must do nobly and well, and doing well means happiness. Was not this, Critias, what we spoke of as the great advantage of wisdom – to know what is known and what is unknown to us?

Very true, he said.

And now you perceive, I said, that no such science is to be found anywhere.

I perceive, he said.

May we assume then, I said, that wisdom, viewed in this new light as a knowledge of knowledge and ignorance, has this advantage: that he who possesses such knowledge will more easily learn anything which he learns; and that everything will be clearer to him, because, in addition to the several objects of knowledge, he sees the science, and this also will better enable him to test the knowledge which others have of what he knows himself; whereas the inquirer who is without this knowledge may be supposed to have a feebler and less effective insight? Are not these, my friend, the real advantages which are to be gained from wisdom? And are not we looking and seeking after something more than is to be found in her?

It may be, he said.

Perhaps it may, I said; or perhaps again we have been inquiring to no purpose; as I am led to infer, because I observe that if this is wisdom, some strange consequences would follow. Let us, if you please, assume the possibility of this science of sciences, and not refuse to allow that, as was originally suggested, wisdom is the knowledge of what we know and do not know. Assuming all this, let us consider more closely, Critias, whether wisdom such as this would do us much good. For we were wrong, I think, in supposing, as we were saying just now, that such wisdom ordering the government of house or state would be a great benefit.

How so? he said.

Why, I said, we were far too ready to admit the great benefits which mankind would obtain from their severally doing the things which they knew, and committing the things of which they are ignorant to those who were better acquainted with them.

Were we not right in making that admission?

I think not.

How very strange, Socrates!

There, I said, I most emphatically agree with you; and I was thinking as much just now when I said that strange consequences would follow, and that I was afraid we were on the wrong track; for however sure we may be that this is wisdom, I certainly cannot make out what good this sort of thing does to us.

What do you mean? he said; I wish that you could make me understand what you mean.

I dare say that what I am saying is nonsense, I replied; and yet if a man has any feeling of what is due to himself, he cannot let the thought which comes into his mind pass away unheeded and unexamined.

I like that, he said.

Hear, then, I said, my own dream; whether coming through the horn or the ivory gate, I cannot tell. The dream is this: let us suppose that wisdom is such as we are now defining, and that she has absolute sway over us; then each action will be done according to the arts or sciences, and no one professing to be a pilot when he is not, no physician or general or anyone else pretending to know matters of which he is ignorant,

54

will deceive or elude us; our health will be improved; our safety at sea, and also in battle, will be assured; our coats and shoes, and all other instruments and implements will be skilfully made, because the workmen will be good and true. Aye, and if you please, you may suppose that prophecy will be a real knowledge of the future, and will be under the control of wisdom, who will deter deceivers and set up the true prophets in their place as the revealers of the future. Now I quite agree that mankind, thus provided, would live and act according to knowledge, for wisdom would watch and prevent ignorance from intruding on us in our work. But whether by acting according to knowledge we shall act well and be happy, my dear Critias – this is a point which we have not yet been able to determine.

Yet I think, he replied, that if you discard knowledge, you will hardly find the crown of happiness in anything else.

Well, just answer me one small question, I said. Of what is this knowledge? Do you mean a knowledge of shoe-making?

God forbid.

Or of working in brass?

Certainly not.

Or in wool, or wood, or anything of that sort?

No, I do not.

Then, I said, we are giving up the doctrine that he who lives according to knowledge is happy, for these live according to knowledge, and yet they are not allowed by you to be happy; but I think that you mean to confine happiness to those who live according to knowledge of some particular thing, such for example as the prophet, who, as I was saying, knows the future. Is it of him you are speaking or of someone else?

Yes, I mean him, but there are others as well.

Who? I said. Evidently someone who knows the past and present as well as the future, and is ignorant of nothing. Let us suppose that there is such a person, and if there is, you will allow that he is the most knowing of all living men.

Certainly he is.

Yet I should like to know one thing more: which of the different kinds of knowledge makes him happy? Or do all equally make him happy?

Not all equally, he replied.

But which most tends to make him happy? The knowledge of what past, present, or future thing? Is it, for example, the knowledge of the game of draughts?

Nonsense: draughts indeed!

Or of computation?

No.

Or of health?

That is nearer the truth, he said.

And that knowledge which is nearest of all, I said, is the knowledge of what?

The knowledge with which he discerns good and evil.

You villain! I said; you have been carrying me round in a circle, and all this time hiding from me the fact that it is not the life according to knowledge which makes men act rightly and be happy, not even if it be knowledge of all the sciences, but one science only, that of good and evil. For, let me ask you, Critias, whether, if you take away this science from the others, medicine will not equally give health, and shoemaking equally produce shoes, and the art of the weaver clothes – whether the art of the pilot will not equally save our lives at sea, and the art of the general in war?

Equally.

And yet, my dear Critias, none of these things will be well or beneficially done, if the science of the good be wanting.

True.

But this science, it seems, is not wisdom or temperance, but a science of human advantage; not a science of other sciences, or of ignorance, but of good and evil: and if this be of advantage, then wisdom or temperance must be something else.

And why, he replied, will not wisdom be of advantage? For, however much we assume that wisdom is a science of sciences, and has a sway over other sciences, surely she will have this particular science of the good under her control, and in this way will benefit us.

And will wisdom give health? I said; is not this rather the effect of medicine? Or does wisdom do the work of any of the other arts – do they not each of them do their own work? Have we not long ago asseverated that wisdom is only the knowledge of knowledge and of ignorance, and of nothing else?

It seems so.

Then wisdom will not be the producer of health?

Certainly not.

We found that health belonged to a different art?

Yes.

Nor does wisdom give advantage, my good friend; for that again we have just now been attributing to another art.

Very true.

How then can wisdom be advantageous, when it produces no advantage?

Apparently it cannot, Socrates.

You see, then, Critias, that I was not far wrong in

fearing that I was making no sound inquiry into wisdom; I was quite right in depreciating myself; for that which is admitted to be the best of all things would never have seemed to us useless, if I had been good for anything at an inquiry. But now I have been utterly defeated, and have failed to discover what that is to which the lawgiver gave this name of temperance or wisdom. And yet many more admissions were made by us than could be fairly granted; for we admitted that there was a science of science, although the argument said No, and protested against us; and we admitted further, that this science knew the works of the other sciences (although this too was denied by the argument), because we wanted to show that the wise man had knowledge of what he knew and of what he did not know; we generously made the concession, and never even considered the impossibility of a man knowing in a sort of way that which he does not know at all; according to our admission, he knows that which he does not know – than which nothing, as I think, can be more irrational. And yet, after finding us so easy and good-natured, the inquiry is still unable to discover the truth; but mocks us to a degree, and has insolently proved the inutility of temperance or wisdom if truly described by a definition such as we have spent all this time in discussing and fashioning together: which result, as far as I am concerned, is not so much to be lamented, I said. But for your sake, Charmides, I am very sorry – that you, having such beauty and such wisdom and temperance of soul, should have no profit nor good in life from your wisdom and temperance. And still more am I grieved about the charm which I learned with so much pain, and to so little profit, from the Thracian, in order to produce a thing which is nothing worth. I think indeed that there is a mistake, and that I must be a bad inquirer, for wisdom or temperance I believe to be really a great good; and happy are you, Charmides, if you possess it. Wherefore examine yourself, and see whether you have this gift and can do without the charm; for if you can, I would rather advise you to regard me simply as a fool who is never able to reason out anything; and to rest assured that the more wise and temperate you are, the happier you will be.

Charmides said: I am sure that I do not know, Socrates, whether I have or have not this gift of wisdom and temperance; for how can I know whether I have a thing, of which even you and Critias are, as you say, unable to discover the nature? Yet I do not quite believe you, and I am sure, Socrates, that I do need the charm, and as far as I am concerned, I shall be willing to be charmed by you daily, until you say that I have had enough.

Very good, Charmides, said Critias; if you do this I shall have a proof of your temperance, that is, if you allow yourself to be charmed by Socrates, and never desert him in things great or small.

You may depend on my following and not deserting him, said Charmides: if you who are my guardian command me, I should be very wrong not to obey you.

And I do command you, he said.

Then I will do as you say, and begin this very day.

You sirs, I said, what are you conspiring about?

We are not conspiring, said Charmides, we have conspired already.

And you are about to use violence, without even giving me a hearing in court?

Yes, I shall use violence, he replied, since he orders

me; and therefore you had better consider what you will do.

But the time for consideration has passed, I said; when you are determined on anything, and in the mood of violence, you are irresistible.

Do not you resist me then, he said.

I shall not resist you then, I replied.

PLATO
LYSIS

LYSIS
or Friendship

Persons of the dialogue
SOCRATES, *who is the narrator*
MENEXENUS
HIPPOTHALES
LYSIS
CTESIPPUS

SCENE: *A newly-erected palaestra outside
the walls of Athens*

I was going from the Academy straight to the Lyceum
by the outer road, which is close under the wall. When
I came to the postern gate of the city, which is by the
fountain of Panops, I fell in with Hippothales, the son of
Hieronymus, and Ctesippus, from the deme of Paeania,
and a company of young men who were standing with
them. Hippothales, seeing me approach, asked whence
I came and whither I was going.

I am going, I replied, from the Academy straight to
the Lyceum.

Then come straight to us, he said, and turn in here;
you may as well.

Who are you, I said; and where am I to come?

Here, he said, showing me an enclosed space and an
open door over against the wall. This is the place
where we all meet: and a goodly company we are.

And what is this place, I asked; and what sort of
entertainment have you?

It is a newly-erected palaestra, he replied; and the

entertainment is generally conversation, to which you are welcome.

Thank you, I said; and who is your teacher?

Your old friend and admirer, Miccus, he said.

Indeed, I replied; he is a very eminent professor.

Are you disposed, he said, to go with me and see them?

Yes, I said; but I should like to know first, what is expected of me, and who is the favourite among you?

Some persons have one favourite, Socrates, and some another, he said.

And who is yours? I asked: tell me that, Hippothales.

At this question he blushed; and I said to him, O Hippothales, son of Hieronymus! You need not say that you are, or that you are not, in love; the confession is too late; for I see that you are not only in love, but are already far gone in your love. Unintelligent and unpractical as I am, the gods have given me the power of quickly detecting a lover and his beloved.

Whereupon he blushed more and more.

Ctesippus said: I like to see you blushing, Hippothales, and hesitating to tell Socrates the name; why, if he is with you but a very short time, you will have plagued him to death by talking about nothing else. Indeed, Socrates, he has deafened us and stopped our ears with talking of Lysis; and if he is a little intoxicated, there is every likelihood that we shall be woken up, thinking we hear the name of Lysis. His talk, bad as it is, might be worse; but when he drenches us with his poems and his prose, it is unbearable; and worse still is his manner of singing them to his love; he has a voice which is truly appalling, and we are forced to endure it: and now being asked straight out by you, he is blushing.

I suppose, I said, this Lysis must be quite young; for the name does not recall anyone to me.

Why, he said, his father being a very well-known man, he is known as his father's son, and is not as yet commonly called by his own name; but, although you do not know his name, I am sure that you must know his face, for that is quite enough to distinguish him.

But tell me whose son he is, I said.

He is the eldest son of Democrates, of the deme of Aexone.

Ah, Hippothales, I said; what a noble and wholly ingenuous love you have found! I wish that you would favour me with the exhibition which you have been giving to the rest of the company, and then I shall be able to judge whether you know what a lover ought to say about his love, either to the youth himself, or to others.

Nay, Socrates, said Hippothales; you surely do not attach any importance to what Ctesippus is saying.

Do you mean, I said, that you disown the love of the person whom he says that you love?

No; but I deny that I make verses or write prose compositions to him.

He is not in his right mind, said Ctesippus; he is talking nonsense, and is stark mad.

O Hippothales, I said, I do not want to hear any verses or songs you have composed in honour of your favourite; but I want to know the purport of them, that I may be able to judge of your mode of approaching your beloved.

Ctesippus will be able to tell you, he said; for if, as he avers, the sound of my words is always dinning in his ears, he must have a very accurate knowledge and recollection of them.

Yes, indeed, said Ctesippus; I know only too well, and very ridiculous the tale is: for although he is a lover, and most devotedly in love, he has nothing particular to talk about to his beloved which a child might not say. Now is not that ridiculous? He can only speak of what the whole city celebrates, the wealth of Democrates, and of Lysis, the boy's grand-father, and of all the other ancestors of the youth, and their stud of horses, and their victories at the Pythian games, and at the Isthmus, and at Nemea in chariot and horse races – these are the tales which he composes and repeats, and even more prehistoric stories still. Only the day before yesterday he made a poem in which he described the entertainment of Heracles, telling how in virtue of his relationship to the family he was hospitably received by an ancestor of Lysis; for this ancestor was himself begotten by Zeus of the daughter of the founder of the deme. And these are the sort of old wives' tales which he sings and recites to us, and compels us to listen to him.

When I heard this, I said: O ridiculous Hippothales! how can you be making and singing hymns in honour of yourself before you have won?

But my songs and verses, he said, are not in honour of myself, Socrates.

You think not?

What do you mean?

Most assuredly, I said, those songs are all in your own honour; for if you win your beautiful love, your discourses and songs will be a glory to you, and may be truly regarded as hymns of praise composed in honour of yourself who have conquered and won such a love; but if he slips away from you, the more you have praised him, the more ridiculous you will look at having lost this fairest and best of blessings; and therefore the wise lover does not praise his beloved until he has won him, because he is afraid of what may come. There is also another danger; the fair, when anyone praises or magnifies them, are filled with the spirit of pride and vainglory. Do you not agree with me?

Yes, he said.

And the more vainglorious they are, the more difficult is the capture of them?

Naturally.

What should you say of a hunter who frightened the animals away, and made the capture of his prey more difficult?

He would be a bad hunter, undoubtedly.

Yes; and to infuriate a lover instead of soothing him with words and songs, would show a great want of art: do you not agree?

Yes.

And now reflect, Hippothales, and see whether you are not guilty of all these errors in writing your poetry. For I can hardly suppose that you will affirm a man to be a good poet who injures himself by his poetry.

Assuredly not, he said; such a poet would be a fool. And this is the reason why I take you into my counsels, Socrates, and I shall be glad of any further advice which you may have to offer. Will you tell me by what words or actions a man might become endeared to his love?

That is not easy to determine, I said; but if you will enable me to talk with your love, I may perhaps be able to show you how to converse with him, instead of singing and reciting in the fashion of which you are accused.

There will be no difficulty there, he replied; if you will only go with Ctesippus into the palaestra, and sit down and talk, I believe that he will come of his own accord; for he is very fond of listening, Socrates. And as this is the festival of the Hermaea, the young men and boys are all together. He will be sure to come: but if he does not come of himself, let Ctesippus call him; for he knows him well, and his cousin Menexenus is Lysis' great friend.

That will be the way, I said. Thereupon I led Ctesippus into the palaestra, and the rest followed.

Upon entering we found that the boys had just been sacrificing; and the ceremony was nearly at an end. They were all in their best array, and games at dice were going on among them. Most of them were in the outer court amusing themselves; but some were in a corner of the apodyterium playing at odd and even with a number of dice, which they took out of little wicker baskets. There was also a circle of lookers-on; among them was Lysis. He was standing with the other boys and youths, having a wreath upon his head, lovely to look at, and not less worthy of praise for his look of gentle breeding than for his beauty. We left them, and went over to the opposite side of the room, where, finding a quiet place, we sat down; and then we began to talk. This attracted Lysis, who was constantly turning round to look at us – he was evidently wanting to come to us. For a time he hesitated and had not the courage to come alone; but afterwards, his friend Menexenus, in the course of his game, entered the palaestra from the court, and when he saw Ctesippus and myself proceeded to take a seat by us; and then Lysis, seeing him, followed, and sat down by his side; and the other boys joined. And Hippothales too, when

68

he saw the crowd standing by us, got behind them, where he thought that he would be out of sight of Lysis, lest he should anger him; and there he stood and listened.

I turned to Menexenus, and said: Son of Demophon, which of you two youths is the elder?

That is a matter of dispute between us, he said.

And which is the nobler? Is that also a matter of dispute?

Yes, certainly.

And do you also dispute which is the fairer?

The two boys laughed.

I shall not ask which is the richer of the two, I said; for you are friends, are you not?

Certainly, they replied.

And friends have all things in common, so that one of you can be no richer than the other, if you say truly that you are friends.

They assented. I was about to ask which was the juster and which the wiser of the two; but at this moment Menexenus was called away by someone who came and said that the gymnastic-master wanted him. I supposed that he had to offer sacrifice. So he went away, and I asked Lysis some more questions. I dare say, Lysis, I said, that your father and mother love you very much.

Certainly, he said.

And they would wish you to be as happy as possible.

Yes.

But do you think that anyone is happy who is in the condition of a slave, and who could not do what he liked?

I should think not indeed, he said.

And if your father and mother love you, and desire

that you should be happy, it is quite clear that they are eager to promote your happiness.

Certainly, he replied.

And do they then permit you to do what you like, and never rebuke you or hinder you from doing what you desire?

Yes, indeed, Socrates; there are a great many things which they hinder me from doing.

What do you mean? I said. Do they want you to be happy, and yet hinder you from doing what you like? For example, if you want to mount one of your father's chariots, and take the reins at a race, would they refuse to allow you to do so and prevent you?

Certainly, he said, they would not allow me to do so.

Whom then will they allow?

There is a charioteer, whom my father pays for driving.

And do they trust a hireling more than you to do what he likes with the horses? And do they pay him for this as well?

They do.

But I dare say that you may take the whip and guide the mule-cart if you like – they would permit that?

Permit me! Indeed they would not.

Then, I said, may no one else use the whip to the mules?

Yes, the muleteer.

And is he a slave or a free man?

A slave.

And do they esteem a slave of more value than you who are their son? And do they entrust their property to him rather than to you? And allow him to do what he likes, when they prohibit you? Answer me now: are you your own master, or do they not even allow that?

Nay, he said; of course they do not allow it.

Then you have a master?

Yes, my tutor; there he is.

And is he a slave?

To be sure; he is our slave, he replied.

Surely, I said, this is a strange thing, that a free man should be governed by a slave. And what does he do with you?

He takes me to my teachers.

You do not mean to say that your teachers also rule over you?

Of course they do.

Then I must say that your father is pleased to inflict many lords and masters on you. But at any rate when you go home to your mother, she lets you have your own way, and does not interfere with your happiness; her wool, or the piece of cloth which she is weaving, is at your disposal: I am sure that she does not hinder you from touching her wooden spathe, or her comb, or any other of her spinning implements.

Nay, Socrates, he replied, laughing; not only does she hinder me, but I should be beaten if I were to touch one of them.

Well, I said, this is amazing. And did you ever behave ill to your father or your mother?

No, indeed, he replied.

But why then are they so terribly anxious to prevent you from being happy, and doing as you like – keeping you all day long in subjection to another, and, in a word, allowing you to do nothing which you desire; so that you get no good, as would appear, out of their great possessions, which are under the control of anybody rather than of you, and have no use of your own fair person, which is tended and taken care of by another; while you, Lysis, are master of nobody, and can do nothing you wish?

Why, he said, Socrates, the reason is that I am not of age.

I doubt whether that is the real reason, I said; for I should imagine that your father Democrates, and your mother, do permit you to do some things already, and do not wait until you are of age: for example, if they want anything read or written, you, I presume, would be the first person in the house set to that task.

Very true.

And you would be allowed to write or read the letters in any order which you please, or to take up the lyre and tighten or loosen any of the strings and play it with your fingers or strike it with the plectrum, exactly as you please, and neither father nor mother would interfere with you.

That is true, he said.

Then what can the reason be, Lysis, I said, why they allow you to do the one and not the other?

I suppose, he said, because I understand the one, and not the other.

Yes, my dear youth, I said, then the reason is not any deficiency of years, but a deficiency of knowledge; and the very day when your father thinks that you are wiser than he is, he will instantly commit himself and his possessions to you.

I expect so.

Aye, I said; and your neighbour, too, will he not observe the same rule about you as your father? As soon as he is satisfied that you know more about the management of family business than he does, will he continue to administer his affairs himself, or will he commit them to you?

I think that he will commit them to me.

Will not the Athenian people, too, entrust their affairs to you when they see that you have wisdom enough to manage them?

Yes.

And oh! let me put another case, I said: There is the great king, and he has an eldest son, who is the Prince of Asia – suppose that you and I go to him and establish to his satisfaction that we are better cooks than his son, will he not entrust to us the prerogative of making soup, and putting in anything that we like while the pot is boiling, rather than to his son?

To us, clearly.

And we shall be allowed to throw in salt by handfuls, whereas the son will not be allowed to put in even a pinch?

Of course.

Or suppose again that the son has bad eyes, would he allow him, or not, to touch his own eyes if he thinks that he has no knowledge of medicine?

He would not allow him.

Whereas, if he supposed us to have a knowledge of medicine, he would allow us to do what we like with him – even to open the eyes wide and sprinkle ashes upon them, because he supposed that we knew the right treatment?

That is true.

And everything in which we appear to him to be wiser than himself or his son he would commit to us?

Of course, Socrates, he replied.

This then is how it stands, my dear Lysis; in things which we know everyone will trust us – Hellenes and barbarians, men and women; we may do as we please about them, and no one if he can help it will interfere with us; we shall be free, and masters of others; and these things will be really ours, for we shall be benefited by them. But in things of which we have no understanding, no one will trust us to do as seems good to us – they will hinder us as far as they can; and not only strangers, but father and mother, and even a nearer relation if there be one, and in these matters we shall be subject to others; and these things will not be ours, for we shall not be benefited by them. Do you agree?

He assented.

And shall we be friends to others, and will any others love us, in matters where we are useless to them?

Certainly not.

Then neither does your father love you, nor does anybody love anybody else, in so far as he is useless to him?

It seems not.

And therefore, my boy, if you become wise, all men will be your friends and kindred, for you will be useful and good; but if you are not wise, neither father, nor mother, nor kindred, nor anyone else, will be your friends. And in matters of which one has as yet no knowledge, can he have any conceit of knowledge?

That is impossible, he replied.

And you, Lysis, if you require a teacher, have not yet attained to wisdom.

True.

And therefore you are not conceited, having no knowledge of which to be conceited.

Indeed, Socrates, I think not.

When I heard him say this, I turned to Hippothales, and was very nearly making a blunder, for I was going to say to him: That is the way, Hippothales, in which you should talk to your beloved, humbling and lowering him, and not as you do, puffing him up and spoiling him. But I saw that he was in great distress and confusion at what had been said, and I remembered that, although he was in the neighbourhood, he did not want to be seen by Lysis; so upon second thoughts I refrained.

In the meantime Menexenus came back and sat down in his place by Lysis; and Lysis, in a childish and affectionate manner, whispered privately in my ear, so that Menexenus should not hear: Do, Socrates, tell Menexenus what you have been telling me.

Suppose that you tell him yourself, Lysis, I replied; for I am sure that you were attending.

Certainly, he replied.

Try, then, to remember the words, and be as exact as you can in repeating them to him, and if you have forgotten anything, ask me again the next time that you see me.

I will be sure to do so, Socrates; but do tell him something new, and let me listen till it is time to go home.

I certainly cannot refuse, I said, since you ask me; but then, as you know, Menexenus is very pugnacious, and therefore you must come to the rescue if he attempts to upset me.

Yes, indeed, he said; he is very pugnacious, and that is the reason why I want you to argue with him.

That I may make a fool of myself?

No, indeed, he said; but I want you to put him down.

That is no easy matter, I replied; for he is a terrible fellow – a pupil of Ctesippus. And there is Ctesippus himself: do you not see him?

Never mind, Socrates, please start arguing with him.

Well, I suppose that I must, I replied.

Hereupon Ctesippus complained that we were talking in secret, and keeping the feast to ourselves.

I shall be happy, I said, to let you have a share. Here is Lysis, who does not understand something that I was saying, and wants me to ask Menexenus, who, as he thinks, is likely to know.

And why do you not ask him? he said.

Very well, I said, I will; and do you, Menexenus, answer. But first I must tell you that I am one who from my childhood upward have set my heart upon a certain possession. All people have their fancies; some desire horses, and others dogs; and some are fond of gold, and others of honour. Now, I have no violent desire of any of these things; but I have a passion for friends; and I would rather have a good friend than the best cock or quail in the world: I would even go further, and say the best horse or dog. Yea, by the dog of Egypt, I should greatly prefer a real friend to all the gold of Darius, or even to Darius himself: I am such a lover of friends as that. And when I see you and Lysis, at your early age, so easily possessed of this treasure and so soon, he of you, and you of him, I am amazed and reckon you happy, seeing that I myself am so far from having made a similar acquisition that I do not even know in what way a friend is acquired. But this is just what I want to ask you about, for you have experience. Tell me then, when one loves another, is the lover or the beloved the friend; or may either be the friend?

Either may, I should think, be the friend of either.

Do you mean, I said, that when only one of them loves the other, they are mutual friends?

Yes, he said; that is my meaning.

But what if the lover is not loved in return – which is a very possible case?

Yes.

Or is, perhaps, even hated? For this does sometimes seem to happen to lovers in relation to their beloved. Nothing can exceed their love; and yet they imagine either that they are not loved in return, or even that they are hated. Is not that true?

Yes, he said, quite true.

In that case, the one loves, and the other is loved?

Yes.

Then which is the friend of which? Is the lover the friend of the beloved, whether he be loved in return, or hated; or is the beloved the friend; or is there no friendship at all on either side, unless they both love one another?

This is what I think is the case.

Then this notion is not in accordance with our previous one. We were saying that both were friends, if one only loved; but now, unless they both love, neither is a friend.

That appears to be so.

Then nothing which does not love in return is beloved by a lover?

I think not.

Then they are not lovers of horses, whom the horses do not love in return; nor lovers of quails, nor of dogs, nor of wine, nor of gymnastic exercises, who have no return of love; no, nor of wisdom, unless wisdom loves them in return. Or shall we say that they do love them, although they are not beloved by their friends; and that the poet was wrong who sings – 'Happy the man to whom his children are dear, and steeds having single hoofs, and dogs of chase, and the stranger of another land'?

I do not think that he is wrong.

You think that he was right?

Yes.

Then, Menexenus, the conclusion is, that what is beloved, whether loving or hating, may be dear to the lover of it: for example, very young children, too young to love, or even hating their father or mother when they are punished by them, are never dearer to them than at the time when they are hating them.

I think that what you say is true.

And, if so, not the lover, but the beloved, is the friend or dear one?

Yes.

And the hated one, and not the hater, is the enemy?

It seems so.

Then many men are loved by their enemies and hated by their friends, and are the friends of their enemies and the enemies of their friends, seeing that it is the beloved and not the lover who is the friend. Yet how absurd, my dear friend, or indeed impossible is this paradox of a man being an enemy to his friend or a friend to his enemy.

What you say, Socrates, does seem to be true.

But if this cannot be, the lover will be the friend of that which is loved?

So it appears.

And the hater will be the enemy of that which is hated?

Certainly.

Well then, we must reach the same conclusion and acknowledge in this as in the preceding instance, that a man may often be the friend of one who is not his friend or who may be his enemy, when he loves that which does not love him or which even hates him. And he may be the enemy of one who is not his enemy, and is even his friend: for example, when he hates that which does not hate him, or which even loves him.

That appears to be true.

But if the lover is not a friend, nor the beloved a friend, nor those who both love and are loved, what are we to say? Whom are we to call friends to one another? Are there any others?

Indeed, Socrates, I cannot think of any.

But, O Menexenus! I said, may we not have been altogether wrong in our line of search?

I am sure we have been wrong, Socrates, said Lysis. And he blushed as he spoke, the words seeming to come from his lips involuntarily, because his whole mind was taken up with the argument; there was no mistaking his attentive look while he was listening.

I was pleased at the interest which was shown by Lysis, and I wanted to give Menexenus a rest, so I turned to him and said, I think, Lysis, that what you say is true, and that, if we were right in our line of search, we should never be wandering as we are; let us proceed no further in this direction (for the road seems to be getting difficult), but take the other path into which we turned, and follow the poets' road; for they are to us in a manner our fathers and guides in wisdom, and in their account of the essence of friendship they make a very lofty claim; god himself, they say, creates friends and draws them to one another; and this they express, if I am not mistaken, in the following words: 'God is ever drawing like towards like, and so making them acquainted.' I dare say that you have heard the verse.

Yes, he said; I have.

And have you not also met with the writings of wise men who say just the same, that like must love like? they are the people who argue and write about nature and the universe.

Very true, he replied.

And are they right in saying this?

They may be.

Perhaps, I said, about half, or possibly altogether, right, if their meaning were correctly apprehended by us. For the more a bad man has to do with a bad man, and the more nearly he is brought into contact with him, the more he will be likely to be at enmity with him, for he injures him; and injurer and injured cannot be friends. Is not that true?

Yes, he said.

Then one half of the saying is untrue, if the wicked are like one another?

That is true.

But the real meaning of the saying, as I imagine, is, that the good are like one another, and friends to one another; and that the bad, as is often said of them, are never at unity with one another or with themselves; for they are passionate and restless, and anything which is at variance and enmity with itself can scarcely be like, and therefore friendly to, any other thing. Do you not agree?

Yes, I do.

Then, my friend, those who say that the like is friendly to the like mean to intimate, if I rightly apprehend them, that the good man only is the friend of the good, and of him only; but that the evil man never attains to any real friendship, either with a good man or an evil one. Do you agree?

He nodded assent.

Then now we know how to answer the question 'Who are friends?' for the argument declares that 'the good are friends'.

Yes, he said, I think so.

Yes, I replied; and yet I am not quite satisfied with this answer. For heaven's sake, let us face what I suspect. Assuming that like, inasmuch as he is like, is the friend of like, and useful to him – or rather let me try another way of putting the matter: can like do any good or harm to like which he could not do to himself, or suffer anything from his like which he would not suffer from himself? And if neither can be of any use to the other, how can they feel affection for one another? Can they now?

They cannot.

And can that be dear to you, for which you feel no affection?

Certainly not.

Then the like is not the friend of the like in so far as he is like; but perhaps the good may be the friend of the good in so far as he is good?

Perhaps.

But then again, will not the good, in so far as he is good, be sufficient for himself? Certainly he will. And he who is sufficient wants nothing – that is implied in the word sufficient.

Of course not.

And he who wants nothing will feel affection for nothing?

He will not.

Neither can he love that for which he has no affection?

He cannot.

And he who loves not is not a lover or friend?

Clearly not.

What place then is there for any friendship at all between good men, if, when absent, they do not feel the loss of one another (for even when alone they are sufficient for themselves), and when present have no use of one another? How can such persons ever value one another?

They cannot.

And friends they cannot be, unless they value one another?

Very true.

But see now, Lysis, where we are mistaken in all this – are we not on the wrong tack?

How so? he replied.

I have heard someone say, as I just now recollect, that the like is the greatest enemy of the like, the good of the good – yes, and he quoted the authority of Hesiod, who says: 'Potter quarrels with potter, bard with bard, beggar with beggar'; and of all other things he affirmed, in like manner, that 'of necessity the most like are most full of envy, strife, and hatred of one another, and the most unlike, of friendship. For the poor man is compelled to be the friend of the rich, and the weak requires the aid of the strong, and the sick man of the physician; and everyone who is ignorant feels affection for, and loves, him who knows.' And indeed he went on to say, even more impressively, that the idea of friendship existing between similars is not the truth, but the very reverse of the truth, and that the most opposed are the most friendly; for that everything desires not like but that which is most unlike: for example, the dry desires the moist, the cold the hot, the bitter the sweet, the sharp the blunt, the void the full, the full the void, and so of all other things; for the opposite is the food of the opposite, whereas like gets no profit from like. And I thought that he who said this was a clever man, and that he spoke well. What do the rest of you say?

I should say, at first hearing, that he is right, said Menexenus.

Then we are to say that the greatest friendship is of opposites?

Exactly.

Well, Menexenus, will not that be a monstrous answer? And will not those omniscient lovers of disputation be down upon us in triumph, and ask whether friendship is not the very opposite of enmity; and what answer shall we make to them – must we not admit that they speak the truth?

We must.

Is then the enemy (they will proceed) the friend of the friend, or the friend the friend of the enemy?

Neither, he replied.

Again, is a just man the friend of the unjust, or the temperate of the intemperate, or the good of the bad?

I do not see how that is possible.

And yet, I said, if friendship goes by contraries, these contraries must be friends.

They must.

Then neither like and like nor unlike and unlike are friends.

I suppose not.

Let us ask a further question: may not all these notions of friendship be erroneous? But may not that which is neither good nor evil still in some cases be the friend of the good?

How do you mean? he said.

83

Why really, I said, the truth is that I do not know; but my head is dizzy with the puzzles of the argument, and therefore I hazard the conjecture, that 'the beautiful is the friend', as the old proverb says. Beauty is certainly a soft, smooth, slippery thing, and therefore of a nature which easily slips through our hands and escapes us. Well, I affirm that the good is beautiful. You will agree to that?

Yes.

I say then, as a kind of inspiration, that what is neither good nor evil is the friend of the beautiful and the good, and I will tell you how I get this inspiration: I assume that there are three categories – the good, the bad, and that which is neither good nor bad. You would agree – would you not?

I agree.

And neither is the good the friend of the good, nor the evil of the evil, nor the good of the evil – these alternatives are excluded by the previous argument; and therefore, if there be such a thing as friendship or love at all, we must infer that what is neither good nor evil must be the friend, either of the good, or of that which is neither good nor evil, for nothing can be the friend of the bad.

True.

But neither can like be the friend of like, as we were just now saying.

True.

And if so, that which is neither good nor evil can have no friend which is neither good nor evil.

It seems not.

It follows that only that which is neither good nor evil is the friend of the good, and of the good alone.

That may be assumed to be certain.

And does not this seem to lead us in the right way? Just remark, that the body which is in health requires neither medical nor any other aid, but has what it needs; and the healthy man has no love of the physician, because he is in health.

He has none.

But the sick loves him, because he is sick?

Certainly.

And sickness is an evil, and the art of medicine a good and useful thing?

Yes.

But the human body, regarded as a body, is neither good nor evil?

True.

And the body is compelled by reason of disease to court and make friends with the art of medicine?

Yes.

Then that which is neither good nor evil becomes the friend of good, by reason of the presence of evil?

So we may infer.

And clearly this must have happened before it had become evil through the evil in it. When once it had become evil, it could no longer desire and love the good; for, as we were saying, evil cannot be the friend of good.

Impossible.

Further, I must observe that some substances are assimilated to others when these others are present with them; and there are some which are not assimilated; take, for example, the case of a colour which is put on another substance; the colour is then present with it.

Very good.

At such a time, is the thing itself which is painted, really of the same colour as the paint which is on it?

What do you mean? he said.

This is what I mean: suppose that I were to cover your auburn locks with white lead, would they be really white, or would they only appear to be white?

They would only appear to be white, he replied.

And yet whiteness would be present in them?

True.

But that would not make them at all the more white; notwithstanding the presence of white in them, they would not be white any more than black?

No.

But when old age infuses whiteness into them, then they become assimilated, and are white by the presence of white.

Certainly.

Now I want to know whether in all cases a substance is assimilated by the presence of another substance; or must the presence be after a peculiar sort?

The latter, he said.

Then that which is neither good nor evil may be in the presence of evil, but not as yet evil, or it may already have become evil?

Yes.

And when anything is in the presence of evil, not being as yet evil, the presence of evil in this sense arouses the desire of good in that thing; but the presence which actually makes a thing evil, takes away the desire and friendship of the good; for that which was once neither good nor evil has now become evil, and the good was supposed to have no friendship with the evil?

None.

And therefore we say that those who are already wise, whether gods or men, are no longer lovers of wisdom; nor can they be lovers of wisdom who are ignorant to the extent of being evil, for no evil or ignorant person is a lover of wisdom. There remain those who suffer from the evil of ignorance, but are not yet hardened in their ignorance or void of understanding, and are still aware that they do not know what they do not know: and therefore those who are as yet neither good nor bad are the lovers of wisdom. But the bad do not love wisdom any more than the good; for, as we have already seen, neither is unlike the friend of unlike, nor like of like. You remember that?

Yes, they both said.

And so, Lysis and Menexenus, we have discovered the nature of friendship – there can be no doubt of it: friendship is the love which the neither good nor evil, when it is in the presence of evil, has for that which is good, either in soul, in body, or in any other way.

They both agreed and entirely assented, and for a moment I rejoiced and was satisfied like a huntsman just holding fast his prey. But then a most unaccountable suspicion came across me, and I felt that the conclusion was untrue. I was pained, and said, Alas! Lysis and Menexenus, I am afraid that we have been grasping at a shadow only.

Why do you say so? said Menexenus.

I am afraid, I said, that our arguments about friendship have, like some men, proved impostors.

How do you mean? he asked.

Well, I said; look at the matter in this way: a friend is the friend of someone, is he not?

Certainly he is.

And has he a motive and object in being a friend, or has he no motive and object?

He has a motive and object.

And is the object which makes him a friend, dear to him, or neither dear nor hateful to him?

I do not quite follow you, he said.

I do not wonder at that, I said. But perhaps, if I put the matter in another way, you will be able to follow me, and my own meaning will be clearer to myself. The sick man, as I was just now saying, is the friend of the physician – is he not?

Yes.

And he is the friend of the physician because of disease, and for the sake of health?

Yes.

And disease is an evil?

Certainly.

And what of health? I said. Is that good or evil, or neither?

Good, he replied.

And we were saying, I believe, that the body being neither good nor evil, because of disease, that is to say because of evil, is the friend of medicine, and medicine is a good: and medicine has entered into this friendship for the sake of health, and health is a good.

True.

And is health a friend, or not a friend?

A friend.

And disease is an enemy?

Yes.

Then that which is neither good nor evil is the friend of the good because of the evil and hateful, and for the sake of the good and the friend?

So it seems.

Then it is for the sake of the friend, and because of the enemy, that the friend is a friend of the friend?

That is to be inferred.

Very well, said I, then at this point, my boys, let us take heed, and be on our guard against deceptions. I will pass over the difficulty that the friend is the friend of the friend, and therefore the like of the like, which has been declared by us to be an impossibility; but in order that this new statement may not delude us, let us attentively examine another point: medicine, as we were saying, is a friend, or dear to us, for the sake of health?

Yes.

And health is also dear?

Certainly.

And if dear, then dear for the sake of something?

Yes.

And surely this object must also be dear, as is implied in our previous admissions?

Yes.

And that something dear involves something else dear?

Yes.

But then, must we not either continue in this way till our strength fails, or arrive at some first principle of friendship or dearness which is not capable of being referred to any other, for the sake of which, as we maintain, all other things are dear.

We must.

My fear is that all those other things, which, as we say, are dear for the sake of another, are illusions and deceptions only, but where that first principle is, there is the true ideal of friendship. Let me put the matter thus: suppose the case of a great treasure (this may be a son, who is more precious to his father than all his other treasures); would not the father, who values his son above all things, value other things also for the sake of his son? I mean, for instance, if he knew that his son had drunk hemlock, and the father thought that wine would save him, he would value the wine?

Of course.

And also the vessel which contains the wine?

Certainly.

But does he therefore value the three measures of wine, or the earthen vessel which contains them, equally with his son? Is not this rather the true state of the case? All his anxiety has regard not to the means which are provided for the sake of an object, but to the object for the sake of which they are provided. And although we may often say that gold and silver are highly valued by us, that is not the truth; for there is a further object, whatever it may be, which we value most of all, and for the sake of which gold and all our other possessions are acquired by us. Am I not right?

Yes, certainly.

And may not the same be said of the friend? That which is only dear to us for the sake of something else is improperly said to be dear, but the truly dear is that in which all these so-called dear friendships terminate.

That, he said, appears to be true.

Then that which is truly dear is not dear for the sake of something else which is dear.

True.

Then we have done with the notion that that which is dear, is so on account of something else which is dear. Now, may we take it that the good is dear?

I think so.

Well then, is the good loved because of the evil? Let me put the case in this way: suppose that of the three categories, good, evil, and that which is neither good nor evil, there remained only the good and the neutral, and that evil were banished far away, and in no way affected soul or body, nor ever at all that class of things which, as we say, are neither good nor evil in themselves – would the good be of any use, or other than useless to us? For if there were nothing to hurt us any longer, we should have no need of anything that would do us good. Then it would be clearly seen that we did but love and desire the good because of the evil, and as the remedy of the evil, which was the disease; but if there is no disease, there is no need of a remedy. Is it true that of its nature the good is loved because of the evil by us who are placed between the two, and that there is no use in the good for its own sake?

It does look like this.

Then that final principle of friendship in which all other friendships terminated, those, I mean, which are relatively dear and for the sake of something else, is of another and a different nature from them. For they are called dear because of another dear or friend. But with the true friend or dear, the case is quite the reverse; for that is proved to be dear because of the hated, and if the hated were away it would be no longer dear.

Very true, he replied: at any rate not if our present view holds good.

But, oh! will you tell me, I said, whether if evil were to perish, we should hunger any more, or thirst any more, or have any similar desire? Or may we suppose that hunger will remain while men and animals remain, but not so as to be hurtful? And the same of thirst and the other desires – that they will remain, but will not be evil because evil has perished? Or rather shall I say, that to ask what either will be then or will not be is ridiculous, for who knows? This we do know, that in our present condition hunger may injure us, and may also benefit us – is not that true?

Yes.

And in like manner thirst or any similar desire may sometimes be an advantage and sometimes a disadvantage to us, and sometimes neither one nor the other?

To be sure.

But is there any reason why, because evil perishes, that which is not evil should perish with it?

None.

Then, even if evil perishes, the desires which are neither good nor evil will remain?

So it seems.

And must not a man love that which he desires and longs for?

He must.

Then, even if evil perishes, there may still remain some things which are dear?

Yes.

But not if evil is the cause of friendship: for in that case nothing will be the friend of any other thing after the destruction of evil; for the effect cannot remain when the cause is destroyed.

True.

And have we not admitted already that the friend loves something, and that for a reason? And at the time of making the admission we were of opinion that the neither good nor evil loves the good because of the evil?

Very true.

But now our view is changed, and we conceive that there must be some other cause of friendship?

I suppose so.

May not the truth be rather, as we were saying just now, that desire is the cause of friendship; for that which desires is dear to that which is desired at the time of desiring it? And may not the other theory have been only a long story about nothing?

Likely enough.

But surely, I said, he who desires, desires that of which he is in want?

Yes.

And that of which he is in want is dear to him?

True.

And he is in want of that of which he is deprived?

Certainly.

Then love and desire and friendship would appear to be of the natural or congenial. Such, Lysis and Menexenus, is the inference.

They assented.

Then if you are friends, you must have natures which are congenial to one another?

Certainly, they both said.

And I say, my boys, that no one who loves or desires another would ever have loved or desired or longed for him if he had not been in some way congenial to him, either in his soul, or in his character, or in his manners, or in his form.

Yes, yes, said Menexenus. But Lysis was silent.

Then, I said, the conclusion is, that what is of a congenial nature must be loved.

It follows, he said.

Then the lover, who is true and no counterfeit, must of necessity be loved by his love.

Lysis and Menexenus gave a reluctant assent to this; and Hippothales changed into all manner of colours with delight.

Here, intending to review the argument, I said: Can we point out any difference between the congenial and the like? For if that is possible, then I think, Lysis and Menexenus, there may be some sense in our argument about friendship. But if the congenial is only the like, how will you get rid of the other argument, of the uselessness of like to like in as far as they are like? (for to allow that what is useless is dear, would be absurd). Suppose, then, that we agree to distinguish between the congenial and the like – in the intoxication of argument, that may perhaps be allowed.

Very true.

And shall we further say that the good is congenial, and the evil uncongenial to everyone? Or again that the evil is congenial to the evil, and the good to the good; and that which is neither good nor evil to that which is neither good nor evil?

They agreed to the latter alternative.

Then, my boys, we have again fallen into the old discarded error; for the unjust will be the friend of the unjust, and the bad of the bad, just as much as the good of the good.

That appears to be the result.

But again, if we say that the congenial is the same as the good, in that case the good and he only will be the friend of the good.

True.

But that too was a position of ours which, as you will remember, has been already refuted by ourselves.

We remember.

Then what is to be done? Or rather is there anything to be done? I can only, like the wise men who argue in courts, sum up the arguments – if neither the beloved, nor the lover, nor the like, nor the unlike, nor the good,

nor the congenial, nor any other of whom we spoke –
for there were such a number of them that I cannot
remember all – if none of these are friends, I know not
what remains to be said.

Here I was going to invite the opinion of some older
person, when suddenly we were interrupted by the
bodyguards of Lysis and Menexenus, who came upon
us, like tutelary genii, bringing with them the boys'
brothers, and bade them go home, as it was getting
late. At first, we and the bystanders tried to drive them
off; but afterwards, as they would not mind, and only
went on shouting in their foreigners' Greek, and got
angry, and kept calling the boys – they appeared to us
to have been drinking rather too much at the
Hermaea, which made them difficult to manage – we
fairly gave way and broke up the company.

I said, however, a few words to the boys at parting:
O Menexenus and Lysis, how ridiculous that you two
boys, and I, an old man, who venture to range myself
with you, should imagine ourselves to be friends – this
is what the bystanders will go away and say – and as yet
we have not been able to discover what is a friend!

PLATO
LACHES

LACHES

or Courage

Persons of the dialogue
LYSIMACHUS, *son of Aristides*
NICIAS
MELESIAS, *son of Thucydides*
LACHES
Their Sons
SOCRATES

LYSIMACHUS: You have seen the exhibition of the man fighting in armour, Nicias and Laches, but we did not tell you at the time the reason why my friend Melesias and I asked you to go with us and see him. I think that we may as well confess what this was, for we certainly ought not to have any reserve with you. Some laugh at the very notion of consulting others, and when they are asked will not say what they think. They guess at the wishes of the person who asks them, and answer according to his, and not according to their own, opinion. But as we know that you are good judges, and will say exactly what you think, we have taken you into our counsels. The matter about which I am making all this preface is as follows: Melesias and I have each a son; that is his son, and he is named Thucydides, after his grandfather; and this is mine, who is also called after his grandfather, my father, Aristides. Now, we are resolved to take the greatest care of the youths, and not, like most fathers, to let them do as they please when they are no longer children, but we mean to begin at once and do the utmost that we can for them. And knowing you to have sons of your own, we thought that you of all men were most likely to have attended to their training and improvement, and, if perchance you have seldom given any thought to the subject, we may remind you that you ought to have done so, and would invite you to assist us in the fulfilment of a common duty. I will tell you, Nicias and Laches, even at the risk of being tedious, how we came to think of this. Melesias and I live together, and our sons live with us; and now, as I was saying at first, we are going to be open with you. Both of us often talk to the lads about the many noble deeds which our own fathers did in war and peace – in managing the affairs of the allies, and those of the city; but neither of us has any deeds of his own which he can show. The truth is that we are ashamed of this contrast being seen by them, and we blame our fathers for letting us be spoiled in the days of our youth, while they were occupied with the concerns of others; and we urge all this upon the lads, pointing out to them that they will not grow up to honour if they are rebellious and take no pains about themselves; but that if they take pains they may, perhaps, become worthy of the names which they bear. They, on their part, promise to comply with our wishes; and our care is to discover what studies or pursuits are likely to be most improving to them. Someone commended to us the art of fighting in armour, which he thought an excellent accomplishment for a young man to learn; and he praised the man whose exhibition you have seen, and told us to go and see him. And we determined that we would go, and get you to accompany us to see the sight; intending at the same time to ask you to advise us, and, if you wish, to share in our project for the education of our sons. That is the matter which we wanted to talk over with you; and we hope that you will give us your opinion about this art of fighting in armour, and about any other studies or pursuits which you would or would not recommend for a young man, and will tell us whether you would like to join in our proposal.

NICIAS: As far as I am concerned, Lysimachus and Melesias, I applaud your purpose, and will gladly join with you; and I believe that you, Laches, will be equally glad.

LACHES: Certainly, Nicias; and I quite approve of the remark which Lysimachus made about his own father and the father of Melesias, and which is applicable, not only to them, but to us, and to everyone who is occupied with public affairs. As he says, such persons are too apt to be negligent and careless of their own children and their private concerns. There is much truth in that remark of yours, Lysimachus. But why, besides consulting us, do you not consult our friend Socrates about the education of the youths? He is of the same deme with you, and is always passing his time in places where the youth have any noble study or pursuit, such as you are inquiring after.

LYSIMACHUS: Why, Laches, has Socrates ever attended to matters of this sort?

LACHES: Certainly, Lysimachus.

NICIAS: That I have the means of knowing as well as Laches; for quite lately he supplied me with a teacher of music for my son – Damon, the pupil of Agathocles, who is a most accomplished man in every way, as well as a musician, and a companion of inestimable value for young men at their age.

LYSIMACHUS: Those who have reached my time of life, Socrates and Nicias and Laches, fall out of acquaintance with the young, because they are generally detained at home by old age; but you, O son of Sophroniscus, should let your fellow demesman have the benefit of any advice which you are able to give. Moreover, I have a claim upon you as an old friend of your father; for I and he were always companions and friends, and to the hour of his death there never was a difference between us; and now it comes back to me, at the mention of your name, that I have heard these lads talking to one another at home, and often speaking of Socrates in terms of the highest praise; but I have never thought to ask them whether the son of Sophroniscus was the person whom they meant. Tell me, my boys, whether this is the Socrates of whom you have often spoken?

SON: Certainly, father, this is he.

LYSIMACHUS: I am delighted to hear, Socrates, that you maintain the name of your father, who was a most excellent man; and I further rejoice at the prospect of our family ties being renewed.

LACHES: Indeed, Lysimachus, you ought not to give him up; for I can assure you that I have seen him maintaining, not only his father's, but also his country's name. He was my companion in the retreat from Delium, and I can tell you that if others had only been like him, the honour of our country would have been upheld, and the great defeat would never have occurred.

LYSIMACHUS: That praise is truly honourable to you, Socrates, given as it is by witnesses entitled to all credit and for such qualities as those which they ascribe to you. Let me tell you the pleasure which I feel in hearing of your fame; and I hope that you will regard me as one of your warmest friends. You ought to have visited us long ago, and made yourself at home with us; but now, from this day forward, as we have at last found one another out, do as I say – come and make acquaintance with me, and with these young men, that you and yours may continue as my friends. I shall expect you to do so, and shall venture at some future time to remind you of your duty. But what say you all of the matter of which we were beginning to speak – the art of fighting in armour? Is that a practice in which the lads may be advantageously instructed?

SOCRATES: I will endeavour to advise you, Lysimachus, as far as I can in this matter, and also in every way will comply with your wishes; but as I am younger and not so experienced, I think that I ought certainly to hear first what my elders have to say, and to learn of them, and if I have anything to add, then I may venture to give my opinion and advice to them as well as to you. Suppose, Nicias, that one or other of you begin.

NICIAS: I have no objection, Socrates; and my opinion is that the acquirement of this art is in many ways useful to young men. It is an advantage to them that instead of the favourite amusements of their leisure hours they should have one which tends to improve their bodily health. No gymnastics could be better or harder exercise; and this, and the art of riding, are of all arts most befitting to a freeman; for they who are thus exercised in the use of arms are the only persons being trained for the contest in which we are engaged, and in the accomplishments which it requires. Moreover in actual battle, when you have to fight in a line with a number of others, such an acquirement will be of some use, and will be of the greatest service whenever the ranks are broken and you have to fight singly, either in pursuit, when you are attacking someone who is defending himself, or in flight, when you have to defend yourself against an assailant. Certainly he who possessed the art could not meet with any harm at the hands of a single person, or perhaps of several; and in every case he would have a great advantage. Further, this sort of skill inclines a man to the love of other noble lessons; for every man who has learned how to fight in armour will desire to learn the proper arrangement of an army, which is the sequel of the lesson: and when he has learned this, and his ambition is once fired, he will go on to learn the complete art of the general. There is no difficulty in seeing that the knowledge and practice of other military arts will be honourable and valuable to a man; and this lesson may be the beginning of them. Let me add a further advantage, which is by no means a slight one – that this science will make any man a great deal more daring and resolute in the field. And I will not disdain to mention, what by some may be thought to be a small matter – he will have a more impressive appearance at the right time; that is to say, at the time when his appearance will strike terror into his enemies. My opinion then, Lysimachus, is, as I say, that the youths should be instructed in this art, and for the reasons which I have given. But Laches may take a different view; and I shall be very glad to hear what he has to say.

LACHES: I should not like to maintain, Nicias, that any kind of knowledge is not to be learned; for all knowledge appears to be a good: and if, as the teachers of the art affirm, this use of arms is really a species of knowledge, and if it is such as Nicias describes, then it ought to be learned; but if not, and if those who profess to teach it are deceivers only, or if it be knowledge, but not of a valuable sort, then what is the use of learning

it? I say this, because I think that if it had been really
valuable, the Lacedaemonians, whose whole life is
passed in finding out and practising the arts which give
them an advantage over other nations in war, would
have discovered this one. And even if they have not,
still these professors of the art cannot have failed to
discover that of all the Hellenes the Lacedaemonians
have the greatest interest in such matters, and that a
master of the art who was honoured among them
would be sure to make his fortune among other
nations, just as a tragic poet would who is honoured
among ourselves; which is the reason why he who
fancies that he can write a tragedy does not go about
exhibiting in the states outside Attica, but rushes
hither straight, and exhibits at Athens; and this is
natural. Whereas I perceive that these fighters in
armour regard Lacedaemon as a sacred inviolable
territory, which they do not touch with the point of
their foot; but they make a circuit of the neighbouring
states, and would rather exhibit to any others than to
the Spartans; and particularly to those who would
themselves acknowledge that they are by no means
first-rate in the arts of war. Further, Lysimachus, I
have encountered a good many of these gentlemen in
actual service, and have taken their measure, which I
can give you at once; for none of these masters of fence
have ever been distinguished in war – there has been a
sort of fatality about them: while in all other arts the
men of note have been always those who have practised the art, these appear to be a most unfortunate
exception. For example, this very Stesilaus, whom you
and I have just witnessed exhibiting in all that crowd
and making such great professions of his powers, I had
a better opportunity of seeing at another time making

in actual battle a real exhibition of himself involuntarily. He was a marine on board a ship which charged a transport vessel, and was armed with a weapon, half spear, half scythe; the weapon was as singular as its owner. To make a long story short, I will only tell you what happened to this notable invention of the scythe-spear. He was fighting, and the scythe was caught in the rigging of the other ship, and stuck fast; and he tugged, but was unable to get his weapon free. The two ships were passing one another. He first ran along his own ship holding on to the spear; but as the other ship passed by and drew him after as he was holding on to the spear, he let it slip through his hand until he retained only the end of the handle. The people in the transport clapped their hands, and laughed at his ridiculous figure; and when someone threw a stone, which fell on the deck at his feet, and he quitted his hold of the scythe-spear, the crew of his own trireme also burst out laughing; they could not refrain when they beheld the weapon waving in the air, suspended from the transport. Now I do not deny that there may be something in such an art, as Nicias asserts, but I tell you my experience; and, as I said at first, whether this be an art of which the advantage is so slight, or not an art at all but only an imposition, in either case such an acquirement is not worth having. For my opinion is that if the professor of this art be a coward, he will be likely to become rash, and his character will be only more clearly revealed; or if he be brave, and fail ever so little, other men will be on the watch, and he will be greatly traduced; for there is a jealousy of such pre-tenders; and unless a man be pre-eminent in valour, he cannot help being ridiculous, if he says that he has this sort of skill. Such is my judgment, Lysimachus, on the study of this art; but, as I said at first, ask Socrates, and do not let him go until he has given you his opinion of the matter.

LYSIMACHUS: I am going to ask this favour of you, Socrates; as is the more necessary because the two counsellors disagree, and someone is in a manner still needed who will decide between them. Had they agreed, no arbiter would have been required. But as Laches has voted one way and Nicias another, I should like to hear with which of our two friends you agree.

SOCRATES: What, Lysimachus, are you going to accept the opinion of the majority?

LYSIMACHUS: Why, yes, Socrates; what else am I to do?

SOCRATES: And would you do so too, Melesias? If you were deliberating about the gymnastic training of your son, would you follow the advice of the majority of us, or the opinion of the one who had been trained and exercised under a skilful master?

MELESIAS: The latter, Socrates; as would surely be reasonable.

SOCRATES: His one vote would be worth more than the vote of all us four?

MELESIAS: Presumably.

SOCRATES: And for this reason, as I imagine – because a good decision is based on knowledge and not on numbers?

MELESIAS: To be sure.

SOCRATES: Now too, then, must we not first of all ask whether there is any one of us who is an expert in that about which we are deliberating? If there is, let us take his advice, though he be one only, and not mind the rest; if there is not, let us seek further counsel. Is this a trifle which you and Lysimachus have at stake? Are you not risking the greatest of your possessions? For children are your riches; and upon their turning out well or ill depends the whole order of their father's house.

MELESIAS: That is true.

SOCRATES: Great care, then, is required in this matter?

MELESIAS: Certainly.

SOCRATES: Suppose, as I was just now saying, that we were considering, or wanting to consider, which of us had the best knowledge of gymnastics. Should we not select him who had learnt and practised the art, and had good teachers?

MELESIAS: I think that we should.

SOCRATES: But would there not arise a prior question about the nature of the art of which we want to find the teachers?

MELESIAS: I do not understand.

SOCRATES: Let me try to make my meaning plainer then. I do not think that we have as yet decided what that is about which we are consulting, when we ask which of us is or is not skilled in the art, and has or has not had teachers of the art.

NICIAS: Why, Socrates, is not the question whether young men ought or ought not to learn the art of fighting in armour?

SOCRATES: Yes, Nicias; but there is also a prior question, which I may illustrate in this way: when a person considers about applying a medicine to the eyes, would you say that he is consulting about the medicine or about the eyes?

NICIAS: About the eyes.

SOCRATES: And when he considers whether he shall set a bridle on a horse and at what time, he is thinking of the horse and not of the bridle?

NICIAS: True.

SOCRATES: And in a word, when he considers anything for the sake of another thing, he thinks of the end and not of the means?

NICIAS: Certainly.

SOCRATES: And when you call in an adviser, you should see whether he too is skilful in the accomplishment of the end which you have in view?

NICIAS: Most true.

SOCRATES: And at present we have in view some knowledge, of which the end is the soul of youth?

NICIAS: Yes.

SOCRATES: And we must inquire whether any of us is skilful or successful in the treatment of the soul, and which of us has had good teachers?

LACHES: Well but, Socrates; did you never observe that some persons who have had no teachers are more skilful than those who have, in some things?

SOCRATES: Yes, Laches, I have observed that; but you would not be very willing to trust them if they professed to be masters of their art, unless they could show some proof of their skill or excellence in one or more works.

LACHES: That is true.

SOCRATES: And therefore, Laches and Nicias, as Lysimachus and Melesias, in their anxiety to improve the minds of their sons, have asked our advice about them, we likewise should tell them, if we can, what teachers we know of who were in the first place men of merit and experienced trainers of the minds of youth, and then taught also ourselves. Or if any of us says that he has had no teacher but that he has works of his own to show, then he should point out to them what Athenians or strangers, bond or free, he is generally acknowledged to have improved. But if we can show neither teachers nor works, then we should tell them to look out for other advisers; we should not run the risk of spoiling the children of friends, and thereby incurring the most formidable accusation which can be brought against anyone by those nearest to him. As for myself, Lysimachus and Melesias, I am the first to confess that I have never had a teacher of the art of virtue; although I have always from my earliest youth desired to have one. But I am too poor to give money to the sophists, who are the only professors of moral improvement; and to this day I have never been able to discover the art myself, though I should not be surprised if Nicias or Laches has discovered or learned it; for they are far wealthier than I am, and may therefore have learnt of others, and they are older too, so that they have had more time to make the discovery. And I really believe that they are able to educate a man; for unless they had been confident in their own knowledge, they would never have spoken thus unhesitatingly of the pursuits which are advantageous or hurtful to a young man. I repose confidence in both of them; but I am surprised to find that they differ from one another. And therefore, Lysimachus, as Laches suggested that you should detain me, and not let me go until I answered, I in turn earnestly beseech and advise you to detain Laches and Nicias, and question them. I would have you say to them: Socrates avers that he has no knowledge of the matter – he is unable to decide which of you speaks truly; neither discoverer nor student is he of anything of the kind. But you, Laches and Nicias, should each of you tell us who is the most skilful educator whom you have ever known; and whether you invented the art yourselves, or learned of another; and if you learned, who were your respective teachers, and who were their brothers in the art; and then, if you are too much occupied in politics to teach us yourselves, let us go to them, and present them with gifts, or make interest with them, or both, in the hope that they may be induced to take charge of our children and of yours; and then they will not grow up to be worthless, and disgrace their ancestors. But if you are yourselves original discoverers in that field, give us some proof of your skill. Who are they who, having been worthless persons, have become under your care good and noble? For if this is your first attempt at education, there is a danger that you may be trying the experiment, not on the *vile corpus* of a Carian slave, but on your own sons or the sons of your friends, and, as the proverb says, 'break the large vessel in learning to make pots'. Tell us then, what qualifications you claim or do not claim. Make them tell you that, Lysimachus, and do not let them off.

LYSIMACHUS: I very much approve of the words of Socrates, my friends; but you, Nicias and Laches, must determine whether you will be questioned, and give an explanation about matters of this sort. Assuredly, I and Melesias would be greatly pleased to hear you answer the questions which Socrates asks, if you will: for I began by saying that we took you into our counsels because we thought that no doubt you had attended to the subject, especially as you have children who, like our own, are nearly of an age to be educated. Well then, if you have no objection, suppose that you take Socrates into partnership; and do you and he ask and answer one another's questions: for, as he has well said, we are deliberating about the most important of our concerns. I hope that you will see fit to comply with our request.

NICIAS: I see very clearly, Lysimachus, that you have only known Socrates' father, and have no acquaintance with Socrates himself: at least, you can only have known him when he was a child, and may have met him among his fellow demesmen, in company with his father, at a sacrifice or at some other gathering. You clearly show that you have never known him since he arrived at manhood.

LYSIMACHUS: Why do you say that, Nicias?

NICIAS: Because you seem not to be aware that anyone who is close to Socrates and enters into conversation with him is liable to be drawn into an argument; and whatever subject he may start, he will be continually carried round and round by him, until at last he finds that he has to give an account both of his present and past life; and when he is once entangled, Socrates will not let him go until he has completely and thoroughly sifted him. Now I am used to his ways; and I know that he will certainly do as I say, and also that I myself shall be the sufferer; for I am fond of his conversation, Lysimachus. And I think that there is no harm in being reminded of any wrong thing which we are, or have been, doing: he who does not fly from reproof will be sure to take more heed of his after-life; as Solon says, he will wish and desire to be learning so long as he lives, and will not think that old age of itself brings wisdom. To me, to be cross-examined by Socrates is neither unusual nor unpleasant; indeed, I was fairly certain all along that where Socrates was, the subject of discussion would soon be ourselves, not our sons; and therefore, I say for my part, I am quite willing to discourse with Socrates in his own manner; but you had better ask our friend Laches what his feeling may be.

LACHES: I have but one feeling, Nicias, or (shall I say?)

two feelings, about discussions. Some would think
that I am a lover, and to others I may seem to be a hater
of discourse; for when I hear a man discoursing of
virtue, or of any sort of wisdom, who is a true man and
worthy of his theme, I am delighted beyond measure:
and I compare the man and his words, and note the
harmony and correspondence of them. And such a
one I deem to be the true musician, attuned to a fairer
harmony than that of the lyre, or any pleasant instrument of music; for he truly has in his own life a
harmony of words and deeds arranged, not in the
Ionian, or in the Phrygian mode, nor yet in the Lydian,
but in the true Hellenic mode, which is the Dorian,
and no other. Such a one makes me merry with the
sound of his voice, and when I hear him I am thought
to be a lover of discourse; so eager am I in drinking in
his words. But a man whose actions do not agree with
his words is an annoyance to me; and the better he
speaks the more I hate him, and then I seem to be a
hater of discourse. As to Socrates, I have no knowledge of his words, but of old, as appears, I have had
experience of his deeds; and his deeds show that he is
entitled to noble sentiments and complete freedom of
speech. And if his words accord, then I am of one
mind with him, and shall be delighted to be interro-
gated by a man such as he is, and shall not be annoyed
at having to learn of him: for I too agree with Solon,
'that I would fain grow old, learning many things'. But
I must be allowed to add 'from the good only'.
Socrates must be willing to allow that the teacher
himself is a good man, or I shall be a dull and reluctant
pupil: but that the teacher is rather young, or not as yet
in repute – anything of that sort is of no account with
me. And therefore, Socrates, I invite you to teach and

confute me as much as ever you like, and also learn of me anything which I know. So high is the opinion which I have entertained of you ever since the day on which you were my companion in danger, and gave a proof of your valour such as only the man of merit can give. Therefore, say whatever you like, and do not mind about the difference of our ages.

SOCRATES: I cannot say that either of you show any reluctance to take counsel and advise with me.

LYSIMACHUS: But this is our proper business; and yours as well as ours, for I reckon you as one of us. Please then to take my place, and find out from Nicias and Laches what we want to know, for the sake of the youths, and talk and consult with them: for I am old, and my memory is bad; and I do not remember the questions which I intend to ask, or the answers to them; and if there is any digression I lose the thread. I will therefore beg of you to carry on the proposed discussion by yourselves; and I will listen, and Melesias and I will act upon your conclusions.

SOCRATES: Let us, Nicias and Laches, comply with the request of Lysimachus and Melesias. There will be no harm in asking ourselves the question which was proposed to us just now: 'Who have been our own instructors in this sort of training, or whom have we ourselves made better?' But another mode of carrying on the inquiry will bring us equally to the same point, and perhaps starts nearer to first principles. For if we know that the addition of something would improve some other thing, and are able to make the addition, then, clearly, we must know how that about which we are advising may be best and most easily attained. Perhaps you do not understand what I mean. Then let me make my meaning plainer in this way. Suppose we know that the addition of sight makes better the eyes which possess this gift, and also are able to impart sight to the eyes, then, clearly, we know the nature of sight, and should be able to advise how this gift of sight may be best and most easily attained; but if we knew neither what sight is, nor what hearing is, we should not be very good medical advisers about the eyes or the ears, or about the best mode of giving sight and hearing to them.

LACHES: That is true, Socrates.

SOCRATES: And are not our two friends, Laches, at this very moment inviting us to consider in what way the gift of virtue may be imparted to their sons for the improvement of their minds?

LACHES: Very true.

SOCRATES: Then must we not first know the nature of virtue? For how can we advise anyone about the best mode of attaining something of whose nature we are wholly ignorant?

LACHES: I do not think that we can, Socrates.

SOCRATES: We say then, Laches, that we know the nature of virtue.

LACHES: Yes.

SOCRATES: And that which we know we must surely be able to tell?

LACHES: Certainly.

SOCRATES: I would not have us begin, my friend, with inquiring about the whole of virtue, for that may be more than we can accomplish; let us first consider whether we have a sufficient knowledge of a part; the inquiry will thus probably be made easier to us.

LACHES: Let us do as you wish, Socrates.

SOCRATES: Then which of the parts of virtue shall we select? Must we not select that to which the art of fighting in armour is supposed to conduce? And is not that generally thought to be courage?

LACHES: Yes, certainly.

SOCRATES: Then, Laches, suppose that we first set about determining the nature of courage, and in the second place proceed to inquire how the young men may attain this quality by the help of studies and pursuits. Tell me, if you can, what is courage.

LACHES: Indeed, Socrates, I see no difficulty in answering; he is a man of courage who does not run away, but remains at his post and fights against the enemy; there can be no mistake about that.

SOCRATES: Very good, Laches; and yet I fear that I did not express myself clearly; and therefore you have answered not the question which I intended to ask, but another.

LACHES: What do you mean, Socrates?

SOCRATES: I will endeavour to explain; you would call a man courageous who remains at his post, and fights with the enemy?

LACHES: Certainly I should.

SOCRATES: And so should I; but what would you say of another man, who fights flying, instead of remaining?

LACHES: How flying?

SOCRATES: Why, as the Scythians are said to fight, flying as well as pursuing; and as Homer says in praise of the horses of Aeneas, that they knew 'how to pursue, and fly quickly hither and thither'; and he passes an encomium on Aeneas himself, as having a knowledge of fear or flight, and calls him 'a deviser of fear or flight'.

LACHES: Yes, Socrates, and there Homer is right: for he was speaking of chariots, as you were speaking of the Scythian cavalry; now cavalry have that way of fighting, but the heavy-armed soldier fights, as I say, remaining in his rank.

SOCRATES: And yet, Laches, you must except the Lacedaemonians at Plataea, who, when they came upon the light shields of the Persians, are said not to have been willing to stand and fight, and to have fled; but when the ranks of the Persians were broken, they turned upon them like cavalry, and won the battle of Plataea.

LACHES: That is true.

SOCRATES: That was my meaning when I said that I was to blame in having put my question badly, and that this was the reason of your answering badly. For I meant to ask you not only about the courage of the heavy-armed soldiers, but about the courage of cavalry and every other style of soldier; and not only who are courageous in war, but who are courageous in perils by sea, and who in disease, or in poverty, or again in politics, are courageous; and not only who are courageous against pain or fear, but mighty to contend against desires and pleasures, either fixed in their rank or turning upon their enemy. There is this sort of courage – is there not, Laches?

LACHES: Certainly, Socrates.

SOCRATES: Now all these are courageous, but some have courage in pleasures and some in pains, some in desires and some in fears: and some are cowards under the same conditions, as I should imagine.

LACHES: Very true.

SOCRATES: I was asking about courage and cowardice in general. And I will begin with courage, and once more ask, what is that common quality, which is the same in all these cases, and which is called courage? Do you now understand what I mean?

LACHES: Not over-well.

SOCRATES: I mean this: as I might ask what is that quality which is called quickness, and which is found in running, in playing the lyre, in speaking, in learning, and in many other similar actions, or rather which we possess in nearly every action that is worth mentioning of arms, legs, mouth, voice, mind – would you not apply the term quickness to all of them?

LACHES: Quite true.

SOCRATES: And suppose I were to be asked by someone: what is that common quality, Socrates, which, in all these activities, you call quickness? I should say the quality which accomplishes much in a little time – whether in running, speaking, or in any other sort of action.

LACHES: You would be quite correct.

SOCRATES: And now, Laches, do you try and tell me in like manner, what is that common quality which is called courage, and which includes all the various uses of the term when applied both to pleasure and pain, and in all the cases to which I was just now referring?

LACHES: I should say that courage is a sort of endurance of the soul, if I am to speak of the universal nature which pervades them all.

SOCRATES: But that is what we must do if we are to answer our own question. And yet I cannot say that every kind of endurance is, in my opinion, to be deemed courage. Hear my reason: I am sure, Laches, that you would consider courage to be a very noble quality.

LACHES: Most noble, certainly.

SOCRATES: And you would say that a wise endurance is also good and noble?

LACHES: Very noble.

PLATO: LACHES

SOCRATES: But what would you say of a foolish endurance? Is not that, on the other hand, to be regarded as evil and hurtful?

LACHES: True.

SOCRATES: And is anything noble which is evil and hurtful?

LACHES: I ought not to say that, Socrates.

SOCRATES: Then you would not admit that sort of endurance to be courage – for it is not noble, but courage is noble?

LACHES: You are right.

SOCRATES: Then, according to you, only the wise endurance is courage?

LACHES: It seems so.

SOCRATES: But as to the epithet 'wise' – wise in what? In all things small as well as great? For example, if a man shows the quality of endurance in spending his money wisely, knowing that by spending he will acquire more in the end, do you call him courageous?

LACHES: Assuredly not.

SOCRATES: Or, for example, if a man is a physician, and his son, or some patient of his, has inflammation of the lungs, and begs that he may be allowed to eat or drink something, and the other is inflexible and refuses; is that courage?

LACHES: No; that is not courage at all, any more than the last.

SOCRATES: Again, take the case of one who endures in war, and is willing to fight, and wisely calculates and knows that others will help him, and that there will be fewer and inferior men against him than there are with him; and suppose that he has also advantages in position – would you say of such a one who endures with all this wisdom and preparation, that he or some man in the opposing army who is in the opposite circumstances to these and yet endures and remains at his post, is the braver?

LACHES: I should say that the latter, Socrates, was the braver.

SOCRATES: But, surely, this is a foolish endurance in comparison with the other?

LACHES: That is true.

SOCRATES: Then you would say that he who in an engagement of cavalry endures, having a knowledge of horsemanship, is not so courageous as he who endures, having no such knowledge?

LACHES: So I should say.

SOCRATES: And he who endures, having a knowledge of the use of the sling, or the bow, or of any other art, is not so courageous as he who endures, not having such a knowledge?

LACHES: True.

SOCRATES: And he who descends into a well, and dives, and holds out in this or any similar action, having no skill in diving or the like, is, as you would say, more courageous than those who have this skill?

LACHES: Why, Socrates, what else can a man say?

SOCRATES: Nothing, if that be what he thinks.

LACHES: But that is what I do think.

SOCRATES: And yet men who thus run risks and endure are foolish, Laches, in comparison of those who do the same things, having the skill to do them.

LACHES: That is true.

SOCRATES: But foolish boldness and endurance appeared before to be base and hurtful to us?

LACHES: Quite true.

SOCRATES: Whereas courage was acknowledged to be a noble quality.

LACHES: True.

SOCRATES: And now on the contrary we are saying that the foolish endurance, which was before held in dishonour, is courage.

LACHES: So we are.

SOCRATES: And are we right in saying so?

LACHES: Indeed, Socrates, I am sure that we are not right.

SOCRATES: Then according to your statement, you and I, Laches, are not attuned to the Dorian mode, which is a harmony of words and deeds; for our deeds are not in accordance with our words. Anyone would say that we had courage who saw us in action, but not, I imagine, he who heard us talking about courage just now.

LACHES: That is most true.

SOCRATES: And is this condition of ours satisfactory?

LACHES: Quite the reverse.

SOCRATES: Suppose, however, that we admit the principle of which we are speaking to a certain extent?

LACHES: To what extent and what principle do you mean?

SOCRATES: The principle of endurance. If you agree, we too must endure and persevere in the inquiry, and then courage will not laugh at our faint-heartedness in searching for courage; which after all may frequently be endurance.

LACHES: I am ready to go on, Socrates; and yet I am unused to investigations of this sort. But the spirit of controversy has been aroused in me by what has been said; and I am really grieved at being thus unable to express my meaning. For I fancy that I do know the nature of courage; but, somehow or other, she has slipped away from me, and I cannot get hold of her and tell her nature.

SOCRATES: But, my dear friend, should not the good sportsman follow the track, and not give up?

LACHES: Certainly, he should.

SOCRATES: Shall we then invite Nicias to join us? He may be better at the sport than we are. What do you say?

LACHES: I should like that.

SOCRATES: Come then, Nicias, and do what you can to help your friends, who are tossing on the waves of argument, and at the last gasp: you see our extremity, and may save us and also settle your own opinion, if you will tell us what you think about courage.

NICIAS: I have been thinking, Socrates, that you and Laches are not defining courage in the right way; for you have forgotten an excellent saying which I have heard from your own lips.

SOCRATES: What is it, Nicias?

NICIAS: I have often heard you say that 'Every man is good in that in which he is wise, and bad in that in which he is unwise'.

SOCRATES: That is certainly true, Nicias.

NICIAS: And therefore if the brave man is good, he is also wise.

SOCRATES: Do you hear him, Laches?

LACHES: Yes, I hear him, but I do not very well understand him.

SOCRATES: I think that I understand him; and he appears to me to mean that courage is a sort of wisdom.

LACHES: What sort of wisdom, Socrates?

SOCRATES: That is a question which you must ask of himself.

LACHES: Yes.

SOCRATES: Tell him then, Nicias, what sort of wisdom

you think courage to be; for you surely do not mean the
wisdom which plays the flute?

NICIAS: Certainly not.

SOCRATES: Nor the wisdom which plays the lyre?

NICIAS: No.

SOCRATES: But what is this knowledge then, and of
what?

LACHES: I think that you put the question to him very
well, Socrates; and I would like him to say what is the
nature of this knowledge or wisdom.

NICIAS: I mean to say, Laches, that courage is the
knowledge of that which inspires fear or confidence in
war, or in anything.

LACHES: How strangely he is talking, Socrates.

SOCRATES: Why do you say so, Laches?

LACHES: Why, surely courage is one thing, and wisdom another.

SOCRATES: That is just what Nicias denies.

LACHES: Yes, that is what he denies; that is where he is
so silly.

SOCRATES: Suppose that we instruct instead of abusing
him?

NICIAS: Certainly, Socrates; but having been proved
to be talking nonsense himself, Laches wants to prove
that I have been doing the same.

LACHES: Very true, Nicias; and you are talking nonsense, as I shall endeavour to show. Let me ask you a
question: do not physicians know the dangers of
disease? Or do the courageous know them? Or are the
physicians the same as the courageous?

NICIAS: Not at all.

LACHES: No more than the husbandmen who know
the dangers of husbandry, or than other craftsmen,
who have a knowledge of that which inspires them

with fear or confidence in their own arts, and yet they are not courageous a whit the more for that.

SOCRATES: What do you think of Laches' argument, Nicias? He appears to be saying something of importance.

NICIAS: Yes, he is saying something, but it is not true.

SOCRATES: How so?

NICIAS: Why, because he thinks that the physician's knowledge of illness extends beyond the nature of health and disease. But in fact the physician knows no more than this; do you imagine, Laches, that he knows whether health or illness is the more terrible to a man? Had not many a man better never get up from a sick bed? I should like to know whether you think that life is always better than death. May not death often be the better of the two?

LACHES: Yes, certainly so in my opinion.

NICIAS: And do you think that the same things are terrible to those who had better die, and to those who had better live?

LACHES: Certainly not.

NICIAS: And do you suppose that the physician knows this, or indeed any other specialist, except the man who is skilled in the grounds of fear and hope? And him I call the courageous.

SOCRATES: Do you understand his meaning, Laches?

LACHES: Yes; I suppose that, in his way of speaking, the soothsayers are the courageous men. For who but one of them can know to whom to die or to live is better? And yet, Nicias, would you allow that you are yourself a soothsayer, or are you neither a soothsayer nor courageous?

NICIAS: What! Do you mean to say that the soothsayer ought to know the grounds of hope or fear?

LACHES: Indeed I do: who but he?

NICIAS: Much rather I should say he of whom I speak; for the soothsayer ought to know only the signs of things that are about to come to pass, whether it be death or disease, or loss of property, or victory, or defeat in war or in any sort of contest; but whether the suffering or not suffering of these things will be best for a man, is a question which is no more for a soothsayer to decide than for anyone else.

LACHES: I cannot understand what Nicias would be at, Socrates, for he represents the courageous as neither a soothsayer, nor a physician, nor in any other character; unless he means to say that he is a god. My opinion is that he does not like honestly to confess that he is talking nonsense, but that he shuffles up and down in order to conceal the difficulty into which he has got himself. You and I, Socrates, might have practised a similar shuffle just now, if we had only wanted to avoid the appearance of inconsistency. And if we had been arguing in a court of law there might have been reason in so doing; but why should a man deck himself out with vain words at a meeting of friends such as this?

SOCRATES: I quite agree with you, Laches, that he should not. But perhaps Nicias is serious, and not merely talking for the sake of talking. Let us ask him just to explain what he means, and if he has reason on his side we will agree with him; if not, we will instruct him.

LACHES: Do you ask him, Socrates, if you will: I think that I have asked enough.

SOCRATES: I do not see why I should not; and my questioning will do for both of us.

LACHES: Very good.

SOCRATES: Then tell me, Nicias, or rather tell us, for Laches and I are partners in the argument: Do you mean to affirm that courage is the knowledge of the grounds of hope and fear?

NICIAS: I do.

SOCRATES: And not every man has this knowledge; the physician and the soothsayer have it not, and they will not be courageous unless they acquire it – that is what you were saying?

NICIAS: I was.

SOCRATES: Then this is certainly not a thing which every sow would know, as the proverb says, and therefore she could not be courageous.

NICIAS: I think not.

SOCRATES: Clearly not, Nicias; not even the sow of Crommyon would be called by you courageous. And this I say not as a joke, but because I think that he who assents to your doctrine cannot allow that any wild beast is courageous, unless he admits that a lion, or a leopard, or perhaps a boar, has such a degree of wisdom that he knows things which but a few human beings ever know by reason of their difficulty. He who takes your view of courage must affirm that a lion is not naturally more disposed to courage than a stag, nor a bull than a monkey.

LACHES: Capital, Socrates; upon my word, that is truly good. And I hope, Nicias, that you will tell us whether you really mean that those animals which we all admit to be courageous are in fact wiser than mankind; or whether you will have the boldness, in the face of universal opinion, to deny their courage.

NICIAS: Why, Laches, I do not describe as courageous animals or any other creatures which have no fear of dangers because they are devoid of understanding, but only as fearless and senseless. Do you imagine that I should call all little children courageous, who fear no dangers because they have no understanding? There is a difference, to my way of thinking, between fearlessness and courage. I am of opinion that thoughtful courage is a quality possessed by very few, but that rashness and boldness, and fearlessness which has no forethought, are very common qualities possessed by many men, many women, many children, many animals. And you, and men in general, call by the term 'courageous' actions which I call rash – my courageous actions are wise actions.

LACHES: Behold, Socrates, how admirably, as he thinks, he dresses himself out in words, while seeking to deprive of the honour of courage those whom all the world acknowledges to be courageous.

NICIAS: Not you, Laches, so do not be alarmed; I am quite willing to say of you, and also of Lamachus and of many other Athenians, that you are wise, being courageous.

LACHES: I could answer that; but I would not have you cast in my teeth that I am a haughty Aexonian.

SOCRATES: Do not answer him, Laches; I rather fancy that you are not aware of the source from which his wisdom is derived. He has got all this from my friend Damon, and Damon is always with Prodicus, who, of all the sophists, is considered to be the best at analysing the meaning of words of this sort.

LACHES: Yes, Socrates; and the examination of such niceties is a much more proper employment for a sophist than for a great statesman whom the city chooses to preside over her affairs.

SOCRATES: Yes, my sweet friend, but great affairs and great minds properly go together. And I think that

Nicias deserves that we should see what he has in view when he so defines courage.

LACHES: Then see for yourself, Socrates.

SOCRATES: That is what I am going to do, my dear friend. Do not, however, suppose I shall let you out of the partnership; for I shall expect you to apply your mind, and join with me in the consideration of the question.

LACHES: I will if you think that I ought.

SOCRATES: Yes, I do; but I must beg of you, Nicias, to begin again. You remember that we originally considered courage to be a part of virtue.

NICIAS: Very true.

SOCRATES: And you yourself said that it was a part; and there were many other parts, all of which taken together are called virtue.

NICIAS: Certainly.

SOCRATES: Do you agree with me about the parts? For I say that justice, temperance, and the like, are all of them parts of virtue as well as courage. Would you not say the same?

NICIAS: Certainly.

SOCRATES: Well then, so far we are agreed. And now let us proceed a step, and try to arrive at a similar agreement about the fearful and the hopeful: I do not want you to be thinking one thing and us another. Let me then tell you our opinion, and if I am wrong you shall set us right: in our opinion the terrible and the hopeful are the things which do and do not create fear, and fear is not of the present nor of the past, but is of future and expected evil. Do you not agree to that, Laches?

LACHES: Yes, Socrates, entirely.

SOCRATES: That is our view, Nicias; the terrible things,

as I should say, are the evils which are future; and the hopeful are the good or not evil things which are future. Do you or do you not agree with me?

NICIAS: I agree.

SOCRATES: And the knowledge of these things you call courage?

NICIAS: Precisely.

SOCRATES: And now let me see whether you agree with Laches and myself as to a third point.

NICIAS: What is that?

SOCRATES: I will tell you. He and I have a notion that there is not one knowledge or science of the past, another of the present, a third of what may and will be best in the future; but that of all three there is one science only: for example, there is one science of medicine which is concerned with the superintendence of health equally in all times, present, past, and future; and one science of husbandry in like manner, which is concerned with the productions of the earth in all times. As to the military art, you yourselves will be my witnesses that it makes excellent provision for the future as well as the present, and that the general claims to be the master and not the servant of the soothsayer, because he knows better what is happening or is likely to happen in war: and accordingly the law places the soothsayer under the general, and not the general under the soothsayer. Am I not correct in saying so, Laches?

LACHES: Quite correct.

SOCRATES: And do you, Nicias, also acknowledge that the same science has understanding of the same things, whether future, present, or past?

NICIAS: Yes, indeed, Socrates; that is my opinion.

SOCRATES: And courage, my friend, is, as you say, a knowledge of the fearful and of the hopeful?

NICIAS: Yes.

SOCRATES: And the fearful, and the hopeful, are admitted to be future goods and future evils?

NICIAS: True.

SOCRATES: And the same science has to do with the same things in the future or at any time?

NICIAS: That is true.

SOCRATES: Then courage is a science which is concerned not only with the fearful and hopeful, for they are future only; courage, like the other sciences, is concerned not only with good and evil of the future, but of the present and past, and of any time?

NICIAS: That, as I suppose, is true.

SOCRATES: Then the answer which you have given, Nicias, includes only a third part of courage; but our question extended to the whole nature of courage: and according to your view, that is, according to your present view, courage is not only the knowledge of the hopeful and the fearful, but seems to include nearly every good and evil without reference to time. What do you say to that alteration in your statement?

NICIAS: I agree, Socrates.

SOCRATES: But then, my dear friend, if a man knew all good and evil, and how they are and have been and will be produced, would he not be perfect, and wanting in no virtue, whether justice or temperance or holiness? He alone would be competent to distinguish between what is to be feared and what is not (whether it be supernatural or natural), and would take the proper precautions to secure that all shall be well; for he would know how to deal aright both with gods and with men.

NICIAS: I think, Socrates, that there is a great deal of truth in what you say.

SOCRATES: But then, Nicias, courage, according to this new definition of yours, instead of being only a part of virtue, will be all virtue?

NICIAS: It would seem so.

SOCRATES: But we were saying that courage is one of the parts of virtue?

NICIAS: Yes, that was what we were saying.

SOCRATES: And that is in contradiction with our present view?

NICIAS: That appears to be the case.

SOCRATES: Then, Nicias, we have not discovered what courage is.

NICIAS: It seems not.

LACHES: And yet, friend Nicias, I imagined that you would have made the discovery, when you were so contemptuous of the answers which I made to Socrates. I had very great hopes that you would have been led to it by the wisdom of Damon.

NICIAS: I perceive, Laches, that you think nothing of having displayed your ignorance of the nature of courage, but you look only to see whether I have not made a similar display; and if we are both equally ignorant of the things which a man with any self-respect should know, that, I suppose, will be of no consequence. You certainly appear to me very like the rest of the world, looking at your neighbour and not at yourself. I am of opinion that enough has been said on the subject which we have been discussing; and if the treatment has been in any way inadequate, that may be hereafter corrected with the help of Damon, whom you think to laugh down although you have never seen him, and of others. And when I am satisfied myself, I will freely impart my satisfaction to you, for I think that you are very much in want of knowledge.

LACHES: You are a philosopher, Nicias, of that I am aware: nevertheless I would recommend Lysimachus and Melesias not to take you and me as advisers about the education of their children; but, as I said at first, they should ask Socrates and not let him off; if my own sons were old enough, I should do the same.

NICIAS: To that I quite agree, if Socrates is willing to take them under his charge. I should not wish for anyone else to be the tutor of Niceratus. But I observe that whenever I mention the matter to him he recommends to me some other tutor and refuses himself. Perhaps he may be more ready to listen to you, Lysimachus.

LYSIMACHUS: He ought, Nicias: for certainly I would do things for him which I would not do for many others. What do you say, Socrates – will you comply? And are you ready to give assistance in the improvement of the youths?

SOCRATES: Indeed, Lysimachus, I should be very wrong in refusing to aid in the improvement of anybody. And if I had shown in this conversation that I had a knowledge which Nicias and Laches have not, then I admit that you would be right in inviting me to perform this duty; but as we are all in the same perplexity, why should one of us be preferred to another? I certainly think that no one should; and under these circumstances, let me offer you a piece of advice (and this need not go further than ourselves). I maintain, my friends, that every one of us should seek out the best teacher whom he can find, first for ourselves who are greatly in need of one, and then for the youths, regardless of expense or anything. But I cannot advise that we remain as we are. And if anyone laughs at us for going to school at our age, I would quote to them the authority of Homer, who says that 'Modesty is not good for a needy man.' Let us then, regardless of what may be said of us, concern ourselves both with our own education and that of the youths, together.

LYSIMACHUS: I like your proposal, Socrates; and as I am the oldest, I am also the most eager to go to school with the boys. Let me beg a favour of you: come to my house tomorrow at dawn, and we will advise about these matters. For the present, let us make an end of the conversation.

SOCRATES: I will come to you tomorrow, Lysimachus, as you propose, god willing.

PLATO
SYMPOSIUM

SYMPOSIUM

Persons of the dialogue
APOLLODORUS, *who repeats to his companion*
the dialogue which he had heard from Aristo-
demus, and had already once narrated to Glaucon
PAUSANIAS
ERYXIMACHUS
ARISTOPHANES
AGATHON
SOCRATES
ALCIBIADES
PHAEDRUS
A troop of revellers

SCENE: *The house of Agathon*

Concerning the things about which you ask to be informed I believe that I am not ill prepared with an answer. For the day before yesterday I was coming from my own home at Phalerum to the city, and one of my acquaintance, who had caught a sight of me from behind, calling out playfully in the distance, said: Man of Phalerum, by name Apollodorus, halt! I did as I was bid; and then he said, I was looking for you, Apollodorus, only just now, that I might ask you about the speeches in praise of love, which were delivered by Socrates, Alcibiades, and others, at Agathon's supper. Phoenix, the son of Philip, told another person who told me of them; his narrative was very indistinct, but he said that you knew, and I wish that you would give me an account of them. Who, if not you, should be the reporter of the words of your friend? And first tell me, he said, were you present at this meeting?

Your informant, Glaucon, I said, must have been very indistinct indeed, if you imagine that the occasion was recent; or that I could have been of the party.

Why, yes, he replied, I thought so.

Impossible: I said. Are you ignorant that for many years Agathon has not resided at Athens; and not three have elapsed since I became acquainted with Socrates, and have made it my daily business to know all that he says and does. There was a time when I was running about the world, fancying myself to be well employed, but I was really a most wretched being, no better than you are now. I thought that I ought to do anything rather than be a philosopher.

Well, he said, jesting apart, tell me when the meeting occurred.

In our boyhood, I replied, when Agathon won the prize with his first tragedy, on the day after that on which he and his chorus offered the sacrifice of victory.

Then it must have been a long while ago, he said; and who told you – did Socrates?

No indeed, I replied, but the same person who told Phoenix; he was a little fellow, who never wore any shoes, Aristodemus, of the deme of Cydathenaeum. He had been at Agathon's feast; and I think that in those days there was no one who was a more devoted admirer of Socrates. Moreover, I have asked Socrates about the truth of some parts of his narrative, and he confirmed them. Then, said Glaucon, let us have the tale over again; is not the road to Athens just made for conversation? And so we walked, and talked of the discourses on love; and therefore, as I said at first, I am not ill prepared to comply with your request, and if you want another rehearsal of them, you shall have it. For to speak or to hear others speak of philosophy always gives me the greatest pleasure, to say nothing of the profit. But when I hear another strain, especially that of you rich business men, such conversation displeases me; and I pity you who are my companions, because you think that you are doing something when in reality you are doing nothing. And I dare say that you pity me in return, whom you regard as an unhappy creature, and very probably you are right. But I certainly know of you what you only think of me – there is the difference.

COMPANION: I see, Apollodorus, that you are just the same – always speaking evil of yourself, and of others; and I do believe that you think all mankind unhappy with the exception of Socrates, yourself first of all. I cannot imagine how you acquired the name of Apollodorus the mild; for you are always the same, raging against yourself and everybody but Socrates.

APOLLODORUS: Yes, friend, and since I have these notions of myself and you, of course no other evidence is required to show that I am out of my wits and crazy!

COMPANION: We need not wrangle about that just now, Apollodorus; but let me renew my request that you would repeat the conversation.

APOLLODORUS: Well, the tale of love was on this wise – but perhaps I had better begin at the beginning, and endeavour to give you the exact words of Aristodemus:

He said that he met Socrates fresh from the bath and sandalled; and as the sight of the sandals was unusual, he asked him whither he was going that he had been converted into such a beau.

To a banquet at Agathon's, he replied, whose

invitation to his sacrifice of victory I refused yesterday, fearing a crowd, but promising that I would come today instead; and so I have put on my finery, because he is such a fine man. What say you to going with me unasked?

I will do as you bid me, I replied.

Follow then, he said, and let us demolish the proverb: 'To the feasts of inferior men the good unbidden go'; instead of which our proverb will run: 'To the feasts of the good the good unbidden go'; and this alteration may be supported by the authority of Homer himself, who not only demolishes but literally outrages the proverb. For, after picturing Agamemnon as the most valiant of men, he makes Menelaus, who is 'a faint-hearted warrior', come unbidden to the banquet of Agamemnon, who is feasting and offering sacrifices; not the better going to the worse, but the worse to the better.

I rather fear, Socrates, said Aristodemus, lest this may still be my case; and that, like Menelaus in Homer, I shall be the inferior person, who 'To the feasts of the wise unbidden goes.' But I shall say that I was bidden of you; so have your excuse ready. 'Two going together', he replied, in Homeric fashion, one or other of us will invent an excuse by the way. Come: let us start.

As they went along after a conversation of this style, Socrates dropped behind in a fit of abstraction, and desired Aristodemus, who was waiting, to go on before him. When he reached the house of Agathon he found the doors wide open, and a comical thing happened. A servant coming out met him, and led him at once into the banqueting-hall in which the guests were reclining, for the banquet was about to begin. Welcome, Aristodemus, said Agathon, as soon as he appeared –

you are just in time to sup with us; if you come on any other matter put it off, and make one of us, as I was looking for you yesterday and meant to have asked you, if I could have found you. But what have you done with Socrates?

I turned round, but Socrates was nowhere to be seen; and I had to explain that he had been with me a moment before, and that I came by his invitation to the supper.

You were quite right in coming, said Agathon; but where is he himself?

He was behind me just now, as I entered, he said, and I cannot think what has become of him.

Go and look for him, boy, said Agathon, and bring him in; and do you, Aristodemus, meanwhile take the place by Eryximachus.

The servant then assisted him to wash, and he lay down, and presently another servant came in and reported that our friend Socrates had retired into the portico of the neighbouring house. 'There he is fixed,' said he, 'and when I call to him he will not stir.'

How strange, said Agathon; then you must call him again, and keep calling him.

Let him alone, said my informant; he has a way of going off sometimes by himself, and standing still anywhere he happens to be. I believe that he will soon appear; do not therefore disturb him.

Well, if you think so, I will leave him, said Agathon. And then, turning to the servants, he added, 'Let us have supper without waiting for him. Serve up whatever you please, for there is no one to give you orders; hitherto I have never left you to yourselves. But on this occasion imagine that you are our hosts, and that I and the company are your guests; treat us well, and then we shall commend you.' After this, supper was served, but still no Socrates; and during the meal Agathon several times expressed a wish to send for him, but Aristodemus objected; and at last when the feast was about half over – for the fit, as usual, was not of long duration – Socrates entered. Agathon, who was reclining alone at the end of the table, begged that he would take the place next to him; that 'I may touch you', he said, 'and have the benefit of that wise thought which came into your mind in the portico, and is now in your possession; for I am certain that you would not have come away until you had found what you sought.'

How I wish, said Socrates, taking his place as he was desired, that wisdom could be infused by touch, out of the fuller into the emptier man, as water runs through wool out of a fuller cup into an emptier one; if that were so, how greatly should I value the privilege of reclining at your side! For you would have filled me full with a stream of wisdom plenteous and fair; whereas my own is of a very mean and questionable sort, no better than a dream. But yours is bright and full of promise, and was manifested forth in all the splendour of your youth the day before yesterday, in the presence of more than thirty thousand Hellenes.

You are mocking, Socrates, said Agathon, and ere long you and I will have to determine who bears off the palm of wisdom – of this Dionysus shall be the judge; but at present you are better occupied with supper.

Socrates took his place on the couch, and supped with the rest; and then libations were offered, and after a hymn had been sung to the god, and there had been the usual ceremonies, they were about to commence drinking, when Pausanias said, And now, my friends, how can we drink with least injury to ourselves? I can assure you that I feel severely the effect of yesterday's potations, and must have time to recover; and I suspect that most of you are in the same predicament, for you were of the party yesterday. Consider then: how can the drinking be made easiest?

I entirely agree, said Aristophanes, that we should, by all means, avoid hard drinking, for I was myself one of those who were deeply dipped yesterday.

I think that you are right, said Eryximachus, the son of Acumenus; but I should still like to hear one other person speak: is Agathon able to drink hard?

I am not equal to it, said Agathon.

It is a blessing, said Eryximachus, for the weak heads like myself, Aristodemus, Phaedrus, and others who never can drink, to find that the stronger ones are not in a drinking mood. (I do not include Socrates, who is able either to drink or to abstain, and will not mind, whichever we do.) Well, as none of the company seem disposed to drink much, I may be forgiven for speaking the truth about deep drinking. My experience as a physician has convinced me that it is a bad practice, which I never follow, if I can help, and certainly do not recommend to another, least of all to anyone who still feels the effects of yesterday's carouse.

I always do what you advise, and especially what you prescribe as a physician, rejoined Phaedrus the Myrrh-inusian, and the rest of the company, if they are wise, will do the same.

It was agreed that heavy drinking was not to be the order of the day, but that they were all to drink only so much as they pleased.

Then, said Eryximachus, as you are all agreed that drinking is to be voluntary, and that there is to be no compulsion, I move, in the next place, that the flute-girl, who has just made her appearance, be told to go away and play to herself, or, if she likes, to the women who are within. Today let us have conversation instead; and, if you will allow me, I will tell you what sort of conversation. This proposal having been welcomed unanimously, Eryximachus proceeded as follows.

I will begin, he said, after the manner of Melanippe in Euripides: 'Not mine the word' which I am about to speak, but that of Phaedrus here. For he is always saying to me in an indignant tone: 'What a strange thing it is, Eryximachus, that, whereas other gods have poems and hymns made in their honour, the ancient and mighty god, Love, has never had a single encomiast among all the poets who are so many. There are the worthy sophists too – the excellent Prodicus for example – who have descanted in prose on the virtues of Heracles and other heroes; which after all is not so extraordinary, considering that I have come across a philosophical work in which the utility of salt has been made the theme of an eloquent discourse; and many other like things have had a like honour bestowed upon them. And only to think that there should have been an eager interest created about them, and yet that to this day no one has ever dared worthily to hymn Love's praises! So entirely has this great deity been neglected.' Now in this Phaedrus seems to me to be quite right, and therefore I want to offer him a contribution; also I think that at the present moment we who are here assembled cannot do better than honour the god Love. If you agree with me, there will be no lack of conversation; for I mean to propose that each of us in turn, going from left to right, shall make a speech in honour of Love. Let him give us the best which he can; and Phaedrus, because he is sitting first on the left hand, and because he is the father of the theme, shall begin.

No one will vote against you, Eryximachus, said Socrates. How can I oppose your motion, who profess to understand nothing but matters of love; nor, I presume, will Agathon and Pausanias; and there can be no doubt of Aristophanes, whose whole concern is with Dionysus and Aphrodite; nor will any one disagree of those whom I see around me. The proposal, as I am aware, may seem rather hard upon us whose place is last; but we shall be contented if we hear some good speeches first. Let Phaedrus begin the praise of Love, and good luck to him. All the company expressed their assent, and desired him to do as Socrates bade him.

Aristodemus did not recollect all the individual speeches, nor do I recollect all that he related to me; but I will tell you what I thought most worthy of remembrance, and what the chief speakers said.

Phaedrus began by affirming that Love is a mighty god, and wonderful among gods and men on many accounts, but especially wonderful in his birth. For he is the eldest of the gods, which is an honour to him; and a proof of his claim to this honour is, that of his parents there is no memorial; neither poet nor prose-writer has ever affirmed that he had any. As Hesiod says: 'First Chaos came, and then broad-bosomed Earth, the everlasting seat of all that is, and Love.' In other words, after Chaos, the Earth and Love, these two, came into being. Also Parmenides sings of Generation: 'First in the train of gods, she fashioned Love'.

And Acusilaus agrees with Hesiod. Thus numerous are the authorities who acknowledge Love to be the eldest of the gods. And not only is he the eldest, he is also the source of the greatest benefits to us. For I know not any greater blessing to a young man who is beginning life than a virtuous lover, or to the lover than a beloved youth. For the principle which ought to be the guide of men who would nobly live – that principle, I say, neither kindred, nor honour, nor wealth, nor any other influence is able to implant so well as love. Of what am I speaking? Of the sense of honour and dishonour, without which neither states nor individuals ever do any good or great work. And I say that a lover who is detected in doing any dishonourable act, or submitting through cowardice when any dishonour is done to him by another, will be more pained at being detected by his beloved than at being seen by his father, or by his companions, or by anyone else. The beloved too, when he is found in any disgraceful situation, has the same feeling about his lover. And if there were only some way of contriving that a state or an army should be made up of lovers and their loves, they would be the very best governors of their own city, abstaining from all dishonour, and emulating one another in honour; and it is scarcely an exaggeration to say that when fighting at each other's side, although a mere handful, they would overcome the world. For what lover would not choose rather to be seen by all mankind than by his beloved, either when abandoning his post or throwing away his arms? He would be ready to die a thousand deaths rather than endure this. Or who would desert his beloved or fail him in the hour of danger? The veriest coward would become an inspired hero, equal to the bravest, at such a time; Love would inspire him. That courage which, as Homer says, the god breathes into the souls of some heroes, Love of his own bounty infuses into the lover.

Love will make men dare to die for their beloved –
love alone; and women as well as men. Of this,
Alcestis, the daughter of Pelias, is a monument to all
Hellas; for she was willing to lay down her life on behalf
of her husband, when no one else would, although he
had a father and mother; but the tenderness of her love
so far exceeded theirs, that she made them seem to be
strangers in blood to their own son, and in name only
related to him; and so noble did this action of hers
appear to the gods, as well as to men, that among the
many who have done virtuously she is one of the very
few to whom, in admiration of her noble action, they
have granted the privilege of returning alive to earth;
such exceeding honour is paid by the gods to the
devotion and virtue of love. But Orpheus, the son of
Oeagrus, the harper, they sent empty away, having
presented to him an apparition only of her whom he
sought, but herself they would not relinquish, because
he showed no spirit; he was only a harp-player, and did
not dare like Alcestis to die for love, but was contriving
how he might enter Hades alive; therefore they afterwards caused him to suffer death at the hands of
women, as the punishment of his cowardliness. Very
different was the reward of the true love of Achilles
towards his lover Patroclus – his lover and not his love
(the notion that Patroclus was the beloved one is a
foolish error into which Aeschylus has fallen, for
Achilles was the fairer of the two, fairer also than all the
other heroes; and, as Homer informs us, he was still
beardless, and younger far). And greatly as the gods
honour the virtue of love, still the return of love on the
part of the beloved to the lover is more admired and
valued and rewarded by them; for the lover is more
divine, because he is inspired by god. Now Achilles

was quite aware, for he had been told by his mother, that he might avoid death and return home, and live to a good old age, if he abstained from slaying Hector. Nevertheless he gave his life to revenge his friend, and dared to die for him, not only in his defence, but after he was dead. Wherefore the gods honoured him even above Alcestis, and sent him to the Islands of the Blest. These are my reasons for affirming that Love is the eldest and noblest and mightiest of the gods, and the chiefest author and giver of virtue and happiness, alike in life and after death.

This, or something like this, was the speech of Phaedrus; and some other speeches followed which Aristodemus did not remember; the next which he repeated was that of Pausanias. Phaedrus, he said, the argument has not been set before us, I think, quite in the right form – we should not be called upon to praise Love in such an indiscriminate manner. If there were only one Love, then what you said would be well enough; but since there are more Loves than one, you should have begun by determining which of them was to be the theme of our praises. I will try to amend this defect; and first of all I will tell you which Love is deserving of praise, and then try to hymn the praise-worthy one in a manner worthy of him. For we all know that Love is inseparable from Aphrodite, and if there were only one Aphrodite there would be only one Love; but as there are two goddesses there must be two Loves. And am I not right in asserting that there are two goddesses? The elder one, having no mother, who is called the heavenly Aphrodite – she is the daughter of Uranus; the younger, who is the daughter of Zeus and Dione – her we call common; and the Love who is her fellow-worker is rightly named common, as the other

Love is called heavenly. All the gods ought to have praise given to them, but not without distinction of their natures; and therefore I must try to distinguish the characters of the two Loves. Now actions vary according to the manner of their performance. Take, for example, that which we are now doing, drinking, singing, and talking – these actions are not in themselves either good or evil, but they turn out in this or that way according to the mode of performing them; and when well done they are good, and when wrongly done they are evil; and in like manner not every kind of loving nor every Love is noble and worthy of praise, but only that which inspires men to love nobly. The Love who is the offspring of the common Aphrodite is essentially common, and has no discrimination, being such as moves the meaner sort of men. They are apt to love women as well as youths, and the body rather than the soul – the most foolish beings they can find are the objects of this love which desires only to gain an end, but never thinks of accomplishing the end nobly, and therefore does good and evil quite indiscriminately. The goddess who is the mother of this love is far younger than the other, and she was born of the union of the male and female, and partakes of both. But the offspring of the heavenly Aphrodite is derived from a mother in whose birth the female has no part – she is from the male only; this is that love which is of youths, and the goddess being older, there is nothing of wantonness in her. Those who are inspired by this love turn to the male, and delight in him who is the more valiant and intelligent nature; anyone may recognize the pure enthusiasts in the very character of their attachments. For they love not boys, but intelligent beings whose reason is beginning to be developed, much about the time at which their beards begin to grow. And starting from such a choice, they are ready, I apprehend, to be faithful to their companions, and pass their whole life with them, not to take them in their inexperience, and deceive them, and make fools of them, and then run away to others of them. But the love of young boys should be forbidden by law, because their future is uncertain; they may turn out good or bad, either in body or soul, and much noble enthusiasm may be thrown away upon them. The good impose this law upon themselves of their own free will; and the coarser sort of lovers ought to be restrained by force, as we restrain or attempt to restrain them from fixing their affections on women of free birth. These are the persons who bring such reproach on love that seeing their impropriety and evil some people go so far as to hold up such attachments to shame; for surely nothing that is decorously and lawfully done can justly be censured. Now here and in Lacedaemon the rules about love are perplexing, but in most cities they are simple and easily intelligible. In Elis and Boeotia, and in countries having no gifts of eloquence, they are very straightforward; the law is simply in favour of these connexions, and no one, whether young or old, has anything to say to their discredit; the reason being, as I suppose, that they are men of few words in those parts, and therefore the lovers do not like the trouble of pleading their suit. In Ionia and other places, and generally in countries which are subject to the barbarians, the custom is held to be dishonourable; because of their despotic governments, loves of youths share the evil repute in which philosophy and gymnastics are held, for the interests of the rulers require, I suppose, that their subjects should be poor in spirit, and that there should be no strong bond of friendship or society among them, which love, above all other motives, is likely to inspire – a lesson that our Athenian tyrants learned by experience, since the love of Aristogeiton and the constancy of Harmodius had a strength which undid their power. And, therefore, the ill repute into which these attachments have fallen is to be ascribed to the evil condition of those who make them to be ill reputed, that is to say, to the self-seeking of the governors and the cowardice of the governed; on the other hand, the indiscriminate honour which is given to them in some countries is attributable to the mental laziness of those who hold this opinion of them. In our own country a far better principle prevails, but, as I was saying, the explanation of it is not easy to grasp. For, observe that open loves are held to be more honourable than secret ones, and that the love of the noblest and highest, even if their persons are less beautiful than others, is especially honourable. Consider, too, how great is the encouragement which all the world gives to the lover, not treating him as though he were doing something dishonourable; but if he succeeds he is praised, and if he fails he is blamed. And in the pursuit of his love the custom of mankind allows him to do many strange things, which philosophy would bitterly censure if they were done from any other interest or motive, such as the desire for money or office or some other kind of power. He may pray, and entreat, and supplicate, and vow upon oath, and lie on a mat at the door, and endure a slavery worse than that of any slave – in any other case friends and enemies would be equally ready to prevent him, but now there is no friend who will be ashamed of him

and admonish him, and no enemy will charge him
with meanness or flattery; the actions of a lover have a
grace which ennobles them; and custom has decided
that they are open to no reproach, because they have
a noble purpose: and, what is strangest of all, he only
may swear and forswear himself (so men say), and the
gods will forgive his transgression, for there is no such
thing as a lover's oath. Such is the entire liberty which
gods and men have allowed the lover, according to the
custom which prevails in our part of the world – from
this point of view a man might fairly argue that in
Athens to love and to be loved is held to be a most
honourable thing. But when parents forbid their sons
to talk with their lovers, and place them under a
tutor's care who is instructed to that effect, and their
companions and equals cast in their teeth anything of
the sort which they may observe, and their elders
refuse to silence the reprovers and do not rebuke this
mistaken censure – anyone who reflects on all this will,
on the contrary, think that we hold these practices to
be most disgraceful. But the truth as I imagine is, that
judgment on such practices cannot be absolute; in
themselves they are neither honourable nor dishonourable, as was said at the beginning; they are
honourable to him who follows them honourably,
dishonourable to him who follows them dishonour-
ably. There is dishonour in yielding to the evil, or in an
evil manner; but there is honour in yielding to the
good, or in an honourable manner. Evil is the vulgar
lover who loves the body rather than the soul, inasmuch as he is not even stable, because he loves a thing
which is in itself unstable, and therefore when the
bloom of youth which he was desiring is over, he takes
wing and flies away, dishonouring all his words and

promises; whereas the love of the noble disposition is lifelong, for it becomes one with the perdurable. The custom of our country would have both of them proven well and truly, and would have us yield to the one sort of lover and avoid the other; and therefore encourages some to pursue, and others to fly, testing both the lover and beloved in contests and trials, until they show to which of the two classes they respectively belong. And this is the reason why, in the first place, a hasty attachment is held to be dishonourable, because time is the true test of this as of most other things; and secondly there is dishonour in being overcome by the love of money or political power, whether one is frightened into surrender by much hardship or, living in enjoyment of the advantages they offer, is unable to rise above their seductions. For none of these things are of a permanent or lasting nature; not to mention that no generous friendship ever sprang from them. There remains, then, only one road of honourable attachment which our custom allows the beloved to follow; for it is our rule that as any menial service which the lover does to him is not to be accounted flattery or a reproach to himself, so the beloved has one way only of voluntary service which is not open to reproach, and this is service directed to virtue.

For you know it is our custom that anyone who does service to another under the idea that he will be improved by him either in wisdom, or in some other particular of virtue – such a voluntary service, I say, is not to be regarded as a dishonour, and is not open to the charge of flattery. And these two customs, one the love of youth, and the other the practice of philosophy and virtue in general, ought to meet in one, and then the beloved may honourably indulge the lover. For when the lover and beloved come together, having each of them an inner law, the lover thinking that he is right in doing any service which he can to his gracious love, and the other that he is right in showing any kindness which he can to him who is making him wise and good; the one capable of communicating understanding and virtue, the other seeking to acquire them with a view to education and wisdom; when the two laws of love are fulfilled and meet in one – then, and then only, may the beloved yield with honour to the lover. Nor when love is of this disinterested sort is there any disgrace in being deceived, but in every other case there is equal disgrace in being or not being deceived. For he who is gracious to his lover under the impression that he is rich, and is disappointed of all gain because he turns out to be poor, is disgraced all the same: for he has done his best to show that he would give himself up to anyone's 'uses base' for the sake of money; but this is not honourable. And on the same principle he who gives himself to a lover because he is a good man and in the hope that he will be improved by his company, shows himself to be virtuous, even though the object of his affection turn out to be a villain, and to have no virtue; and though he is deceived he has committed a noble error. For he has proved that for his part he will do anything for anybody with a view to virtue and improvement, than which there can be nothing nobler. Thus noble in every case is the acceptance of another, if it be for the sake of virtue. This is that love which comes from the heavenly goddess, and is heavenly, and of great price to individuals and cities, making the lover and the beloved alike eager in the work of their own improvement. But all other loves are the offspring of the other, who is the common goddess. To you, Phaedrus, I offer this my contribution in praise of love, which is as good as I could make extempore.

Pausanias came to a pause – this is the balanced way in which I have been taught by the wise to speak; and Aristodemus said that the turn of Aristophanes was next, but either he had eaten too much, or from some other cause he had the hiccough, and was unable to speak. So he turned to Eryximachus the physician, who was reclining on the couch below him, and said, Eryximachus, you ought either to stop my hiccough, or to speak in my turn until I have left off.

I will do both, said Eryximachus: I will speak in your turn, and do you speak in mine; and while I am speaking let me recommend you to hold your breath, and if after you have done so for some time the hiccough is no better, then gargle with a little water; and if it is still violent, tickle your nose with something and sneeze; if you sneeze once or twice, even the most violent hiccough is sure to stop. I will do as you prescribe, said Aristophanes, and now get on.

Eryximachus spoke as follows: Seeing that Pausanias made a fair beginning, and but a lame ending, I must endeavour to supply his deficiency. I think that he has rightly distinguished two kinds of love. But my art further informs me that the double love is not merely an affection of the soul of man towards human beauty, but is an affection directed to many other objects, and is to be found in other things, in the bodies of all animals and in productions of the earth, and I may say in all that is; such is the conclusion which I seem to have gathered from my own art of medicine, whence I learn how great and wonderful and universal is the deity of love, whose empire extends over all things, divine as well as human. And from medicine I will begin that I may do honour to my art. In the body there are by its nature these two kinds of love; the state of bodily health and the state of sickness are confessedly different and unlike, and being unlike, they have loves and desires which are unlike; so the desire of the healthy is one, and the desire of the diseased is another. As Pausanias was just now saying, to indulge good men is honourable, and bad men dishonourable; so it is with the body. In each body it is right and proper to favour the good and healthy elements (and this is what is called the practice of medicine), and the bad elements and the elements of disease are not to be indulged, but discouraged. This is what the physician has to do, and in this the art of medicine consists: for medicine may be briefly described as the knowledge of the loves and desires of the body, and how to satisfy them or mortify them; and the best physician is he who is able to separate fair love from foul, or to convert one into the other; and he who knows how to eradicate and how to implant love, whichever is required, and can reconcile the most hostile elements in the constitution and make them loving friends, is a skilful practitioner. Now the most hostile are the most opposite, such as hot and cold, bitter and sweet, moist and dry, and the like. And our father, Aesculapius, knowing how to implant friendship and accord in these elements, was the creator of our art, as our friends the poets here tell us, and I believe them; and not only medicine in every branch, but the arts of gymnastic and husbandry are likewise under his dominion. Anyone who pays the least attention to the subject will also perceive that in music there is the same reconciliation of opposites; and I suppose that this must have been the meaning of Heracleitus, although his words are not accurate; for he

says that the One is united by disunion, like the
harmony of the bow and the lyre. Now it is the height of
absurdity to say that harmony is discord or is composed of elements which are still in a state of discord.
But what he probably meant was, that harmony is
attained through the art of music by the reconciliation
of differing notes of higher or lower pitch which once
disagreed; for if the higher and lower notes still
disagreed, there could be no harmony – clearly not.
For harmony is a symphony, and symphony is a kind
of agreement; but an agreement of disagreements
while they disagree there cannot be; you cannot, I
repeat, harmonize that which disagrees. In like manner
rhythm is compounded of elements short and long,
once differing and now in accord; which accordance,
as in the former instance medicine, so in all these other
cases music implants, making love and concord to
grow up among them; and thus music, too, is a science
of the phenomena of love in their application to
harmony and rhythm. Again, in the constitution of a
harmony as of a rhythm there is no difficulty in
discerning love, and as yet there is no sign of its
duality. But when you want to use them in actual life,
either in the kind of composition to which the term
'lyrical' is applied or in the correct employment of airs
or metres composed already, which latter is called
education, then indeed the difficulty begins, and the
good artist is needed. Then the old tale has to be
repeated of fair and heavenly love – the love that comes
from Urania the fair and heavenly muse – and of the
duty of gratifying the temperate, and those who are as
yet intemperate only that they may become temperate,
and of preserving their love; and again, of the common
love that comes from Polyhymnia, that must be used

with circumspection in order that the pleasure be enjoyed, but may not generate licentiousness; just as in our own art it is a great matter so to regulate the desires of the epicure that he may attain his pleasure without the attendant evil of disease. Whence I infer that in music, in medicine, in all other things human as well as divine, both loves ought to be watched as far as may be, for they are both present.

The course of the seasons is also full of both these principles; and when, as I was saying, the elements of hot and cold, moist and dry, attain the temperate love of one another and blend in chastened harmony, they bring to men, animals, and plants health and plenty, and do them no harm; whereas the wanton love, getting the upper hand and affecting the seasons of the year, is very destructive and injurious, being the source of pestilence, and bringing many different kinds of diseases on animals and plants; and also hoar-frost and hail and blight are wont to spring from the mutual disproportions and disorders caused by this love, which to know in relation to the revolutions of the heavenly bodies and the seasons of the year is termed astronomy. Moreover all sacrifices and the activities that are the province of divination, which constitute the communion between gods and men – these, I say, are concerned only with the preservation of the good and the cure of the evil love. For all manner of impiety is likely to ensue if, instead of gratifying and honouring and reverencing the temperate love in all his actions, a man honours the other love, whether in his relations with gods or parents, with the living or the dead. Wherefore the business of divination is to watch over these lovers and to heal them, and divination is the peacemaker between gods and men, working by a knowledge of the tendencies to religion and piety which exist in human loves. Such is the great and mighty, or rather omnipotent, force of love in general. And the love, more especially, which is concerned with the good and which is perfected in company with temperance and justice, whether among gods or men, has the greatest power, and is the source of all our happiness, and gives us communion and friendship with the gods who are above us, and with one another. I dare say that I, too, have omitted much that might be said in praise of Love, but this was not intentional, and you, Aristophanes, may now supply the omission or take some other line of commendation; for I perceive that you are rid of the hiccough.

Yes, said Aristophanes, who followed, the hiccough is gone; not, however, until I applied the sneezing; and I wonder whether the orderly system of the body has a love of such noises and ticklings, for I no sooner applied the sneezing than I was cured.

Eryximachus said: Beware, friend Aristophanes; although you are going to speak, you are making fun of me; and I shall have to watch and see whether I cannot have a laugh at your expense, when you might speak in peace.

You are quite right, said Aristophanes, laughing, and I unsay my words. But do you please not to watch me, as I fear that in the speech which I am about to make, instead of others laughing with me, which is the natural work of our muse and would be satisfactory, I shall only be laughed at by them.

Do you expect to shoot your bolt and escape, Aristophanes? Well, perhaps if you are very careful and bear in mind that you will be called to account, I may be induced to let you off.

Aristophanes professed to open another vein of discourse; he had a mind to praise Love in another way, unlike that of either Pausanias or Eryximachus. Mankind, he said, judging by their neglect of him, have never, as I think, at all understood the power of Love. For if they had understood him they would surely have built noble temples and altars, and offered solemn sacrifices in his honour; but this is not done, and most certainly ought to be done: since of all the gods he is the best friend of men, the helper and the healer of the ills which are the great impediment to the happiness of the race. I will try to describe his power to you, and you shall teach the rest of the world what I am teaching you. In the first place, let me treat of the nature of man and what has happened to it. The original human nature was not like the present, but different. The sexes were not two as they are now, but originally three in number; there was man, woman, and the union of the two, of which the name survives but nothing else. Once it was a distinct kind, with a bodily shape and a name of its own, constituted by the union of the male and the female: but now only the word 'androgynous' is preserved, and that as a term of reproach. In the second place, the primeval man was round, his back and sides forming a circle; and he had four hands and the same number of feet, one head with two faces, looking opposite ways, set on a round neck and precisely alike; also four ears, two privy members, and the remainder to correspond. He could walk upright as men now do, backwards or forwards as he pleased, and he could also roll over and over at a great pace, turning on his four hands and four feet, eight in all, like tumblers going over and over with their legs in the air; this was when he wanted to run fast. Now the sexes were three, and such as I have described them, because the sun, moon, and earth are three; and the man was originally the child of the sun, the woman of the earth, and the man-woman of the moon, which is made up of sun and earth, and they were all round and moved round and round because they resembled their parents. Terrible was their might and strength, and the thoughts of their hearts were great, and they made an attack upon the gods; of them is told the tale of Otys and Ephialtes who, as Homer says, attempted to scale heaven, and would have laid hands upon the gods. Doubt reigned in the celestial councils. Should they kill them and annihilate the race with thunderbolts, as they had done the giants, then there would be an end of the sacrifices and worship which men offered to them; but, on the other hand, the gods could not suffer their insolence to be unrestrained. At last, after a good deal of reflection, Zeus discovered a way. He said: 'Methinks I have a plan which will enfeeble their strength and so extinguish their turbulence; men shall continue to exist, but I will cut them in two and then they will be diminished in strength and increased in numbers; this will have the advantage of making them more profitable to us. They shall walk upright on two legs, and if they continue insolent and will not be quiet, I will split them again and they shall hop about on a single leg.' He spoke and cut men in two, like a sorb-apple which is halved for pickling, or as you might divide an egg with a hair; and as he cut them one after another, he bade Apollo give the face and the half of the neck a turn in order that man might contemplate the section of himself: he would thus learn a lesson of humility. Apollo was also bidden to heal their wounds and compose their forms.

So he gave a turn to the face and pulled the skin from the sides all over that which in our language is called the belly, like the purses which draw tight, and he made one mouth at the centre, which he fastened in a knot (the same which is called the navel); he also moulded the breast and took out most of the wrinkles, much as a shoemaker might smooth leather upon a last; he left a few, however, in the region of the belly and navel, as a memorial of the primeval state. After the division the two parts of man, each desiring his other half, came together, and throwing their arms about one another, entwined in mutual embraces; longing to grow into one, they began to die from hunger and self-neglect, because they did not like to do anything apart; and when one of the halves died and the other survived, the survivor sought another mate, man or woman as we call them – being the sections of entire men or women – and clung to that. Thus they were being destroyed, when Zeus in pity invented a new plan: he turned the parts of generation round to the front, for this had not been always their position, and they sowed the seed no longer as hitherto like grasshoppers in the ground, but in one another; and after the transposition the male generated in the female in order that by the mutual embraces of man and woman they might breed, and the race might continue; or if man came to man they might be satisfied, and rest, and go their ways to the business of life. So ancient is the desire of one another which is implanted in us, reuniting our original nature, seeking to make one of two, and to heal the state of man. Each of us when separated, having one side only, like a flat fish, is but the tally-half of a man, and he is always looking for his other half. Men who are a section of that double nature which was once called androgynous are lovers of women; adulterers are generally of this breed, and also adulterous women who lust after men. The women who are a section of the woman do not care for men, but have female attachments; the female companions are of this sort. But they who are a section of the male follow the male, and while they are young, being slices of the original man, they have affection for men and embrace them, and these are the best of boys and youths, because they have the most manly nature. Some indeed assert that they are shameless, but this is not true; for they do not act thus from any want of shame, but because they are valiant and manly, and have a manly countenance, and they embrace that which is like them. And these when they grow up become our statesmen, and these only, which is a great proof of the truth of what I am saying. When they reach manhood they are lovers of youth, and are not naturally inclined to marry or beget children – if at all, they do so only in obedience to custom; but they are satisfied if they may be allowed to live with one another unwedded; and such a nature is prone to love and ready to return love, always embracing that which is akin to him. And when one of them meets with his other half, the actual half of himself, whether he be a lover of youth or a lover of another sort, the pair are lost in an amazement of love and friendship and intimacy, and one will not be out of the other's sight, as I may say, even for a moment: these are the people who pass their whole lives together, and yet they could not explain what they desire of one another. For the intense yearning which each of them has towards the other does not appear to be the desire of lover's intercourse, but of something else which the soul of either evidently desires and cannot tell, and of which she has only a dark and doubtful presentiment. Suppose Hephaestus, with his instruments, to come to the pair who are lying side by side and to say to them, 'What do you mortals want of one another?' they would be unable to explain. And suppose further, that when he saw their perplexity he said: 'Do you desire to be wholly one; always day and night in one another's company? For if this is what you desire, I am ready to melt and fuse you together, so that being two you shall become one, and while you live live a common life as if you were a single man, and after your death in the world below still be one departed soul, instead of two – I ask whether this is what you lovingly desire and whether you are satisfied to attain this' – there is not a man of them who when he heard the proposal would deny or would not acknowledge that this meeting and melting into one another, this becoming one instead of two, was the very expression of his ancient need. And the reason is that human nature was originally one and we were a whole, and the desire and pursuit of the whole is called love. There was a time, I say, when we were one, but now because of the wickedness of mankind god has dispersed us, as the Arcadians were dispersed into villages by the Lacedaemonians. And if we are not obedient to the gods, there is a danger that we shall be split up again and go about in basso-relievo, like the profile figures showing only one half the nose which are sculptured on monuments, and that we shall be like tallies. Wherefore let us exhort all men to piety in all things, that we may avoid evil and obtain the good, taking Love for our leader and commander. Let no one oppose him – he is the enemy

of the gods who opposes him. For if we are friends of
god and at peace with him we shall find our own true
loves, which rarely happens in this world at present. I
am serious, and therefore I must beg Eryximachus not
to make fun or to find any allusion in what I am saying
to Pausanias and Agathon, who, as I suspect, are both
of the manly nature, and belong to the class which I
have been describing. But my words have a wider
application – they include men and women everywhere; and I believe that if our loves were perfectly
accomplished, and each one returning to his primeval
nature had his original true love, then our race would
be happy. And if this would be best of all, the best in
the next degree must in present circumstances be the
nearest approach to such a union; and that will be the
attainment of a congenial love. Wherefore, if we would
praise him who has given to us the benefit, we must
praise the god Love, who is our greatest benefactor,
both leading us in this life back to our own nature, and
giving us high hopes for the future, for he promises
that if we are pious, he will restore us to our original
state, and heal us and make us happy and blessed.
This, Eryximachus, is my discourse of love, which,
although different to yours, I must beg you to leave
unassailed by the shafts of your ridicule, in order that
each may have his turn; each, or rather either, for
Agathon and Socrates are the only ones left.

Indeed, I am not going to attack you, said
Eryximachus, for I thought your speech charming,
and did I not know that Agathon and Socrates are
masters in the art of love, I should be really afraid that
they would have nothing to say, after the world of
things which have been said already. But, for all that, I
am not without hopes.

Socrates said: You played your part well, Eryximachus; but if you were as I am now, or rather as I shall be when Agathon has added another fine discourse, you would indeed be frightened out of your wits.

You want to cast a spell over me, Socrates, said Agathon, in the hope that I may be disconcerted by the idea that the audience confidently expect a fine discourse from me.

I should be strangely forgetful, Agathon, replied Socrates, of the courage and strength of mind which you showed when your own compositions were about to be exhibited, and you came upon the stage with the actors and faced the vast theatre altogether undismayed, if I thought that your nerves could be fluttered at a small party of friends.

Do you think, Socrates, said Agathon, that my head is so full of the theatre as not to know how much more formidable to a man of sense a few intelligent men are than many fools?

Nay, replied Socrates, I should be very wrong in attributing to you, Agathon, that or any other want of perception; I am quite aware that if you happened to meet with any whom you thought wise, you would care for their opinion much more than for that of the many. But then we, having been a part of the foolish many in the theatre, cannot be regarded as the select wise; and I fancy that if you chanced to be in the presence, not of one of ourselves, but of some really wise man, you would be ashamed of disgracing yourself before him – would you not?

Yes, said Agathon.

But before the many you would not be ashamed, if you thought that you were doing something disgraceful?

Here Phaedrus interrupted them, saying: Do not

answer him, my dear Agathon; for if he can only get a
partner with whom he can talk, especially a good-
looking one, he will no longer care what happens
about the completion of our plan. Now I love to hear
him talk; but just at present I must not forget the
encomium on Love which I ought to receive from him
and from everyone. When you and he have paid your
tribute to the god, then you may talk.

Very good, Phaedrus, said Agathon; I see no
reason why I should not proceed with my speech, as
I shall have many opportunities of conversing with
Socrates. Let me say first how I ought to speak, and
then speak.

The previous speakers, instead of praising the god
Love, and unfolding his nature, appear to have con-
gratulated mankind on the benefits which he confers
upon them. But I would rather praise the god first, and
then speak of his gifts; this is always the right way of
praising everything. May I say without impiety or
offence, that of all the blessed gods he is the most
blessed because he is the fairest and best? And he is the
fairest: for, in the first place, he is the youngest, and of
his youth he is himself the witness, fleeing out of the
way of age, who is swift enough, coming indeed to us
more swiftly than we like. Love has a natural hatred for
him and will not come near him; but youth and love
live and have their being together – like to like, as the
ancient proverb says. Many things were said by
Phaedrus about Love in which I agree with him, but
I cannot agree that he is older than Iapetus and
Cronos – not so; I maintain him to be the youngest
of the gods, and youthful ever. The ancient doings
among the gods of which Hesiod and Parmenides
spoke, if the tradition of them be true, were done of

Necessity and not of Love; had Love been in those days, there would have been no chaining or mutilation of the gods, or other violence, but peace and sweetness, as there is now in heaven since the rule of Love began. Love then is young, and he is also tender; he ought to have a poet like Homer to describe his tenderness, as Homer says of Ate that she is a goddess and tender, at least her feet are tender: 'Her feet are tender, for she sets her steps, not on the ground but on the heads of men': herein is an excellent proof of her tenderness – that she walks not upon the hard but upon the soft. Let us adduce a similar proof of the tenderness of Love; for he walks not upon the earth, nor yet upon the skulls of men, which are not so very soft, but in the hearts and souls of both gods and men, which are of all things the softest: in them he walks and dwells and makes his home. Not in every soul without exception, for where there is hardness he departs, where there is softness there he takes up his abode; and nestling always with his feet and in all manner of ways in the softest of soft places, how can he be other than the most tender of all things? Of a truth he is the tenderest as well as the youngest and also he is of flexile form; for if he were hard and without flexure he could not enfold all things, or wind his way into and out of every soul of man undiscovered. And a proof of his flexibility and symmetry of form is his grace, which is universally admitted to be in an especial manner the attribute of Love; ungracefulness and love are always at war with one another. The beauty of his complexion is revealed by his habitation among the flowers; for he dwells not amid bloomless or fading charms, whether of body or soul or aught else, but in the place of flowers and scents, there he sits and abides. Concerning the beauty of the god I have said enough; and yet there remains much more which I might say. Of his virtue I have now to speak: his greatest glory is that he can neither do nor suffer wrong to or from any god or any man. For he suffers not by force if he suffers – force comes not near him – neither when he acts does he act by force; for all men in all things serve him of their own free will, and where there is voluntary agreement, there, as the laws which are the lords of the city say, is justice. And not only is he just but exceedingly temperate, for Temperance is the acknowledged ruler of the pleasures and desires, and no pleasure ever masters Love; he is their master and they are his servants; and if he conquers them he must be temperate indeed. As to courage, even the god of war stands not up against him; he is the captive and Love is the lord, for love, the love of Aphrodite, masters him, as the tale runs; and the master is stronger than the servant. And if he conquers the bravest of all others, he must be himself the bravest. Of his courage and justice and temperance I have spoken, but I have yet to speak of his wisdom; and according to the measure of my ability I must try to rise to the height of my theme. In the first place he is a poet (and here, like Eryximachus, I magnify my art), and he is also the source of poesy in others, which he could not be if he were not himself a poet. And at the touch of him every one becomes a poet, 'even though he had no music in him before'; this we may properly take as a proof that Love is a good poet and, speaking summarily, accomplished in all the fine arts; for no one can give to another that which he has not himself, or teach that of which he has no knowledge. Who will deny that all living beings are of his creation? Are they not all the works of his wisdom, born and begotten of him? And as to the artists, do we not know that he only who has love for his instructor emerges into the light of fame? He whom Love touches not walks in darkness. The arts of medicine and archery and divination were discovered by Apollo under the guidance of love and desire; so that he too is a disciple of Love. Likewise the arts of the Muses, the metallurgy of Hephaestus, the weaving of Athene, the governance of Zeus over gods and men, are all due to the teaching of Love. And so, you see, Love set in order the empire of the gods – the love of beauty, as is evident, for with deformity Love has no concern. In the days of old, as I began by saying, dreadful deeds were done among the gods, for they were ruled by Necessity; but now since the birth of Love, and from the love of the beautiful, has sprung every good in heaven and earth. Therefore, Phaedrus, I say of Love that he is first the fairest and best in himself, and then the cause of what is fairest and best in all other things. And there comes into my mind a line of poetry in which he is said to be the god who 'Gives peace on earth and calms the stormy deep, who stills the winds and bids the sufferer sleep'. This is he who empties men of disaffection and fills them with affection, who makes them to meet together at gatherings such as sacrifices, feasts, dances, where he is our lord – who sends courtesy and sends away discourtesy, who gives kindness ever and never gives unkindness; gracious and good, the wonder of the wise, the amazement of the gods; desired by those who have no part in him, and precious to those who have the better part in him; parent of delicacy, luxury, desire, fondness, softness, grace; regardful of the good, regardless of the evil: in every word, labour, wish, fear – saviour, pilot, comrade, warrior, glory of gods and men, leader best and brightest: in whose footsteps let every man follow, sweetly singing in his honour and joining in that sweet strain with which love charms the souls of gods and men alike. Such is the speech, Phaedrus, half-playful, yet having a certain measure of seriousness according to my ability, which I dedicate to the god.

When Agathon had done speaking, Aristodemus said that there was a general cheer; the young man was thought to have spoken in a manner worthy of himself, and of the god. And Socrates, looking at Eryximachus, said: Tell me, son of Acumenus, was there not reason in my fears? And was I not a true prophet when I said that Agathon would make a wonderful oration, and that I should be in a strait?

The part of the prophecy which concerns Agathon, replied Eryximachus, appears to me to be true; but not the other part – that you will be in a strait.

Why, my dear friend, said Socrates, must not I or anyone be in a strait who has to speak after he has heard such a rich and varied discourse? It culminated in the beautiful diction and style of the concluding words – who could listen to them without amazement? When I reflected on the immeasurable inferiority of my own powers, I was ready to run away for shame, if there had been a possibility of escape. For I was reminded of Gorgias, and at the end of his speech I fancied in my terror that Agathon was shaking at me the Gorginian or Gorgonian head of the great master of rhetoric, which was simply to turn me and my speech into stone, as Homer says, and strike me dumb. And then I perceived how foolish I had been in consenting to take my turn with you in praising love, and saying that I too was an expert on love, when I really had no conception how anything whatever ought to be praised. For in my simplicity I imagined that the substance of praise should be truth, and that this being presupposed, the speaker was to choose the best topics and set them forth in the best manner. And I felt quite proud, thinking that I knew the true nature of all praise, and should speak well. Whereas I now see that, on the contrary, in order to pay a goodly tribute of praise to anything, you must attribute to it every species of greatness and glory, without regard to truth or falsehood – that doesn't matter; it looks as if the original proposal was not that each of us should really praise Love, but only that we should appear to praise him. And so, I suggest, you attribute to Love every imaginable form of praise which can be gathered anywhere; and you say that 'he is all this', and 'the cause of all that', making him appear a paragon of beauty and excellence to those who know him not, for you cannot impose upon those who know him. And a noble and solemn hymn of praise have you rehearsed. But as I misunderstood the nature of this praise when I said that I would take my turn, I must beg to be absolved from the promise which I made in ignorance; it was (as Euripides would say) a promise of the lips and not of the mind. Farewell then to such a strain, for I do not praise in that way; no, indeed, I cannot. But if you like to hear the truth about love, I am ready to speak in my own manner, though I will not make myself ridiculous by entering into any rivalry with you. Say then, Phaedrus, whether you would like to have the truth about love, spoken in any words and in any order which may happen to come into my mind at the time. Will that be agreeable to you?

Aristodemus said that Phaedrus and the company

bid him speak in any manner which he thought best. Then, he added, let me have your permission first to ask Agathon a few questions, in order that I may take what he accepts as the premises of my discourse.

I grant the permission, said Phaedrus: put your questions. Socrates then proceeded as follows.

In your oration, my dear Agathon, I think that you were certainly right in proposing to speak of the nature of Love first and afterwards of his works – that is a way of beginning which I very much approve. And as you have set forth his nature with such stately eloquence, may I ask you further, whether Love is by his nature the love of something or of nothing. And here I must explain myself: I do not want you to say that Love is the love of a father or the love of a mother – that would be ridiculous; but to answer as you would, if I asked, Is a father a father of something? To which you would find no difficulty in replying 'Of a son or daughter': and the answer would be right.

Very true, said Agathon.

And you would say the same of a mother?

He assented.

Yet let me ask you one more question in order to illustrate my meaning: is not a brother to be regarded essentially as a brother of something?

Certainly, he replied.

That is, of a brother or sister?

Yes, he said.

And now, said Socrates, I will ask about Love: is Love of something or of nothing?

Of something, surely, he replied.

Keep in mind what this is, and tell me what I want to know – whether Love desires that of which love is.

Yes, surely.

And does he possess, or does he not possess, that which he loves and desires?

Probably not, I should say.

Nay, replied Socrates, I would have you consider whether 'necessarily' is not rather the word. The inference that he who desires something is lacking in that thing, and that he who does not desire a thing is not in lack of it, is in my judgment, Agathon, absolutely and necessarily true. What do you think?

I agree with you, said Agathon.

Very good. Would he who is great, desire to be great, or he who is strong, desire to be strong?

That would be inconsistent with our previous admissions.

True. For he who has those qualities cannot be lacking in them?

Very true.

Suppose that a man being strong desired to be strong, or being swift desired to be swift, or being healthy desired to be healthy – since in that case he might be thought to desire something which he already has or is, I refer to the point in order that we may not be led astray – you will see on reflection that the possessors of these qualities must have their respective advantages at the time, whether they choose or not; and who can desire that which he has? Therefore, when a person says, I am well and wish to be well, or I am rich and wish to be rich, and I desire to have exactly what I have – to him we shall reply: 'You, my friend, having wealth and health and strength, want to have the continuance of them; for at this moment, whether you choose or no, you have them. And when you say, I desire that which I have and nothing else, is not your meaning that you want to have in the future what you have at present?' He must agree with us – must he not?

He must, replied Agathon.

Then, said Socrates, he desires that what he has at present may be preserved to him in the future, which is equivalent to saying that he desires something which is non-existent to him, and which as yet he has not got?

Very true, he said.

Then he and everyone who desires, desires that which he has not already, and which is future and not present, and which he has not, and is not, and which he lacks – these are the sort of things which love and desire seek?

Very true, he said.

Then now, said Socrates, let us recapitulate the argument. First, is not love of something, and of something too which is wanting to a man?

Yes, he replied.

Remember further what you said in your speech, or if you like I will remind you: you said that the love of the beautiful set in order the empire of the gods, for that of deformed things there is no love – did you not say something of that kind?

Yes, said Agathon.

Yes, my friend, and the remark was a just one. And if this is true, love is the love of beauty and not of deformity?

He assented.

And the admission has been already made that love is of something which one lacks and has not?

True, he said.

Then Love lacks and has not beauty?

Certainly, he replied.

And would you call that beautiful which lacks beauty and does not possess it in any way?

Certainly not.

Then would you still say that Love is beautiful?

Agathon replied: I fear that I said what I did without understanding.

Indeed, you made a very good speech, Agathon, replied Socrates; but there is yet one small question which I would fain ask – is not the good also the beautiful?

Yes.

Then in lacking the beautiful, love lacks also the good?

I cannot refute you, Socrates, said Agathon: Be it as you say.

Say rather, beloved Agathon, that you cannot refute the truth; for Socrates is easily refuted.

And now, taking my leave of you, I will rehearse a tale of love which I heard from Diotima of Mantinea, a woman wise in this and many other kinds of knowledge, who in the days of old, when the Athenians offered sacrifice before the coming of the plague, delayed the disease ten years. She was my instructress in the art of love, and I shall try to repeat to you what she said to me, beginning with the propositions on which Agathon and I are agreed; I will do the best I can do without any help. As you, Agathon, suggested, it is proper to speak first of the being and nature of Love, and then of his works. (I think it will be easiest for me if in recounting my conversation with the wise woman I follow its actual course of question and answer.) First I said to her in nearly the same words which he used to me, that Love was a mighty god, and likewise fair; and she proved to me, as I proved to him, that by my own showing Love was neither fair nor good. 'What do you mean, Diotima,' I said, 'is Love then evil and foul?' 'Hush,' she cried; 'must that be foul which is not fair?' 'Certainly,' I said. 'And is that which is not wise, ignorant? Do you not see that there is a mean between wisdom and ignorance?' 'And what may that be?' I said. 'Right opinion,' she replied; 'which, as you know, being incapable of giving a reason, is not knowledge (for how can knowledge be devoid of reason?) nor again ignorance (for neither can ignorance attain the truth), but is clearly something which is a mean between ignorance and wisdom.' 'Quite true,' I replied. 'Do not then insist,' she said, 'that what is not fair is of necessity foul, or what is not good evil; or infer that because Love is not fair and good he is therefore foul and evil; for he is in a mean between them.' 'Well,' I said, 'Love is surely admitted by all to be a great god.' 'By those who know or by those who do not know?' 'By all.' 'And how, Socrates,' she said with a smile, 'can Love be acknowledged to be a great god by those who say that he is not a god at all?' 'And who are they?' I said. 'You and I are two of them,' she replied. 'How can that be?' I said. 'It is quite intelligible,' she replied; 'for you yourself would acknowledge that the gods are happy and fair – of course you would – would you dare to say that any god was not?' 'Certainly not,' I replied. 'And you mean by the happy, those who are the possessors of things good and things fair?' 'Yes.' 'And you admitted that Love, because he was in want, desires those good and fair things of which he is in want?' 'Yes, I did.' 'But how can he be a god who has no portion in what is good and fair?' 'Impossible.' 'Then you see that you also deny the divinity of Love.'

'What then is Love?' I asked; 'Is he mortal?' 'No.'

'What then?' 'As in the former instance, he is neither mortal nor immortal, but in a mean between the two.' 'What is he, Diotima?' 'He is a great spirit, and like all spirits he is intermediate between the divine and the mortal.' 'And what,' I said, 'is his power?' 'He interprets between gods and men, conveying and taking across to the gods the prayers and sacrifices of men, and to men the commands of the gods and the benefits they return; he is the mediator who spans the chasm which divides them, and therefore by him the universe is bound together, and through him the arts of the prophet and the priest, their sacrifices and mysteries and charms, and all prophecy and incantation, find their way. For god mingles not with man; but through Love all the intercourse and converse of gods with men, whether they be awake or asleep, is carried on. The wisdom which understands this is spiritual; all other wisdom, such as that of arts and handicrafts, is mean and vulgar. Now these spirits or intermediate powers are many and diverse, and one of them is Love.' 'And who,' I said, 'was his father, and who his mother?' 'The tale,' she said, 'will take time; nevertheless I will tell you. On the day when Aphrodite was born there was a feast of all the gods, among them the god Poros or Plenty, who is the son of Metis or Sagacity. When the feast was over, Penia or Poverty, as the manner is on such occasions, came about the doors to beg. Now Plenty, who was the worse for nectar (there was no wine in those days), went into the garden of Zeus and fell into a heavy sleep; and Poverty considering that for her there was no plenty, plotted to have a child by him, and accordingly she lay down at his side and conceived Love, who partly because he is naturally a lover of the beautiful, and because

Aphrodite is herself beautiful, and also because he was
begotten during her birthday feast, is her follower and
attendant. And as his parentage is, so also are his
fortunes. In the first place he is always poor, and
anything but tender and fair, as the many imagine
him; and he is rough and squalid, and has no shoes,
nor a house to dwell in; on the bare earth exposed he
lies under the open heaven, in the streets, or at the
doors of houses, taking his rest; and like his mother he
is always in distress. Like his father too, whom he also
partly resembles, he is always plotting against the fair
and good; he is bold, enterprising, strong, a mighty
hunter, always weaving some intrigue or other, keen in
the pursuit of wisdom, fertile in resources; a philosopher at all times, terrible as an enchanter, sorcerer,
sophist. He is by nature neither mortal nor immortal,
but alive and flourishing at one moment when he is in
plenty, and dead at another moment in the same day,
and again alive by reason of his father's nature. But
that which is always flowing in is always flowing out,
and so he is never in want and never in wealth; and,
further, he is in a mean between ignorance and
knowledge. The truth of the matter is this: no god is a
philosopher or seeker after wisdom, for he is wise
already; nor does any man who is wise seek after
wisdom. Neither do the ignorant seek after wisdom;
for herein is the evil of ignorance, that he who is
neither a man of honour nor wise is nevertheless
satisfied with himself: there is no desire when there is
no feeling of want.' 'But who then, Diotima,' I said,
'are the lovers of wisdom, if they are neither the wise
nor the foolish?' 'A child may answer that question,'
she replied; 'they are those who are in a mean between
the two; Love is one of them. For wisdom is a most

beautiful thing, and Love is of the beautiful; and therefore Love is also a philosopher or lover of wisdom, and being a lover of wisdom is in a mean between the wise and the ignorant. And of this, too, his birth is the cause; for his father is wealthy and wise, and his mother poor and foolish. Such, my dear Socrates, is the nature of the spirit Love. The error in your conception of him was very natural; from what you say yourself, I infer that it arose because you thought that Love is that which is loved, not that which loves; and for that reason, I think, Love appeared to you supremely beautiful. For the beloved is the truly beautiful, and delicate, and perfect, and blessed; but the active principle of love is of another nature, and is such as I have described.'

I said: 'O thou stranger woman, thou sayest well; but, assuming Love to be such as you say, what is the use of him to men?' 'That, Socrates,' she replied, 'I will attempt to unfold: of his nature and birth I have already spoken; and you acknowledge that love is of the beautiful. But someone will say: What does it consist in, Socrates and Diotima? Or rather let me put the question more clearly, and ask: When a man loves the beautiful, what does his love desire?' I answered her, 'That the beautiful may be his.' 'Still,' she said, 'the answer suggests a further question: what is given by the possession of beauty?' 'To what you have asked,' I replied, 'I have no answer ready.' 'Then,' she said, 'let me put the word "good" in the place of the beautiful, and repeat the question once more: if he who loves loves the good, what is it then that he loves?' 'The possession of the good.' 'And what does he gain who possesses the good?' 'Happiness,' I replied; 'there is less difficulty in answering that question.' 'Yes,' she said, 'the happy are made happy by the acquisition of good things. Nor is there any need to ask why a man desires happiness; the answer is already final.' 'You are right,' I said. 'And is this wish and this desire common to all? Do all men always desire their own good, or only some men? What say you?' 'All men,' I replied; 'the desire is common to all.' 'Why, then,' she rejoined, 'are not all men, Socrates, said to love, but only some of them? Whereas you say that all men are always loving the same things.' 'I myself wonder,' I said, 'why this is.' 'There is nothing to wonder at,' she replied; 'the reason is that one part of love is separated off and receives the name of the whole, but the other parts have other names.' 'Give an illustration,' I said. She answered me as follows: 'There is creative activity which, as you know, is complex and manifold. All that causes the passage of non-being into being is a "poesy" or creation, and the processes of all art are creative; and the masters of arts are all poets or creators.' 'Very true.' 'Still,' she said, 'you know that they are not called poets, but have other names; only that one portion of creative activity which is separated off from the rest, and is concerned with music and metre, is called by the name of the whole and is termed poetry, and they who possess poetry in this sense of the word are called poets.' 'Very true,' I said. 'And the same holds of love. For you may say generally that all desire of good and happiness is only the great and subtle power of love; but they who are drawn towards him by any other path, whether the path of money-making or gymnastics or philosophy, are not called lovers – the name of the whole is appropriated to those whose desire takes one form only – they alone are said to love, or to be lovers.' 'I dare say,' I replied, 'that you are right.' 'Yes,' she added, 'and you hear people say that lovers are seeking for their other half; but I say that they are seeking neither for the half of themselves, nor for the whole, unless the half or the whole be also a good; men will cut off their own hands and feet and cast them away, if they think them evil. They do not, I imagine, each cling to what is his own, unless perchance there be someone who calls what belongs to him the good, and what belongs to another the evil; for there is nothing which men love but the good. Is there anything?' 'Certainly, I should say, that there is nothing.' 'Then,' she said, 'the simple truth is, that men love the good.' 'Yes,' I said. 'To which must be added that they love the possession of the good?' 'Yes, that must be added.' 'And not only the possession, but the everlasting possession of the good?' 'That must be added too.' 'Then love,' she said, 'may be described generally as the love of the everlasting possession of the good?' 'That is most true.'

'Then if this be always the nature of love, can you tell me further,' she went on, 'what is the manner of the pursuit? What are they doing who show all this eagerness and heat which is called love? And what is the object which they have in view? Answer me.' 'Nay, Diotima,' I replied, 'if I knew, I should not be wondering at your wisdom, neither should I come to learn from you about this very matter.' 'Well,' she said, 'I will teach you: the object which they have in view is birth in beauty, whether of body or soul.' 'I do not understand you,' I said; 'the oracle requires an explanation.' 'I will make my meaning clearer,' she replied. 'I mean to say, that all men are bringing to the birth in their bodies and in their souls. There is a certain age at which human nature is desirous of procreation – procreation which must be in beauty and not in deformity. The union of man and woman is a procreation; it is a divine thing, for conception and generation are an immortal principle in the mortal creature, and in the inharmonious they can never be. But the deformed is inharmonious with all divinity, and the beautiful harmonious. Beauty, then, is the destiny or goddess of parturition who presides at birth, and therefore, when approaching beauty, the procreating power is propitious, and expansive, and benign, and bears and produces fruit: at the sight of ugliness she frowns and contracts and has a sense of pain, and turns away, and shrivels up, and not without a pang refrains from procreation. And this is the reason why, when the hour of procreation comes, and the teeming nature is full, there is such a flutter and ecstasy about beauty whose approach is the alleviation of the bitter pain of travail. For love, Socrates, is not, as you imagine, the love of the beautiful only.' 'What then?' 'The love of generation and of birth in beauty.' 'Yes,' I said. 'Yes, indeed,' she replied. 'But why of generation? Because to the mortal creature, generation is a sort of eternity and immortality, and if, as has been already admitted, love is of the everlasting possession of the good, all men will necessarily desire immortality together with good: whence it must follow that love is of immortality.'

All this she taught me at various times when she spoke of love. And I remember her once saying to me, 'What is the cause, Socrates, of love, and the attendant desire? See you not how all animals, birds as well as beasts, in their desire of procreation, are in agony when they take the infection of love, which begins with the desire of union and then passes to the care of offspring, on whose behalf the weakest are ready to battle against the strongest even to the uttermost, and to die for them, and will let themselves be tormented with hunger, or make any other sacrifice, in order to maintain their young. Man may be supposed to act thus from reason; but why should animals have these passionate feelings? Can you tell me why?' Again I replied that I did not know. She said to me: 'And do you expect ever to become a master in the art of love, if you do not know this?' 'But I have told you already, Diotima, that my ignorance is the reason why I come to you, for I am conscious that I want a teacher; tell me then the cause of this and of the other mysteries of love.' 'Marvel not,' she said, 'if you believe that love is of the immortal, as we have several times acknowledged; for here again, and on the same principle too, the mortal nature is seeking as far as is possible to be everlasting and immortal: and this is only to be attained by generation, because generation always leaves behind a new and different existence in the place of the old. Nay, even in the life of the same individual there is succession and not absolute uniformity: a man is called the same, and yet in the interval between youth and age, during which every animal is said to have life and identity, he is undergoing a perpetual process of loss and reparation – hair, flesh, bones, blood, and the whole body are always changing. Which is true not only of the body, but also of the soul, whose habits, tempers, opinions, desires, pleasures, pains, fears, never remain the same in any one of us, but are always coming and going. What is still more surprising, it is equally true of science; not only do some of the sciences come to life in our minds, and others die away, so that we are never the same in regard to them either:

but the same fate happens to each of them individually. For what is implied in the word "recollection", but the departure of knowledge, which is ever being forgotten, and is renewed and preserved by recollection, and appears to be the same although in reality new, according to that law by which all mortal things are preserved, not absolutely the same, but by substitution, the old worn-out mortality leaving another new and similar existence behind – unlike the divine, which is wholly and eternally the same? And in this way, Socrates, the mortal body, or mortal anything, partakes of immortality; but the immortal in another way. Marvel not then at the love which all men have of their offspring; for that universal love and interest is for the sake of immortality.'

I was astonished at her words, and said: 'Is this really true, O most wise Diotima?' And she answered with all the authority of an accomplished sophist: 'Of that, Socrates, you may be assured – think only of the ambition of men, and you will wonder at the senselessness of their ways, unless you consider how they are stirred by the passionate love of fame. They are ready to run all risks, even greater than they would have run for their children, and to pour out money and undergo any sort of toil, and even to die, "if so they leave an everlasting name". Do you imagine that Alcestis would have died to save Admetus, or Achilles to avenge Patroclus, or your own Codrus in order to preserve the kingdom for his sons, if they had not imagined that the memory of their virtues, which still survives among us, would be immortal? Nay,' she said, 'I am persuaded that all men do all things, and the better they are the more they do them, in hope of the glorious fame of immortal virtue; for they desire the immortal.

'Those who are pregnant in the body only, betake themselves to women and beget children – this is the character of their love; their offspring, as they hope, will preserve their memory and give them the blessedness and immortality which they desire for all future time. But souls which are pregnant – for there certainly are men who are more creative in their souls than in their bodies, creative of that which is proper for the soul to conceive and bring forth: and if you ask me what are these conceptions, I answer, wisdom, and virtue in general – among such souls are all creative poets and all artists who are deserving of the name inventor. But the greatest and fairest sort of wisdom by far is that which is concerned with the ordering of states and families, and which is called temperance and justice. And he who in youth has the seed of these implanted in his soul, when he grows up and comes to maturity desires to beget and generate. He wanders about seeking beauty that he may get offspring – for from deformity he will beget nothing – and naturally embraces the beautiful rather than the deformed body; above all, when he finds a fair and noble and well-nurtured soul, he embraces the two in one person, and to such a one he is full of speech about virtue and the nature and pursuits of a good man, and he tries to educate him. At the touch and in the society of the beautiful which is ever present to his memory, even when absent, he brings forth that which he had conceived long before, and in company with him tends that which he brings forth; and they are married by a far nearer tie and have a closer friendship than those who beget mortal children, for the children who are their common offspring are fairer and more immortal. Who, when he thinks of Homer and Hesiod and other great poets, would not rather have their children than ordinary human ones? Who would not emulate them in the creation of children such as theirs, which have preserved their memory and given them everlasting glory? Or who would not have such children as Lycurgus left behind him to be the saviours, not only of Lacedaemon, but of Hellas, as one may say? There is Solon, too, who is the revered father of Athenian laws; and many others there are in many other places, both among Hellenes and barbarians, who have given to the world many noble works, and have been the parents of virtue of every kind; and many temples have been raised in their honour for the sake of children such as theirs; which were never raised in honour of anyone, for the sake of his mortal children.

'These are the lesser mysteries of love, into which even you, Socrates, may enter; to the greater and more hidden ones which are the crown of these, and to which, if you pursue them in a right spirit, they will lead, I know not whether you will be able to attain. But I will do my utmost to inform you, and do you follow if you can. For he who would proceed aright in this matter should begin in youth to seek the company of corporeal beauty; and first, if he be guided by his instructor aright, to love one beautiful body only – out of that he should create fair thoughts; and soon he will of himself perceive that the beauty of one body is akin to the beauty of another; and then if beauty of form in general is his pursuit, how foolish would he be not to recognize that the beauty in every body is one and the same! And when he perceives this he will abate his violent love of the one, which he will despise and deem a small thing, and will become a steadfast lover of all

beautiful bodies. In the next stage he will consider that
the beauty of the soul is more precious than the beauty
of the outward form; so that if a virtuous soul have but
a little comeliness, he will be content to love and tend
him, and will search out and bring to the birth
thoughts which may improve the young, until he is
compelled next to contemplate and see the beauty in
institutions and laws, and to understand that the
beauty of them all is of one family, and that personal
beauty is a trifle; and after institutions his guide will
lead him on to the sciences, in order that, beholding
the wide region already occupied by beauty, he may
cease to be like a servant in love with one beauty only,
that of a particular youth or man or institution, himself
a slave mean and narrow-minded; but drawing towards
and contemplating the vast sea of beauty, he will
create many fair and noble thoughts and discourses in
boundless love of wisdom, until on that shore he grows
and waxes strong, and at last the vision is revealed to
him of a single science, which is the science of beauty
everywhere. To this I will proceed; please to give me
your very best attention.

  'He who has been instructed thus far in the things of
love, and who has learned to see the beautiful in due
order and succession, when he comes toward the end
will suddenly perceive a nature of wondrous beauty
(and this, Socrates, is the final cause of all our former
toils) – a nature which in the first place is everlasting,
knowing not birth or death, growth or decay; secondly,
not fair in one point of view and foul in another, or at
one time or in one relation or at one place fair, at
another time or in another relation or at another place
foul, as if fair to some and foul to others, or in the
likeness of a face or hands or any other part of the

bodily frame, or in any form of speech or knowledge, or existing in any individual being, as for example, in a living creature, whether in heaven, or in earth, or anywhere else; but beauty absolute, separate, simple, and everlasting, which is imparted to the ever growing and perishing beauties of all other beautiful things, without itself suffering diminution, or increase, or any change. He who, ascending from these earthly things under the influence of true love, begins to perceive that beauty, is not far from the end. And the true order of going, or being led by another, to the things of love, is to begin from the beauties of earth and mount upwards for the sake of that other beauty, using these as steps only, and from one going on to two, and from two to all fair bodily forms, and from fair bodily forms to fair practices, and from fair practices to fair sciences, until from fair sciences he arrives at the science of which I have spoken, the science which has no other object than absolute beauty, and at last knows that which is beautiful by itself alone. This, my dear Socrates,' said the stranger of Mantinea, 'is that life above all others which man should live, in the contemplation of beauty absolute; a beauty which if you once beheld, you would see not to be after the measure of gold, and garments, and fair boys and youths, whose presence now entrances you; and you and many a one would be content to live seeing them only and conversing with them without meat or drink, if that were possible – you only want to look at them and to be with them. But what if a man had eyes to see the true beauty – the divine beauty, I mean, pure and clear and unalloyed, not infected with the pollutions of the flesh and all the colours and vanities of mortal life – thither looking, and holding converse with the true beauty simple and divine? Remember how in that communion only, beholding beauty with that by which it can be beheld, he will be enabled to bring forth, not images of beauty, but realities (for he has hold not of an image but of a reality), and bringing forth and nourishing true virtue will properly become the friend of god and be immortal, if mortal man may. Would that be an ignoble life?'

Such, Phaedrus – and I speak not only to you, but to all of you – were the words of Diotima; and I am persuaded of their truth. And being persuaded of them, I try to persuade others, that in the attainment of this end human nature will not easily find a helper better than Love. And therefore, also, I say that every man ought to honour him as I myself honour him, and walk in his ways, and exhort others to do the same, and praise the power and spirit of Love according to the measure of my ability now and ever.

The words which I have spoken, you, Phaedrus, may call an encomium of Love, or anything else which you please.

When Socrates had done speaking, the company applauded, and Aristophanes was beginning to say something in answer to the allusion which Socrates had made to his own speech, when suddenly there was a great knocking at the door of the house, as of revellers, and the sound of a flute-girl was heard. Agathon told the attendants to go and see who were the intruders. 'If they are friends of ours,' he said, 'invite them in, but if not, say that the drinking is over.' A little while afterwards they heard the voice of Alcibiades resounding in the court; he was in a great state of intoxication, and kept roaring and shouting Where is Agathon? Lead me to Agathon, and at length, supported by the flute-girl and some of his attendants, he found his way to them. Hail, friends, he said, appearing at the door crowned with a massive garland of ivy and violets, his head flowing with ribands. Will you have a very drunken man as a companion of your revels? Or shall I crown Agathon, which was my intention in coming, and go away? For I was unable to come yesterday, and therefore I am here today, carrying on my head these ribands, that taking them from my own head, I may crown the head of this fairest and wisest of men, as I may be allowed to call him. Will you laugh at me because I am drunk? Yet I know very well that I am speaking the truth, although you may laugh. Come now, I have stated my terms: am I to come in or not? Yes or no, will you drink with me?

The company were vociferous in begging that he would take his place among them, and Agathon specially invited him. Thereupon he was led in by the people who were with him; and as he was being led, intending to crown Agathon, he took the ribands from his own head and held them in front of his eyes; he was thus prevented from seeing Socrates, who made way for him, and Alcibiades took the vacant place between Agathon and Socrates, and in taking the place he embraced Agathon and crowned him. Take off his sandals, said Agathon, and let him make a third on the same couch.

By all means; but who makes the third partner in our revels? said Alcibiades, turning round and starting up as he caught sight of Socrates. Good heavens, he said, what is this? Why, it is Socrates! Here you are, always laying an ambush for me, and always, as your way is, pouncing out upon me at all sorts of unsuspected places: and now, what have you to say for yourself, and why are you lying here, where I perceive that you have contrived to find a place, not by a joker or lover of jokes like Aristophanes, but by the fairest of the company?

Socrates turned to Agathon and said: I must ask you to protect me, Agathon; for my passion for this man has grown quite a serious matter to me. Since I became his admirer I have never been allowed to speak to any other beauty, or so much as to look at them. If I do, he goes wild with envy and jealousy, and not only abuses me but can hardly keep his hands off me, and at this moment he may do me some harm. Please to see to this, and either reconcile me to him, or, if he attempts violence, protect me, as I am in bodily fear of his mad and passionate attempts.

There can never be reconciliation between you and me, said Alcibiades; but for what you have just said, I will chastise you some other time. At the moment, Agathon, I must beg you to give me some of the ribands that I may crown his head, his marvellous head – I would not have him complain of me for crowning you, and neglecting him, who in his eloquence is the conqueror of all mankind; and this not only once, as you were the day before yesterday, but always. Whereupon, taking some of the ribands, he crowned Socrates, and again reclined.

Then he said: You seem, my friends, to be sober, which is a thing not to be endured; you must drink – for that was the agreement under which I was admitted – and I elect myself master of the feast until you have drunk an adequate amount. Let us have a large goblet, Agathon, if there is one; or rather, he said, addressing the attendant, bring me that wine-cooler. The wine-cooler which had caught his eye was a vessel holding more than two quarts – this he filled and emptied, and bade the attendant fill it again for Socrates. Observe, my friends, said Alcibiades, that this ingenious trick of mine will have no effect on Socrates, for he can drink any quantity of wine and not be at all nearer being drunk. Socrates drank the cup which the attendant filled for him.

Eryximachus said: What is this, Alcibiades? Are we to have neither conversation nor singing over our cups; but simply to drink as if we were thirsty?

Alcibiades replied: Hail, worthy son of a most wise and worthy sire!

The same to you, said Eryximachus; but what shall we do?

That I leave to you, said Alcibiades. 'The wise physician worth a thousand men' ought to prescribe and we to obey. What do you want?

Well, said Eryximachus, before you appeared we had passed a resolution that each one of us in turn should make a speech in praise of love, and as good a one as he could: the turn was passed round from left to right; and as all of us have spoken, and you have not spoken but have well drunken, you ought to speak, and then impose upon Socrates any task which you please, and he on his right hand neighbour, and so on.

That is good, Eryximachus, said Alcibiades; and yet the comparison of a drunken man's speech with those of sober men is hardly fair. Also I should like to know, sweet friend, whether you really believe what Socrates was just now saying; for I can assure you that the very reverse is the fact, and that if I praise anyone but himself in his presence, whether god or man, he will hardly keep his hands off me.

For shame, said Socrates.

Hold your tongue, said Alcibiades, for I swear there is no one else whom I will praise when you are of the company.

Well then, said Eryximachus, if you like – praise Socrates.

What do you think, Eryximachus? said Alcibiades: shall I attack him and inflict the punishment before you all?

What are you about? said Socrates; are you going to raise more laughter, at my expense? Is that the meaning of your praise?

I am going to speak the truth, if you will permit me.

I not only permit, but exhort you to speak the truth.

Then I will begin at once, said Alcibiades, and if I say anything which is not true, you may interrupt me if you will, and say 'that is a lie', though my intention is to speak the truth. But you must not wonder if I speak anyhow as things come into my mind; for the fluent and orderly enumeration of all your singularities is not a task which is easy to a man in my condition.

And now, my boys, I shall praise Socrates in a figure which will appear to him to be a caricature, and yet I speak, not to make fun of him, but only for the truth's sake. I say, that he is exactly like the busts of Silenus, which are set up in the statuaries' shops, holding pipes or flutes in their mouths; and they are made to open in the middle, and have images of gods inside them. I say also that he is like Marsyas the satyr. You yourself will not deny, Socrates, that your face is like that of a satyr. Aye, and there is a resemblance in other points too. For example, you are a bully, as I can prove by witnesses, if you will not confess. And are you not a flute-player? That you are, and a performer far more wonderful than Marsyas. He indeed with instruments used to charm the souls of men by the power of his breath, and the players of his music do so still: for the melodies of Olympus are derived from Marsyas who taught them, and these, whether they are played by a great master or by a miserable flute-girl, have a power which no others have; they alone possess the soul and reveal the wants of those who have need of gods and mysteries, because they are divine. But you produce the same effect with your words only, and do not require the flute: that is the difference between you and him. When we hear any other speaker, even a very good one, he produces absolutely no effect upon us, or not much, whereas the mere fragments of you and your words, even at second hand, and however imperfectly repeated, amaze and possess the souls of every man, woman, and child who comes within hearing of them. And if I were not afraid that you would think me hopelessly drunk, I would have sworn as well as spoken to the influence which they have always had and still have over me. For my heart leaps within me more than that of any Corybantian reveller, and my eyes rain tears when I hear them. And I observe that very many others are affected in the same manner. I have heard Pericles and other great orators, and I thought that they spoke well, but I never had any similar feeling; my soul was not shaken by them, nor was I angry at the thought of my own slavish state. But this Marsyas has often brought me to such a pass, that I have felt as if I could not endure the life which I am leading (this, Socrates, you will admit); and at this very moment I am conscious that if I did not shut my ears against him, and fly as from the voice of the siren, I could not hold out against him, and my fate would be like that of others – he would pin me down, and I should grow old sitting at his feet. For he makes me confess that I ought not to live as I do, neglecting the many wants of my own soul and busying myself with the concerns of the Athenians; therefore I hold my ears and tear myself away from him. And he is the only person who ever made me ashamed, which you might think not to be in my nature, and there is no one else who does the same. For I know that I cannot answer him or say that I ought not to do as he bids, but when I leave his presence the love of popularity gets the better of me. And therefore I steal away and fly from him, and when I see him I am ashamed of what I have confessed to him. Many a time have I wished that he were dead, and yet I know that I should be much more sorry than glad if he were to die: so that I am at my wit's end what to do about the fellow.

And this is what I and many others have suffered from the flute-playing of this satyr. Yet hear me once more while I show you how exact the image is, and how marvellous his power. For be assured of this, none of you know him; but I will reveal him to you, since, having begun, I must go on. See you how fond he is of the fair? He is always with them and is always being smitten by them, and then again he knows nothing and is ignorant of all things – such is the appearance which he puts on. Is he not like a Silenus in this? To be sure he is: his outer mask is the carved head of the Silenus; but, O my companions in drink, when he is opened, what temperance there is residing within! Know you that beauty and wealth and all the other blessings which in popular opinion bring felicity, are of no account with him, and are utterly despised by him: he regards not at all the persons who are gifted with them, nor us ourselves – this is fact; but he spends all his life in teasing mankind, and hiding his true intent. When, however, I opened him, and looked within at his serious purpose, I saw in him divine and golden images of such fascinating beauty that I was ready to do in a moment whatever Socrates commanded: they may have escaped the observation of others, but I saw them. Now I fancied that he was seriously enamoured of my beauty, and I thought it a marvellous piece of luck; I had the means of persuading him to tell me everything that he knew, for I had a wonderful opinion of the attractions of my youth. In the prosecution of this design, when I next went to him, I sent away the attendant who usually accompanied me (I will confess the whole truth, and beg you to listen; and if I speak falsely, do you, Socrates, expose the falsehood). Well, he and I were alone together, and I thought that when there was nobody with us, I should hear him speak the language which lovers use to their loves when they are by themselves, and I was delighted. Nothing of the sort; he conversed as usual, and spent the day with me and then went away. Afterwards I challenged him to the palaestra; and he wrestled and closed with me several times when there was no one present; I fancied that I might succeed in this manner. Not a bit; I made no way with him. Lastly, as I had failed hitherto, I thought that I must take stronger measures and attack him boldly, and, as I had begun, not give him up, but see how matters stood between him and me. So I invited him to sup with me, just as if he were a fair youth, and I a designing lover. He was not easily persuaded to come; he did, however, after a while accept the invitation, and when he came the first time, he wanted to go away at once as soon as supper was over, and I had not the face to detain him. The second time, still in pursuance of my design, after we had supped, I went on conversing far into the night, and when he wanted to go away, I pretended that the hour was late and compelled him to remain. So he lay down on the couch next to me, on which he had reclined at supper, and there was no one but ourselves sleeping in the apartment. All this may be told without shame to anyone, but what follows I could hardly tell you if I were sober; yet as the proverb says, *in vino veritas*, whether there are also the mouths of children or not; and therefore I may speak. Nor should I be justified in concealing a resplendent action of Socrates when I have set out to praise him. Moreover I have felt the serpent's sting; and he who has suffered, as they say, is willing to tell only his fellow sufferers as they alone will be likely to understand him, and will not be extreme in judging of the sayings or doings which have been wrung from his agony. For I have been bitten by a worse than a viper's tooth; I have known in my soul, or in my heart, or however else it ought to be described, that worst of pangs, more violent in ingenuous youth than any serpent's tooth, the pang of philosophy, which will make a man say or do anything. And you whom I see around me, Phaedrus and Agathon and Eryximachus and Pausanias and Aristodemus and Aristophanes, all of you, and I need not say Socrates himself, and multitudes of others, have had experience of the same dionysiac madness and passion of philosophy. Therefore listen and excuse my doings then and my sayings now. But let the attendants and other profane and unmannered persons close tightly the doors of their ears.

When the lamp was put out and the servants had gone away, I thought that I must be plain with him and have no more ambiguity. So I gave him a shake, and I said: 'Socrates, are you asleep?' 'No,' he said. 'Do you know what I am thinking?' 'What is it?' he said. 'I think,' I replied, 'that of all the lovers whom I have ever had you are the only one who is worthy of me, and you appear to be too modest to speak. Now I feel that I should be a fool to refuse you this or any other favour, and therefore I come to lay at your feet all that I have and all that my friends have, in the hope that you will assist me in the way of virtue, which I desire above all things, and in which I believe that you can help me better than anyone else. And I should certainly have more reason to be ashamed of what wise men would say if I were to refuse my favour to such as you, than of what the world, who are mostly fools, would say of me if I granted it.' To these words he replied in the ironical manner which is so characteristic of him: 'Alcibiades, my friend, you have indeed an elevated aim if what you say is true, and if there really is in me any power by which you may become better; truly you must see in me some rare beauty of a kind infinitely higher than the comeliness which I see in you. And therefore, if you mean to share with me and to exchange beauty for beauty, you will have greatly the advantage of me; you will gain true beauty in return for appearance – like Diomede, gold in exchange for brass. But look again, sweet friend, and see whether you are not deceived in me. The mind begins to grow critical when the bodily eye fails, and you are still a long way from that point.' Hearing this, I said: 'I have told you my own thoughts, saying exactly what I mean; and now it is for you to consider what you think best for you and me.' 'That is good,' he said; 'at some other time then we will consider and act as seems best about this and about other matters.' After this interchange, I imagined that he was wounded by my shafts, and so without waiting to hear more I got up, and throwing my coat about him crept under his threadbare cloak, as the time of year was winter, and there I lay during the whole night having this truly superhuman wonder in my arms. This again, Socrates, will not be denied by you. And yet, notwithstanding all, he was so superior to my solicitations, so contemptuous and derisive and disdainful of my beauty – which really, as I fancied, had some attractions – hear, O judges; for judges you shall be of the haughty virtue of Socrates – nothing more happened, but in the morning when I awoke (let all the gods and goddesses be my witnesses) I arose as from the couch of a father or an elder brother.

What do you suppose must have been my feelings, after this rejection, at the thought of my own dishonour? And yet I could not help wondering at his natural temperance and self-restraint and manliness. I never imagined that I could have met with a man such as he is in wisdom and endurance. And therefore, I could not be angry with him or renounce his company, any more than I could find a way to win him. For I well knew that if Ajax could not be wounded by steel, much less he by money; and he had escaped me when I tried the only means by which I thought I might captivate him. So I was at my wit's end; no one was ever more hopelessly enslaved by another. All this happened before he and I went on the expedition to Potidaea; there we messed together, and I had the opportunity of observing his extraordinary power of sustaining fatigue. His endurance was simply marvellous when, being cut off from our supplies, we were compelled to go without food – on such occasions, which often happen in time of war, he was superior not only to me but to everybody; there was no one to be compared to him. Yet at a festival he had no equal in his power of enjoyment; though not willing to drink, he could if compelled beat us all at that – wonderful to relate! no human being had ever seen Socrates drunk; and his powers, if I am not mistaken, will be tested before long. His fortitude in enduring cold was also surprising. There was a most severe frost, for the winter in that region is really tremendous, and everybody else either remained indoors, or if they went out had on an amazing quantity of clothes, and were well shod, and had their feet swathed in felt and fleeces: in the midst of this, Socrates with his bare feet on the ice and in his ordinary dress marched better than the other soldiers who had shoes, and they looked daggers at him because he seemed to despise them.

I have told you one tale, and now I must tell you another, which is worth hearing, 'of the doings and sufferings of the enduring man' while he was on the expedition. One morning he was thinking about something which he could not resolve; he would not give it up, but continued thinking from early dawn until noon – there he stood fixed in thought; and at noon attention was drawn to him, and the rumour ran through the wondering crowd that Socrates had been standing and thinking about something ever since the break of day. At last, in the evening after supper, some Ionians out of curiosity (I should explain that this was not in winter but in summer), brought out their mats and slept in the open air that they might watch him and see whether he would stand all night. There he stood until the following morning; and with the return of light he offered up a prayer to the sun, and went his way. I will also tell, if you please – and indeed I am bound to tell – of his courage in battle; for who but he saved my life? Now this was the engagement in which I received the prize of valour: I was wounded and he would not leave me, but rescued both me and my arms; and he ought to have received the prize of valour which the generals wanted to confer on me on account of my rank, and I told them so (this, again, Socrates will not impeach or deny), but he was more eager than the generals that I and not he should have the prize. There was another occasion on which his behaviour was very remarkable – in the flight of the army after the battle of Delium, where he served among the heavy-armed – I had a better opportunity of seeing him than at Potidaea, for I was myself on horseback, and therefore comparatively out of danger. The troops were scattered in flight and he was retreating in company with Laches; I happened to meet them and told them not to be discouraged, and promised to remain with them; and there you might see him, Aristophanes, as you describe, just as he is in the streets of Athens, stalking like a pelican and rolling his eyes, calmly contemplating enemies as well as friends, and making very intelligible to anybody, even a great way off, that whoever attacked him would be likely to meet with a stout resistance; and in this way he and his companion escaped – for this is the sort of man who is never touched in war; those only are pursued who are running away headlong. I particularly observed how superior he was to Laches in presence of mind. Much else that is extraordinary might be said in praise of Socrates; some of his ways might perhaps be paralleled in another man, but yet his absolute unlikeness to any human being that is or ever has been is perfectly astonishing. You may imagine Brasidas and others to have been like Achilles, or you may imagine Nestor and Antenor to have been like Pericles, and the same may be said of other famous men; but of this strange being, and of his words, you will never be able to find any likeness, however remote, either in the present or in past generations – other than that which I have already suggested of Silenus and the satyrs; and they may represent not only himself, but his words. For, although I forgot to mention this to you before, his discourses are like the images of Silenus which open; they are ridiculous when you first hear them; they are enveloped in words and phrases that are like the skin of the wanton satyr – for his talk is of pack-asses and smiths and cobblers and curriers, and he is always repeating the same things in the same words, so that any stupid or inexperienced person might feel disposed to laugh at him. But he who sees the bust opening and looks into its interior, will find that they are the only words which have a meaning in them, and also are most divine, abounding in fair images of virtue, and of the widest comprehension, or rather comprehending everything which a man should bear in mind if he is to become a man of honour.

This, friends, is my praise of Socrates. I have added my blame of him for his ill treatment of me; and he has ill treated not only me, but Charmides the son of Glaucon, and Euthydemus the son of Diocles, and many others in the same way – beginning as their lover, the deceiver has ended by making them pay their addresses to him. Wherefore I say to you, Agathon, 'be not deceived by him; learn from me and take warning, and do not be a fool and learn by experience, as the proverb says.

When Alcibiades had finished, there was a laugh at his outspokenness; for he seemed to be still in love with Socrates. You are sober, Alcibiades, said Socrates, or you would never have gone so far about to hide the purpose of your satyr's praises; for all this long story is only an ingenious circumlocution, of which the point comes in by the way at the end; you want to get up a quarrel between me and Agathon, and your notion is that I ought to love you and nobody else, and that you and you only ought to love Agathon. But the plot of this Satyric or Silenic drama has been detected, and you must not allow him, Agathon, to score a success, and set us at variance.

I believe you are right, said Agathon; so I infer from the way in which he has placed himself between you and me with the intention of dividing us; but he shall gain nothing by that move, for I will go and lie on the couch next to you.

Yes, yes, replied Socrates, by all means come here and lie on the couch below me.

Alas, said Alcibiades, how the fellow goes on persecuting me; he is determined to get the better of me at every turn. I do beseech you, at least allow Agathon to lie between us.

Certainly not, said Socrates; as you praised me, and I in turn ought to praise my neighbour on the right, he will be out of order in praising me again when he ought rather to be praised by me, and I must entreat you to consent to this, and not be jealous, for I have a great desire to praise the youth.

Hurrah! cried Agathon, I cannot possibly stay here, Alcibiades; I must move instantly, that I may be praised by Socrates.

The usual way, said Alcibiades; where Socrates is,

no one else has any chance with beauty; and now how readily has he invented a specious reason for attracting Agathon to himself.

Agathon arose in order that he might take his place on the couch by Socrates, when suddenly a large band of revellers entered, and spoiled the order of the banquet. Someone who was going out having left the door open, they had found their way in, and made themselves at home; great confusion ensued, and everyone was compelled to drink large quantities of wine. Aristodemus said that Eryximachus, Phaedrus, and others went away – he himself fell asleep, and as the nights were long took a good rest: he was awakened towards daybreak by a crowing of cocks, and when he awoke, the others were either asleep, or had gone away; there remained only Socrates, Aristophanes, and Agathon, who were drinking out of a large goblet which they passed round, and Socrates was discoursing to them. Aristodemus was only half awake, and he did not hear the beginning of the discourse; the chief thing which he remembered was Socrates compelling the other two to acknowledge that the genius of comedy was the same with that of tragedy, and that the true artist in tragedy was an artist in comedy also. To this they were constrained to assent, being drowsy, and not quite following the argument. And first of all Aristophanes dropped off, then, when the day was already dawning, Agathon. Socrates, having laid them to sleep, rose to depart; Aristodemus, as his manner was, following him. At the Lyceum he took a bath, and passed the day as usual. In the evening he retired to rest at his own home.

PLATO
APOLOGY

APOLOGY

How you, O Athenians, have been affected by my accusers, I cannot tell; but I know that they almost made me forget who I was – so persuasively did they speak; and yet they have hardly uttered a word of truth. But of the many falsehoods told by them, there was one which quite amazed me – I mean when they said that you should be upon your guard and not allow yourselves to be deceived by the force of my eloquence. To say this, when they were certain to be detected as soon as I opened my lips and proved myself to be anything but a great speaker, did indeed appear to me most shameless – unless by the force of eloquence they mean the force of truth; for if such is their meaning, I admit that I am eloquent. But in how different a way from theirs! Well, as I was saying, they have scarcely spoken the truth at all; from me you shall hear the whole truth, but not delivered after their manner in a set oration duly ornamented with fine words and phrases. No, by heaven! I shall use the words and arguments which occur to me at the moment, for I am confident in the justice of my cause: at my time of life I ought not to be appearing before you, O men of Athens, in the character of a boy inventing falsehoods – let no one expect it of me. And I must particularly beg of you to grant me this favour: if I defend myself in my accustomed manner, and you hear me using the words which many of you have heard me using habitually in the agora, at the tables of the money-changers, and elsewhere, I would ask you not to be surprised, and not to interrupt me on this account. For

I am more than seventy years of age, and appearing now for the first time before a court of law, I am quite a stranger to the language of the place; and therefore I would have you regard me as if I were really a stranger, whom you would excuse if he spoke in his native tongue, and after the fashion of his country. Am I making an unfair request of you? Never mind the manner, which may or may not be good; but think only of the truth of my words, and give heed to that: let the speaker speak truly and the judge decide justly.

And first, I have to reply to the older charges and to my first accusers, and then I will go on to the later ones. For of old I have had many accusers, who have accused me falsely to you during many years; and I am more afraid of them than of Anytus and his associates, who are dangerous, too, in their own way. But far more dangerous are the others, who began when most of you were children, and took possession of your minds with their falsehoods, telling of one Socrates, a wise man, who speculated about the heaven above, and searched into the earth beneath, and made the worse appear the better cause. The men who have besmeared me with this tale are the accusers whom I dread; for their hearers are apt to fancy that such inquirers do not believe in the existence of the gods. And they are many, and their charges against me are of ancient date, and they were made by them in the days when some of you were more impressible than you are now – in childhood, or it may have been in youth – and the cause went by default, for there was none to answer. And hardest of all, I do not know and cannot tell the names of my accusers, unless in the chance case of a comic poet. All who from envy and malice have persuaded you – some of them having first convinced themselves – all this class of men are most difficult to deal with; for I cannot have them up here, and cross-examine them, and therefore I must simply fight with shadows in my own defence, and argue when there is no one who answers. I will ask you then to take it from me that my opponents are of two kinds; one recent, the other ancient: and I hope that you will see the propriety of my answering the latter first, for these accusations you heard long before the others, and much oftener.

Well, then, I must make my defence, and endeavour to remove from your minds in a short time, a slander which you have had a long time to take in. May I succeed, if to succeed be for my good and yours, or likely to avail me in my cause! The task is not an easy one; I quite understand the nature of it. And so leaving the event with god, in obedience to the law I will now make my defence.

I will begin at the beginning, and ask what is the accusation which has given rise to the slander of me, and in fact has encouraged Meletus to prefer this charge against me. Well, what do the slanderers say? They shall be my prosecutors, and this is the information they swear against me: 'Socrates is an evildoer; a meddler who searches into things under the earth and in heaven, and makes the worse appear the better cause, and teaches the aforesaid practices to others.' Such is the nature of the accusation: it is just what you have yourselves seen in the comedy of Aristophanes, who has introduced a man whom he calls Socrates, swinging about and saying that he walks on air, and talking a deal of nonsense concerning matters of which I do not pretend to know either much or little – not that I mean to speak disparagingly of anyone who is a student of natural philosophy. May Meletus never bring so many charges against me as to make me do that! But the simple truth is, O Athenians, that I have nothing to do with physical speculations. Most of those here present are witnesses to the truth of this, and to them I appeal. Speak then, you who have heard me, and tell your neighbours whether any of you have ever known me hold forth in few words or in many upon such matters . . . You hear their answer. And from what they say of this part of the charge you will be able to judge of the truth of the rest.

As little foundation is there for the report that I am a teacher, and take money; this accusation has no more truth in it than the other. Although, if a man were really able to instruct mankind, this too would, in my opinion, be an honour to him. There is Gorgias of Leontium, and Prodicus of Ceos, and Hippias of Elis, who go the round of the cities, and are able to persuade the young men to leave their own citizens by whom they might be taught for nothing, and come to them whom they not only pay, but are thankful if they may be allowed to pay them. There is at this time a Parian philosopher residing in Athens, of whom I have heard; and I came to hear of him in this way: I came across a man who has spent more money on the sophists than the rest of the world put together, Callias, the son of Hipponicus, and knowing that he had sons, I asked him: 'Callias,' I said, 'if your two sons were foals or calves, there would be no difficulty in finding someone to put over them; we should hire a trainer of horses, or a farmer probably, who would improve and perfect them in the appropriate virtue and excellence; but as they are human beings, whom are you thinking of placing over them? Is there anyone who understands human and civic virtue? You must have thought about the matter, for you have sons; is there anyone?' 'There is,' he said. 'Who is he?' said I; 'and of what country? and what does he charge?' 'Evenus the Parian,' he replied; 'he is the man, and his charge is five minas.' Happy is Evenus, I said to myself, if he really has this wisdom, and teaches at such a moderate charge. Had I the same, I should have been very proud and conceited; but the truth is that I have no knowledge of the kind.

I dare say, Athenians, that someone among you will reply, 'Yes, Socrates, but what *is* your occupation? What is the origin of these accusations which are brought against you; there must have been something strange which you have been doing? All these rumours and this talk about you would never have arisen if you had been like other men: tell us, then, what is the cause of them, for we should be sorry to judge hastily of you.' Now I regard this as a fair challenge, and I will endeavour to explain to you the reason why I am called wise and have such an evil fame. Please to attend then. And although some of you may think that I am joking, I declare that I will tell you the entire truth. Men of Athens, this reputation of mine has come of a certain sort of wisdom which I possess. If you ask me what kind of wisdom, I reply, wisdom such as may perhaps be attained by man, for to that extent I am inclined to believe that I am wise; whereas the persons of whom I was speaking have a kind of superhuman wisdom, which I know not how to describe, because I have it not myself; and he who says that I have, speaks falsely, and is taking away my character. And here, O men of Athens, I must beg you not to interrupt me, even if I seem to say something extravagant. For the word which I will speak is not mine. I will refer you to a witness who is worthy of credit; that witness shall be the god of Delphi – he will tell you about my wisdom, if I have any, and of what sort it is. You must have known Chaerephon; he was early a friend of mine, and also a friend of yours, for he shared in the recent exile of the people, and returned with you. Well, Chaerephon, as you know, was very impetuous in all his doings, and he went to Delphi and boldly asked the oracle to tell him whether – as I was saying, I must beg you not to interrupt – he actually asked the oracle to tell him whether anyone was wiser than I was, and the Pythian prophetess answered that there was no man wiser. Chaerephon is dead himself; but his brother, who is in court, will confirm the truth of what I am saying.

Why do I mention this? Because I am going to explain to you why I have such an evil name. When I heard the answer, I said to myself, What can the god mean? And what is the interpretation of his riddle? For I know that I have no wisdom, small or great. What then can he mean when he says that I am the wisest of men? And yet he is a god, and cannot lie; that would be against his nature. After long perplexity, I thought of a method of trying the question. I reflected that if I could only find a man wiser than myself, then I might go to the god with a refutation in my hand. I should say to him, 'Here is a man who is wiser than I am; but you said that I was the wisest.' Accordingly I went to one who had the reputation of wisdom, and observed him – his name I need not mention, he was a politician; and in the process of examining him and talking with him, this, men of Athens, was what I found. I could not help thinking that he was not really wise, although he was thought wise by many, and still wiser by himself; and thereupon I tried to explain to him that he thought himself wise, but was not really wise; and the consequence was that he hated me, and his enmity was shared by several who were present and heard me. So I left him, saying to myself as I went away: Well, although I do not suppose that either of us knows anything really worth knowing, I am at least wiser than this fellow – for he knows nothing, and thinks that he knows; I neither know nor think that I know. In this one little point, then, I seem to have the advantage of him. Then I went to another who had still higher pretensions to wisdom, and my conclusion was exactly the same. Whereupon I made another enemy of him, and of many others besides him.

Then I went to one man after another, being not unconscious of the enmity which I provoked, and I lamented and feared this: but necessity was laid upon me – the word of god, I thought, ought to be considered first. And I said to myself, Go I must to all who appear to know, and find out the meaning of the oracle. And I swear to you, Athenians – for I must tell you the truth – the result of my mission was just this: I found that the men most in repute were nearly the most foolish; and that others less esteemed were really closer to wisdom. I will tell you the tale of my wanderings and of the 'Herculean' labours, as I may call them, which I endured only to find at last the oracle irrefutable. After the politicians, I went to the poets; tragic, dithyrambic, and all sorts. And there, I said to myself, you will be instantly detected; now you will find out that you are more ignorant than they are. Accordingly, I took them some of the most elaborate passages in their own writings, and asked what was the meaning of them – thinking that they would teach me something. Will you believe me? I am ashamed to confess the truth, but I must say that there is hardly a person present who would not have talked better about their poetry than they did themselves. So I learnt that not by wisdom do poets write poetry, but by a sort of genius and inspiration; they are like diviners or sooth-sayers who also say many fine things, but do not understand the meaning of them. The poets appeared to me to be much in the same case; and I further observed that upon the strength of their poetry they believed themselves to be the wisest of men in other things in which they were not wise. So I departed, conceiving myself to be superior to them for the same reason that I was superior to the politicians.

At last I went to the artisans, for I was conscious that I knew nothing at all, as I may say, and I was sure that they knew many fine things; and here I was not mistaken, for they did know many things of which I was ignorant, and in this they certainly were wiser than I was. But I observed that even the good artisans fell into the same error as the poets: because they were good workmen they thought that they also knew all sorts of high matters, and this defect in them over-shadowed their wisdom; and therefore I asked myself on behalf of the oracle, whether I would like to be as I was, neither having their knowledge nor their igno-rance, or like them in both; and I made answer to myself and to the oracle that I was better off as I was.

This inquisition has led to my having many enemies of the worst and most dangerous kind, and has given rise also to many imputations, including the name of 'wise'; for my hearers always imagine that I myself possess the wisdom which I find wanting in others.

But the truth is, O men of Athens, that god only is wise; and by his answer he intends to show that the wisdom of men is worth little or nothing; although speaking of Socrates, he is only using my name by way of illustration, as if he said, He, O men, is the wisest, who, like Socrates, knows that his wisdom is in truth worth nothing. And so I go about the world, obedient to the god, and search and make inquiry into the wisdom of anyone, whether citizen or stranger, who appears to be wise; and if he is not wise, then in vindication of the oracle I show him that he is not wise; and my occupation quite absorbs me, and I have had no time to do anything useful either in public affairs or in any concern of my own, but I am in utter poverty by reason of my devotion to the god.

There is another thing: young men of the richer classes, who have not much to do, come about me of their own accord; they like to hear people examined, and they often imitate me, and proceed to do some examining themselves; there are plenty of persons, as they quickly discover, who think that they know something, but really know little or nothing; and then those who are examined by them instead of being angry with themselves are angry with me: This confounded Socrates, they say; this villainous mis-leader of youth! And then if somebody asks them, Why, what evil does he practise or teach? they do not know, and cannot tell; but in order that they may not appear to be at a loss, they repeat the ready-made charges which are used against all philosophers about teaching things up in the clouds and under the earth, and having no gods, and making the worse appear the better cause; for they do not like to confess that their pretence of knowledge has been detected – which is the truth; and as they are numerous and ambitious and energetic, and speak vehemently with persuasive tongues, they have filled your ears with their loud and inveterate calumnies. And this is the reason why my three accusers, Meletus and Anytus and Lycon, have set upon me; Meletus, who has a quarrel with me on behalf of the poets; Anytus, on behalf of the craftsmen and politicians; Lycon, on behalf of the rhetoricians: and as I said at the beginning, I cannot expect to get rid of such a mass of calumny all in a moment. And this, O men of Athens, is the truth and the whole truth; I have concealed nothing, I have dissembled nothing. And yet, I feel sure that my plainness of speech is fanning their hatred of me, and what is their hatred but a proof that I am speaking the truth? Hence has arisen the prejudice against me; and this is the reason of it, as you will find out either in this or in any future inquiry.

I have said enough in my defence against the first class of my accusers; I turn to the second class. They are headed by Meletus, that good man and true lover of his country, as he calls himself. Against these, too, I must try to make a defence. Let their affidavit be read; it contains something of this kind: it says that Socrates is a doer of evil, inasmuch as he corrupts the youth, and does not receive the gods whom the state receives, but has a new religion of his own. Such is the charge; and now let us examine the particular counts. He says that I am a doer of evil, and corrupt the youth; but I say, O men of Athens, that Meletus is a doer of evil, in that he is playing a solemn farce, recklessly bringing men to trial from a pretended zeal and interest about matters in which he really never had the smallest interest. And the truth of this I will endeavour to prove to you.

Come hither, Meletus, and let me ask a question of you. You attach great importance to the improvement of youth?

Yes, I do.

Tell the judges, then, who is their improver; for you must know, as you take such interest in the subject, and have discovered their corrupter, and are citing and accusing me in this court. Speak, then, and tell the judges who is the improver of youth. Observe, Meletus, that you are silent, and have nothing to say. But is this not rather disgraceful, and a very considerable proof of what I was saying, that you have no interest in the matter? Speak up, friend, and tell us who their improver is.

The laws.

But that, my good sir, is not my question. Can you not name some person – whose first qualification will be that he knows the laws?

The judges, Socrates, who are present in court.

What, do you mean to say, Meletus, that they are able to instruct and improve youth?

Certainly they are.

What, all of them, or some only and not others?

All of them.

Truly, that is good news! There are plenty of improvers, then. And what do you say of the audience – do they improve them?

Yes, they do.

And the senators?

Yes, the senators improve them.

But perhaps the members of the assembly corrupt them? Or do they too improve them?

They improve them.

Then every Athenian improves and elevates them;

all with the exception of myself; and I alone am their corrupter? Is that what you affirm?

That is what I stoutly affirm.

I am very unfortunate if you are right. But suppose I ask you a question: is it the same with horses? Does one man do them harm and all the world good? Is not the exact opposite the truth? One man is able to do them good, or at least very few – the trainer of horses, that is to say, does them good, but the ordinary man does them harm if he has to do with them? Is not that true, Meletus, of horses, or of any other animals? Most assuredly it is, whether you and Anytus say yes or no. Happy indeed would be the condition of youth if they had one corrupter only, and all the rest of the world were their benefactors. But you, Meletus, have sufficiently shown that you never had a thought about the young: your carelessness is plainly seen in your not caring about the very things which you bring against me.

And now, Meletus, I adjure you to answer me another question: which is better, to live among bad citizens, or among good ones? Answer, friend, I say; the question is one which may be easily answered. Do not the good do their neighbours good, and the bad do them evil?

Certainly.

And is there anyone who would rather be injured than benefited by those who live with him? Answer, my good friend, the law requires you to answer – does anyone like to be injured?

Certainly not.

And when you accuse me of corrupting and deteriorating the youth, do you allege that I corrupt them intentionally or unintentionally?

PLATO: APOLOGY

Intentionally, I say.

But you have just admitted that the good do their neighbours good, and the evil do them evil. Now, is that a truth which your superior wisdom has recognized thus early in life, and am I, at my age, in such darkness and ignorance as not to know that if a man with whom I have to live is corrupted by me, I am very likely to be harmed by him; and yet I corrupt him, and intentionally, too – so you say, although neither I nor any other human being is ever likely to be convinced by you. But either I do not corrupt them, or I corrupt them unintentionally; and on either view of the case you lie. If my offence is unintentional, the law has no cognizance of unintentional offences: you ought to have taken me privately, and warned and admonished me; for if I had had instruction, I should have left off doing what I only did unintentionally – beyond doubt I should; but you would have nothing to say to me and refused to teach me. And now you bring me up in this court, which is a place not of instruction, but of punishment.

It will be very clear to you, Athenians, as I was saying, that Meletus has never had any care, great or small, about the matter. But still I should like to know, Meletus, in what I am affirmed to corrupt the young. I suppose you mean, as I infer from your indictment, that I teach them not to acknowledge the gods which the state acknowledges, but some other new divinities or spiritual agencies in their stead. These are the lessons by which I corrupt the youth, as you say.

Yes, that I say emphatically.

Then, by the gods, Meletus, of whom we are speaking, tell me and the court, in somewhat plainer terms, what you mean! For I do not as yet understand

221

whether you affirm that I teach other men to acknowledge some gods, and therefore that I do believe in
gods, and am not an entire atheist – this you do not lay
to my charge – but only you say that they are not the
same gods which the city recognizes – the charge is
that they are different gods. Or, do you mean that I am
an atheist simply, and a teacher of atheism?

I mean the latter – that you are a complete atheist.

What an extraordinary statement! Why do you
think so, Meletus? Do you mean that I do not believe
in the godhead of the sun or moon, like the rest of
mankind?

I assure you, judges, that he does not: for he says
that the sun is stone, and the moon earth.

Friend Meletus, do you think that you are accusing
Anaxagoras? Have you such a low opinion of the
judges, that you fancy them so illiterate as not to know
that these doctrines are found in the books of
Anaxagoras the Clazomenian, which are full of them?
And so, forsooth, the youth are said to be taught them
by Socrates, when they can be bought in the book-
market for one drachma at most; and they might pay
their money, and laugh at Socrates if he pretends to
father these extraordinary views. And so, Meletus, you
really think that I do not believe in any god?

I swear by Zeus that you verily believe in none at all.

Nobody will believe you, Meletus, and I am pretty
sure that you do not believe yourself. I cannot help
thinking, men of Athens, that Meletus is reckless and
impudent, and that he has brought this indictment in
a spirit of mere wantonness and youthful bravado.
Has he not compounded a riddle, thinking to try
me? He said to himself: I shall see whether the wise
Socrates will discover my facetious self-contradiction,

or whether I shall be able to deceive him and the rest of them. For he certainly does appear to me to contradict himself in the indictment as much as if he said that Socrates is guilty of not believing in the gods, and yet of believing in them – but this is not like a person who is in earnest.

I should like you, O men of Athens, to join me in examining what I conceive to be his inconsistency; and do you, Meletus, answer. And I must remind the audience of my request that they would not make a disturbance if I speak in my accustomed manner.

Did ever man, Meletus, believe in the existence of human things, and not of human beings? . . . I wish, men of Athens, that he would answer, and not be always trying to get up an interruption. Did ever any man believe in horsemanship, and not in horses? Or in flute-playing, and not in flute-players? My friend, no man ever did; I answer to you and to the court, as you refuse to answer for yourself. But now please to answer the next question: can a man believe in the existence of things spiritual and divine, and not in spirits or demigods?

He cannot.

How lucky I am to have extracted that answer, by the assistance of the court! But then you swear in the indictment that I teach and believe in divine or spiritual things (new or old, no matter for that); at any rate, I believe in spiritual things – so you say and swear in the affidavit; and yet if I believe in them, how can I help believing in spirits or demigods – must I not? To be sure I must; your silence gives consent. Now what are spirits or demigods? Are they not either gods or the sons of gods?

Certainly they are.

But this is what I call the facetious riddle invented by you: the demigods or spirits are gods, and you say first that I do not believe in gods, and then again that I do believe in gods; that is, if I believe in demigods. For if the demigods are the illegitimate sons of gods, whether by nymphs, or by other mothers, as some are said to be – what human being will ever believe that there are no gods when there are sons of gods? You might as well affirm the existence of mules, and deny that of horses and asses. Such nonsense, Meletus, could only have been intended by you to make trial of me. You have put this into the indictment because you could think of nothing real of which to accuse me. But no one who has a particle of understanding will ever be convinced by you that a man can believe in the existence of things divine and superhuman, and the same man refuse to believe in gods and demigods and heroes.

I have said enough in answer to the charge of Meletus: any elaborate defence is unnecessary. You know well the truth of my statement that I have incurred many violent enmities; and this is what will be my destruction if I am destroyed – not Meletus, nor yet Anytus, but the envy and detraction of the world, which has been the death of many good men, and will probably be the death of many more; there is no danger of my being the last of them.

Someone will say: And are you not ashamed, Socrates, of a course of life which is likely to bring you to an untimely end? To him I may fairly answer: There you are mistaken; a man who is good for anything ought not to calculate the chance of living or dying; he ought only to consider whether in doing anything he is doing right or wrong – acting the part of a good man or of a bad. Whereas, upon your view, the

heroes who fell at Troy were not good for much, and
the son of Thetis above all, who altogether despised
danger in comparison with disgrace; and when he was
so eager to slay Hector, his goddess mother said to
him that if he avenged his companion Patroclus, and
slew Hector, he would die himself – 'Fate,' she said, in
these or the like words, 'waits for you next after
Hector'; he, receiving this warning, utterly despised
danger and death, and instead of fearing them, feared
rather to live in dishonour, and not to avenge his
friend. 'Let me die forthwith,' he replied, 'and be
avenged of my enemy, rather than abide here by the
beaked ships, a laughing-stock and a burden of the
earth.' Had Achilles any thought of death and danger?
For wherever a man's place is, whether the place
which he has chosen or that in which he has been
placed by a commander, there he ought to remain in
the hour of danger, taking no account of death or of
anything else in comparison with disgrace. And this,
O men of Athens, is a true saying.

Strange, indeed, would be my conduct, O men of
Athens, if I who, when I was ordered by the generals
whom you chose to command me at Potidaea and
Amphipolis and Delium, remained where they placed
me, like any other man, facing death – if now, when, as
I conceive and imagine, god orders me to fulfil the
philosopher's mission of searching into myself and
other men, I were to desert my post through fear of
death, or any other fear; that would indeed be strange,
and I might justly be arraigned in court for denying the
existence of the gods, if I disobeyed the oracle because
I was afraid of death, fancying that I was wise when I
was not wise. For the fear of death is indeed the
pretence of wisdom, and not real wisdom, being a

pretence of knowing the unknown; and no one knows whether death, of which men are afraid because they apprehend it to be the greatest evil, may not be the greatest good. Is not this ignorance of a disgraceful sort, the ignorance which is the conceit that a man knows what he does not know? And in this respect only I believe myself to differ from men in general, and may perhaps claim to be wiser than they are – that whereas I know but little of the world below, I do not suppose that I know: but I do know that injustice and disobedience to a better, whether god or man, is evil and dishonourable, and I will never fear or avoid a possible good rather than a certain evil. And therefore if you let me go now, and are not convinced by Anytus, who said that since I had been prosecuted I must be put to death (or if not that I ought never to have been prosecuted at all); and that if I escape now, your sons will all be utterly ruined by practising what I teach – if you say to me, Socrates, this time we will not mind Anytus, and you shall be let off, but upon one condition, that you are not to inquire and speculate in this way any more, and that if you are caught doing so again you shall die – if this was the condition on which you let me go, I should reply: Men of Athens, I honour and love you; but I shall obey god rather than you, and while I have life and strength I shall never cease from the practice and teaching of philosophy, exhorting any one of you whom I meet and saying to him after my manner: You, my friend – a citizen of the great and mighty and wise city of Athens – are you not ashamed of heaping up the largest amount of money and honour and reputation, and caring so little about wisdom and truth and the greatest improvement of the soul, which you never regard nor heed at all? And if the person with whom I am arguing, says: Yes, but I do care, then I shall not leave him nor let him go at once, but proceed to interrogate and examine and cross-examine him, and if I think that he has no virtue in him but only says that he has, I shall reproach him with undervaluing the most precious, and overvaluing the less. And I shall repeat the same words to everyone whom I meet, young and old, citizen and alien, but especially to you citizens, inasmuch as you are my brethren. For know that this is the command of god; and I believe that no greater good has ever happened in the state than my service to the god. For I do nothing but go about persuading you all, old and young alike, not to take thought for your persons or your properties, but first and chiefly to care about the greatest improvement of the soul. I tell you that virtue is not given by money, but that from virtue comes money and every other good of man, public as well as private. This is my teaching, and if it corrupts the young, it is mischievous; but if anyone says that this is not my teaching, he is speaking an untruth. Wherefore, O men of Athens, I say to you, do as Anytus bids or not as Anytus bids, and either acquit me or not; but whichever you do, understand that I shall never alter my ways, not even if I have to die many times.

Men of Athens, do not interrupt, but hear me; I begged you before to listen to me without interruption, and I beg you now to hear me to the end. I have something more to say, at which you may be inclined to cry out; but I believe that to hear me will be good for you, and therefore I beseech you to restrain yourselves. I would have you know, that if you kill such an one as I am, you will injure yourselves more than you will injure me. Nothing will injure me, not Meletus nor yet

Anytus – they cannot, for a bad man is not permitted to injure a better than himself. I do not deny that Anytus may, perhaps, kill him, or drive him into exile, or deprive him of civil rights; and he may imagine, and others may imagine, that he is inflicting a great injury upon him: but there I do not agree. For the evil of doing as he is doing – the evil of seeking unjustly to take the life of another – is greater far.

And now, Athenians, I am not going to argue for my own sake, as you may think, but for yours, that you may not sin against god by condemning me, who am his gift to you. For if you kill me you will not easily find a successor to me, who, if I may use such a ludicrous figure of speech, am a sort of gadfly, given to the state by god; and the state is a great and noble steed who is tardy in his motions owing to his very size, and requires to be stirred into life. I am that gadfly which god has attached to the state, and all day long and in all places am always fastening upon you, arousing and persuading and reproaching you. You will not easily find another like me, and therefore I would advise you to spare me. I dare say that you may feel out of temper (like a person who is suddenly awakened from sleep), and you think that you might easily strike me dead as Anytus advises, and then you would sleep on for the remainder of your lives, unless god in his care of you sent you another gadfly. When I say that I am given to you by god, the proof of my mission is this: if I had been like other men, I should not have neglected all my own concerns or patiently seen the neglect of them during all these years, and have been doing yours, coming to you individually like a father or elder brother, exhorting you to regard virtue; such conduct, I say, would be unlike human nature. If I gained anything, or if my exhortations were paid, there would be some sense in my doing so; but now, as you see for yourselves, not even the unfailing impudence of my accusers dares to say that I have ever exacted or sought pay of anyone; of that they can produce no witness. And I have a sufficient witness to the truth of what I say – my poverty.

Someone may wonder why I go about in private giving advice and busying myself with the concerns of others, but do not venture to come forward in public and advise the state. I will tell you why. You have heard me speak at sundry times and in divers places of a superhuman oracle or sign which comes to me, and is the divinity which Meletus ridicules in the indictment. This sign, which is a kind of voice, first began to come to me when I was a child; from time to time it forbids me to do something which I am going to do, but never commands anything. This is what deters me from being a politician. And rightly, as I think. For I am certain, O men of Athens, that if I had engaged in politics, I should have perished long ago, and done no good either to you or to myself. And do not be offended at my telling you the truth; for the truth is, that no man who sets himself firmly against you or any other multitude, honestly striving to keep the state from many lawless and unrighteous deeds, will save his life; he who will fight for the right, if he would live even for a brief space, must have a private station and not a public one.

I can give you convincing evidence of what I say, not words only, but what you value far more – actions. Let me relate to you a passage of my own life which will prove to you that to no man should I ever wrongly yield from fear of death, and that I should in fact be willing to perish for not yielding. I will tell you a tale of the courts, not very interesting perhaps, but nevertheless true. The only office of state which I ever held, O men of Athens, was that of senator: the tribe Antiochis, which is my tribe, had the presidency at the trial of the generals who had not taken up the bodies of the slain after the battle of Arginusae; and you proposed to try them in a body, contrary to law, as you all thought afterwards; but at the time I was the only one of the Prytanes who was opposed to the illegality, and I gave my vote against you; and when the orators threatened to impeach and arrest me, and you called and shouted, I made up my mind that I would run the risk, having law and justice with me, rather than take part in your injustice because I feared imprisonment and death. This happened in the days of the democracy. But when the oligarchy of the Thirty was in power, they sent for me and four others into the rotunda, and bade us bring Leon the Salaminian from Salamis, as they wanted to put him to death. This was a specimen of the sort of commands which they were always giving with the view of implicating as many as possible in their crimes; and then I showed again, not in word only but in deed, that, if I may be allowed to use such an expression, I care not a straw for death, and that my great and only care is lest I should do an unrighteous or unholy thing. For the strong arm of that oppressive power did not frighten me into doing wrong; and when we came out of the rotunda the other four went to Salamis and fetched Leon, but I went quietly home. For which I might have lost my life, had not the power of the Thirty shortly afterwards come to an end. And many will witness to my words.

Now do you really imagine that I could have survived

all these years, if I had led a public life, supposing that like a good man I had always maintained the right and had made justice, as I ought, the first thing? No indeed, men of Athens, neither I nor any other man. But I have been always the same in all my actions, public as well as private, and never have I yielded any base compliance to those who are slanderously termed my disciples, or to any other. Not that I have ever had any regular disciples. But if anyone likes to come and hear me while I am pursuing my mission, whether he be young or old, he is not excluded. Nor do I converse only with those who pay; but anyone, whether he be rich or poor, may ask and answer me and listen to my words; and whether he turns out to be a bad man or a good one, neither result can be justly imputed to me; for I never taught nor professed to teach anything. And if anyone says that he has ever learned or heard anything from me in private which all the world has not heard, let me tell you that he is lying.

But I shall be asked, Why do people delight in continually conversing with you? I have told you already, Athenians, the whole truth about this matter: they like to hear the cross-examination of the pretenders to wisdom; there is amusement in it. Now this duty of cross-examining other men has been imposed upon me by god; and has been signified to me by oracles, dreams, and in every way in which the will of divine power was ever intimated to anyone. This is true, O Athenians; or, if not true, can easily be disproved. If I really am or have been corrupting the youth, those of them who are now grown up and have become sensible that I gave them bad advice in the days of their youth should of course come forward as accusers, and take their revenge; or if they do not like to come themselves, some of their relatives, fathers, brothers, or other kinsmen, should think of the evil their families have suffered at my hands. Now is their time. Many of them I see in the court. There is Crito, who is of the same age and of the same deme with myself, and there is Critobulus his son, whom I also see. Then again there is Lysanias of Sphettus, who is the father of Aeschines – he is present; and also there is Antiphon of Cephisus, who is the father of Epigenes; and there are the brothers of several who have associated with me. There is Nicostratus the son of Theodotides, and the brother of Theodotus (now Theodotus himself is dead, and therefore he, at any rate, will not seek to stop him); and there is Paralus the son of Demodocus, who had a brother Theages; and Adeimantus the son of Ariston, whose brother Plato is present; and Aeantodorus, who is the brother of Apollodorus, whom I also see. I might mention a great many others, some of whom Meletus should have produced as witnesses in the course of his speech; and let him still produce them, if he has forgotten – I will make way for him. And let him say, if he has any testimony of the sort which he can produce. Nay, Athenians, the very opposite is the truth. For all these are ready to witness on behalf of the corrupter, of the injurer of their kindred, as Meletus and Anytus call me; not the corrupted youth only – there might have been a motive for that – but their uncorrupted elder relatives. Why should they too support me with their testimony? Why, indeed, except for the sake of truth and justice, and because they know that I am speaking the truth, and that Meletus is a liar.

Well, Athenians, this and the like of this is all the defence which I have to offer. Yet a word more. Perhaps there may be someone who is offended at me, when he calls to mind how he himself on a similar, or even a less serious occasion, prayed and entreated the judges with many tears, and how he produced his children in court to excite compassion, together with a host of relations and friends; whereas I, who am probably in danger of my life, will do none of these things. The contrast may occur to his mind, and he may be set against me, and vote in anger because he is displeased at me on this account. Now if there be such a person among you – mind, I do not say that there is – to him I may fairly reply: My friend, I am a man, and like other men, a creature of flesh and blood, and not 'of wood or stone', as Homer says; and I have a family, yes, and sons, O Athenians, three in number, one almost a man, and two others who are still young; and yet I will not bring any of them hither in order to petition you for an acquittal. And why not? Not from any self-assertion or want of respect for you. Whether I am or am not afraid of death is another question, of which I will not now speak. But when I think of my own good name, and yours, and that of the whole state, I feel that such conduct would be discreditable. One who has reached my years, and has the name I have, ought not to demean himself. Whether this opinion of me be deserved or not, at any rate the world has decided that Socrates is in some way superior to other men. And if those among you who are said to be superior in wisdom or courage, or any other virtue, demean themselves in this way, how shameful is their conduct! I have seen men of reputation behaving in the strangest manner while they were being tried: they seemed to fancy that they were going to suffer something dreadful if they had to die, and that they would live for ever if you spared them; and I think that such are a dishonour to the state, and that any stranger coming in would have said of them that the most eminent men of Athens, to whom the Athenians themselves give office and honour, are no better than women. And I say that these things ought not to be done to you by those who have a reputation in any walk of life; and if they are done, you ought not to permit them; you ought rather to show that you are far more disposed to condemn the man who gets up a doleful scene and makes the city ridiculous, than him who holds his peace.

But, setting aside the question of honour, there seems to be something wrong in asking a favour of a judge, and thus procuring an acquittal, instead of informing and convincing him. For his duty is not to make a present of justice, but to give judgment; and he has sworn that he will judge according to the laws, and not according to his own good pleasure; and we ought not to encourage you, nor should you allow yourselves to be encouraged, in this habit of perjury – there can be no piety in that. Do not then require me to do what I consider dishonourable and impious and wrong, especially now, when I am being tried for impiety on the indictment of Meletus. For if, O men of Athens, by force of persuasion and entreaty I could overpower your oaths, then I should be teaching you to believe that there are no gods, and in defending should simply convict myself of the charge of not believing in them. But that is not so – far otherwise. For I do believe that there are gods, and in a sense higher than that in which any of my accusers believe in them. And to you and to god I commit my cause, to be determined as is best for you and me.

*　　*　　*

There are many reasons why I am not grieved, O men of Athens, at the vote of condemnation. I expected it, and am only surprised that the votes are so nearly equal; for I had thought that the majority against me would have been far larger; but now, had thirty votes gone over to the other side, I should have been acquitted. And I may say, I think, that I have escaped Meletus. I may say more; for without the assistance of Anytus and Lycon, anyone may see that he would not have had a fifth part of the votes, as the law requires, in which case he would have incurred a fine of a thousand drachmas.

And so he proposes death as the penalty. And what shall I propose on my part, O men of Athens? Clearly that which is my due. And what is my due? What ought I to have done to me, or to pay – a man who has never had the wit to keep quiet during his whole life, but has been careless of what the many care for – wealth, and family interests, and military offices, and speaking in the assembly, and magistracies, and plots, and parties. Reflecting that I was really too honest a man to be a politician and live, I did not go where I could do no good to you or to myself, but where I could do privately the greatest good (as I affirm it to be) to everyone of you, thither I went, and sought to persuade every man among you that he must look to himself, and seek virtue and wisdom before he looks to his private interests, and look to the state before he looks to the interests of the state; and that this should be the order which he observes in all his actions. What shall be done to such an one? Doubtless some good thing, O men of Athens, if he has his reward; and the good should be of a kind suitable to him. What would be a reward suitable to a poor man who is your benefactor, and who desires leisure that he may instruct you? There can be no reward so fitting as maintenance in the Prytaneum, O men of Athens, a reward which he deserves far more than the citizen who has won the prize at Olympia in the horse or chariot race, whether the chariots were drawn by two horses or by many. For I am in want, and he has enough; and he only gives you the appearance of happiness, and I give you the reality. And if I am to estimate the penalty fairly, I should say that maintenance in the Prytaneum is the just return.

Perhaps you think that I am braving you in what I am saying now, as in what I said before about the tears and prayers. But this is not so. I speak rather because I am convinced that I never intentionally wronged anyone, although I cannot convince you – the time has been too short; if there were a law at Athens, as there is in other cities, that a capital cause should not be decided in one day, then I believe that I should have convinced you. But I cannot in a moment refute great slanders; and, as I am convinced that I never wronged another, I will assuredly not wrong myself. I will not say of myself that I deserve any evil, nor propose any penalty. Why should I? Because I am afraid of the penalty of death which Meletus proposes? When I do not know whether death is a good or an evil, why should I propose a penalty which would certainly be an evil? Shall I say imprisonment? And why should I live in prison, and be the slave of the magistrates of the year – of the Eleven? Or shall the penalty be a fine, and imprisonment until the fine is paid? There is the same objection. I should have to lie in prison, for money I have none, and cannot pay. And if I say exile (and this may possibly be the penalty which you will affix), I must indeed be blinded by the love of life, if I am so irrational as to expect that when you, who are my own citizens, cannot endure my discourses and arguments, and have found them so grievous and odious that you will have no more of them, others are likely to endure them. No indeed, men of Athens, that is not very likely. And what a life should I lead, at my age, wandering from city to city, ever changing my place of exile, and always being driven out! For I am quite sure that wherever I go, there, as here, the young men will flock to listen to me; and if I drive them away, their elders will drive me out at their request; and if I let them come, their fathers and friends will drive me out for their sakes.

Someone will say: Yes, Socrates, but cannot you hold your tongue, and then you may go into a foreign city, and no one will interfere with you? Now I have great difficulty in making you understand my answer to this. For if I tell you that to do as you say would be a disobedience to god, and therefore that I cannot hold my tongue, you will not believe that I am serious; and if I say again that daily to discourse about virtue, and of those other things about which you hear me examining myself and others, is the greatest good of man, and that the unexamined life is no life for a human being, you are still less likely to believe me. Yet I say what is true, although a thing of which it is hard for me to persuade you. Also, I have never been accustomed to think that I deserve to suffer any harm. Had I money I might have estimated the offence at what I was able to pay, and not have been much the worse. But I have none, and therefore I must ask you to proportion the fine to my means. Well, perhaps I could afford a mina, and therefore I propose that penalty: Plato, Crito, Critobulus, and Apollodorus,

my friends here, bid me say thirty minas, and they will
be the sureties. Let thirty minas be the penalty; for
which sum they will be ample security to you.

*   *   *

Not much time will be gained, O Athenians, in return
for the evil name which you will get from the detractors
of the city, who will say that you killed Socrates, a wise
man; for they will call me wise, even although I am not
wise, when they want to reproach you. If you had
waited a little while, your desire would have been
fulfilled in the course of nature. For I am far advanced
in years, as you may perceive, and not far from death.
I am speaking now not to all of you, but only to those
who have condemned me to death. And I have another
thing to say to them: You think that I was convicted
because I had no words of the sort which would have
procured my acquittal – I mean, if I had thought fit to
leave nothing undone or unsaid. Not so; the deficiency
which led to my conviction was not of words – certainly
not. But I had not the boldness nor impudence nor
inclination to address you as you would have liked me
to do, weeping and wailing and lamenting, and saying
and doing many things, such indeed as you have been
accustomed to hear from others, but I maintain to be
unworthy of myself. I thought at the time that I ought
not to do anything common or mean when in danger:
nor do I now repent of the style of my defence; I would
rather die having spoken after my manner, than speak
in your manner and live. For neither in war nor yet at
law ought I or any man to use every way of escaping
death. Often in battle there can be no doubt that if a
man will throw away his arms, and fall on his knees
before his pursuers, he may escape death; and in other

dangers there are other ways of escaping death, if a man has the hardihood to say and do anything. The difficulty, my friends, is not to avoid death, but to avoid unrighteousness; for that runs faster than death. I am old and move slowly, and the slower runner has overtaken me; my accusers are keen and quick, and the faster runner, who is wickedness, has overtaken them. And now I depart hence condemned by you to suffer the penalty of death – they too go their ways condemned by the truth to suffer the penalty of villainy and wrong; and I must abide by my award – let them abide by theirs. I suppose that these things may be regarded as fated – and I think that they are well.

And now, O men who have condemned me, I would fain prophesy to you; for I am about to die, and in the hour of death men are gifted with prophetic power. And I prophesy to you who are my murderers, that immediately after my departure punishment far heavier than you have inflicted on me surely awaits you. Me you have killed because you wanted to escape the accuser, and not to give an account of your lives. But that will not be as you suppose: far otherwise. For I say that there will be more accusers of you than there are now, accusers whom hitherto I have restrained: and as they are younger they will be more severe with you, and you will be more offended at them. If you think that by killing men you will stop all censure of your evil lives, you are mistaken; that is not a way of escape which is either very possible, or honourable; the easiest and the noblest way is not to be disabling others, but to be improving yourselves. This is the prophecy which I utter before my departure to the judges who have condemned me.

Friends, who would have acquitted me, I would like

also to talk with you about the thing which has come to pass, while the magistrates are busy, and before I go to the place at which I must die. Stay then a little, for we may as well talk with one another while there is time. You are my friends, and I should like to show you the meaning of this event which has happened to me. O my judges – for you I may truly call judges – I should like to tell you of a wonderful circumstance. Hitherto the divine faculty of which the internal oracle is the source has constantly been in the habit of opposing me even about trifles, if I was going to make a slip or error in any matter; and now as you see there has come upon me that which may be thought, and is generally believed to be, the last and worst evil. But the oracle made no sign of opposition, either when I was leaving my house in the morning, or when I was on my way to the court, or while I was speaking, at anything which I was going to say; and yet I have often been stopped in the middle of a speech, but now in nothing I either said or did touching the matter in hand has the oracle opposed me. What do I take to be the explanation of this silence? I will tell you. It is an intimation that what has happened to me is a good, and therefore those of us who think that death is an evil must be in error. I have this conclusive proof; the customary sign would surely have opposed me had I been going to evil and not to good.

Let us reflect in another way, and we shall see that there is great reason to hope that death is a good; for one of two things – either death is a state of nothingness and utter unconsciousness, or, as men say, there is a change and migration of the soul from this world to another. Now if you suppose that there is no consciousness, but a sleep like the sleep of him who is undisturbed even by dreams, death will be an unspeakable gain. For if a person were to select the night in which his sleep was undisturbed even by dreams, and were to compare with this the other days and nights of his life, and then were to tell us how many days and nights he had passed in the course of his life better and more pleasantly than this one, I think that any man, I will not say a private man, but even the great king will not find many such days or nights, when compared with the others. Now if death be of such a nature, I say that to die is gain; for eternity is then only a single night. But if death is the journey to another place, and there, as men say, all the dead abide, what good, O my friends and judges, can be greater than this? If indeed when the pilgrim arrives in the world below, he is delivered from our earthly professors of justice, and finds the true judges who are said to give judgment there, Minos and Rhadamanthus and Aeacus and Triptolemus, and other sons of god who were righteous in their own life, that pilgrimage will be worth making. What would not a man give if he might converse with Orpheus and Musaeus and Hesiod and Homer? Nay, if this be true, let me die again and again. I myself, too, shall find a wonderful interest in there meeting and conversing with Palamedes, and Ajax the son of Telamon, and any other ancient hero who has suffered death through an unjust judgment; and there will be no small pleasure, as I think, in comparing my own experience with theirs. Above all, I shall then be able to continue my search into true and false knowledge, as in this world, so also in the next; and I shall find out who is wise, and who pretends to be wise, and is not. What would not a man give, O judges, to be able to examine the leader of the great Trojan expedition; or Odysseus or Sisyphus, or numberless others, men and women too! What infinite delight would there be in conversing with them and asking them questions! In another world they do not put a man to death for asking questions: assuredly not. For besides being happier than we are, they will be immortal, if what is said is true.

Wherefore, O judges, be of good cheer about death, and know of a certainty that no evil can happen to a good man, either in life or after death, and that he and his are not neglected by the gods. Nor has my own approaching end happened by mere chance; I see clearly that the time had arrived when it was better for me to die and be released from trouble; therefore the oracle gave no sign, and therefore also I am not at all angry with my condemners, or with my accusers. But although they have done me no harm, they intended it; and for this I may properly blame them.

Still I have a favour to ask of them. When my sons are grown up, I would ask you, O my friends, to punish them; I would have you trouble them, as I have troubled you, if they seem to care about riches, or anything, more than about virtue; or if they pretend to be something when they are really nothing – then reprove them, as I have reproved you, for not caring about that for which they ought to care, and thinking that they are something when they are really nothing. And if you do this, I shall have received justice at your hands, and so will my sons.

The hour of departure has arrived, and we go our ways – I to die, and you to live. Which is better god only knows.

PLATO
CRITO

CRITO

Persons of the dialogue
SOCRATES
CRITO

SCENE: *The prison of Socrates*

SOCRATES: WHY have you come at this hour, Crito? It must be quite early?

CRITO: Yes, certainly.

SOCRATES: What is the exact time?

CRITO: The dawn is about to break.

SOCRATES: I wonder that the keeper of the prison would let you in.

CRITO: He knows me, because I often come, Socrates; moreover, I have done him a kindness.

SOCRATES: And are you only just arrived?

CRITO: No, I came some time ago.

SOCRATES: Then why did you sit and say nothing, instead of at once awakening me?

CRITO: Awaken you, Socrates? Certainly not! I wish I were not myself so sleepless and full of sorrow. I have been watching with amazement your peaceful slumbers; and I deliberately refrained from awaking you, because I wished time to pass for you as happily as might be. Often before during the course of your life I have thought you fortunate in your disposition; but never did I see anything like the easy, tranquil manner in which you bear this calamity.

SOCRATES: Why, Crito, when a man has reached my age he ought not to be repining at the approach of death.

245

CRITO: And yet other old men find themselves in similar misfortunes, and age does not prevent them from repining.

SOCRATES: That is true. But you do not say why you come so early.

CRITO: I come to bring you a painful message; not, as I believe, to yourself, but painful and grievous to all of us who are your friends, and most grievous of all to me.

SOCRATES: What? Has the ship come from Delos, on the arrival of which I am to die?

CRITO: No, the ship has not actually arrived, but she will probably be here today, as persons who have come from Sunium tell me that they left her there; and therefore tomorrow, Socrates, must be the last day of your life.

SOCRATES: Very well, Crito; if such is the will of god, I am willing; but my belief is that there will be a delay of a day.

CRITO: Why do you think so?

SOCRATES: I will tell you. I am to die on the day after the arrival of the ship.

CRITO: Yes; that is what the authorities say.

SOCRATES: But I do not think that the ship will be here until tomorrow; this I infer from a vision which I had last night, or rather only just now, when you fortunately allowed me to sleep.

CRITO: And what was the nature of the vision?

SOCRATES: There appeared to me the likeness of a woman, fair and comely, clothed in bright raiment, who called to me and said: 'O Socrates, the third day hence to fertile Phthia shalt thou come.'

CRITO: What a singular dream, Socrates!

SOCRATES: There can be no doubt about the meaning, Crito, I think.

CRITO: Yes; the meaning is only too clear. But, oh! my beloved Socrates, let me entreat you once more to take my advice and escape. For if you die I shall not only lose a friend who can never be replaced, but there is another evil: people who do not know you and me will believe that I might have saved you if I had been willing to spend money, but that I did not care. Now, can there be a worse disgrace than this – that I should be thought to value money more than the life of a friend? For the many will not be persuaded that I wanted you to escape, and that you refused.

SOCRATES: But why, my dear Crito, should we care about the opinion of the many? The best men, and they are the only persons who are worth considering, will think of these things truly as they occurred.

CRITO: But you see, Socrates, that the opinion of the many must be regarded, for what is now happening shows of itself that they can do the greatest evil to anyone who has lost their good opinion.

SOCRATES: I only wish it were so, Crito, and that the many could do the greatest evil; for then they would also be able to do the greatest good – and what a fine thing this would be! But in reality they can do neither; for they cannot make a man either wise or foolish, and they do not care what they make of him.

CRITO: Well, I will not dispute with you; but please to tell me, Socrates, whether you are not acting out of regard to me and your other friends: are you not afraid that if you escape from prison we may get into trouble with the informers for having stolen you away, and lose either the whole or a great part of our property; or that even a worse evil may happen to us? Now, if you fear on our account, be at ease; for in order to save you, we ought surely to run this, or even a greater risk; be persuaded, then, and do as I say.

SOCRATES: Yes, Crito, that is one fear which you mention, but by no means the only one.

CRITO: Fear not – there are persons who are willing to get you out of prison at no great cost; and as for the informers, you know that they are far from being exorbitant in their demands – a little money will satisfy them. My means, which are certainly ample, are at your service, and if out of regard for my interests you have a scruple about spending my money, here are strangers who will give you the use of theirs; and one of them, Simmias the Theban, has brought a large sum for this very purpose; and Cebes and many others are prepared to spend their money in helping you to escape. I say, therefore, do not shirk the effort on our account, and do not say, as you did in the court, that you will have a difficulty in knowing what to do with yourself anywhere else. For men will love you in other places to which you may go, and not in Athens only; there are friends of mine in Thessaly, if you like to go to them, who will value and protect you, and no Thessalian will give you any trouble. Nor can I think that you are at all justified, Socrates, in betraying your own life when you might be saved; in acting thus you are working to bring on yourself the very fate which your enemies would and did work to bring on you, your own destruction. And further I should say that you are deserting your own children; for you might bring them up and educate them; instead of which you go away and leave them, and they will have to take their chance; and if they do not meet with the usual fate of orphans, there will be small thanks to you. No man should bring children into the world who is unwilling to persevere to the end in their nurture and education. But you appear to be choosing the easier part, not the better and manlier, which would have been more becoming in one who professes to care for virtue in all his life, like yourself. And indeed, I am ashamed not only of you, but of us who are your friends, when I reflect that the whole business may be attributed entirely to our want of courage. The trial need never have come on, or might have been managed differently; and this last opportunity will seem (crowning futility of it all) to have escaped us through our own incompetence and cowardice, who might have saved you if we had been good for anything, and you might have saved yourself; for there was no difficulty at all. See now, Socrates, how discreditable as well as disastrous are the consequences, both to us and you. Make up your mind then, or rather have your mind already made up, for the time of deliberation is over, and there is only one thing to be done, which must be done this very night, and if we delay at all will be no longer practicable or possible; I beseech you therefore, Socrates, be persuaded by me, and do not say me nay.

SOCRATES: Dear Crito, your zeal is invaluable, if a right one; but if wrong, the greater the zeal the greater the danger; and therefore we ought to consider whether I shall or shall not do as you say. For I am and always have been one of those natures who must be guided by reason, whatever the reason may be which upon reflection appears to me to be the best; and now that this chance has befallen me, I cannot repudiate my own doctrines, which seem to me as sound as ever: the principles which I have hitherto honoured and revered I still honour, and unless we can at once find other and better principles, I am certain not to agree with you;

no, not even if the power of the multitude could let loose upon us many more imprisonments, confiscations, deaths, frightening us like children with hobgoblin terrors. What will be the fairest way of considering the question? Shall I return to your old argument about the opinions of men? We were saying that some of them are to be regarded, and others not. Now were we right in maintaining this before I was condemned? And has the argument which was once good now proved to be talk for the sake of talking – mere childish nonsense? That is what I want to consider with your help, Crito – whether, under my present circumstances, the argument will appear to me in any way different or not; and whether we shall dismiss or accept it. That argument, which, as I believe, is maintained by many persons of authority, was to the effect, as I was saying, that the opinions of some men are to be regarded, and of other men not to be regarded. Now you, Crito, are not going to die tomorrow – at least, there is no human probability of this – and therefore you are disinterested and not liable to be deceived by the circumstances in which you are placed. Tell me then, I beg you, whether I am right in saying that some opinions, and the opinions of some men only, are to be valued, and that others are to be disregarded. Is not this true?

CRITO: Certainly.

SOCRATES: The good opinions are to be regarded, and not the bad?

CRITO: Yes.

SOCRATES: And the opinions of the wise are good, and the opinions of the unwise are evil?

CRITO: Certainly.

SOCRATES: And what was said about another matter?

Does the pupil who devotes himself to the practice of gymnastics attend to the praise and blame and opinion of any and every man, or of one man only – his physician or trainer, whoever he may be?

CRITO: Of one man only.

SOCRATES: And he ought to fear the censure and welcome the praise of that one only, and not of the many?

CRITO: Clearly so.

SOCRATES: And he ought to act and train, and eat and drink in the way which seems good to his single master who has understanding, rather than according to the opinion of all other men put together?

CRITO: True.

SOCRATES: And if he disobeys and disregards the opinion and approval of the one, and regards the opinion of the many who have no understanding, will he not suffer evil?

CRITO: Certainly he will.

SOCRATES: And what will the evil be, whither tending and what affecting, in the disobedient person?

CRITO: Clearly, affecting the body; that is what is ruined by the evil.

SOCRATES: Very good; and is not this true, Crito, of other things which we need not separately enumerate? In questions of just and unjust, fair and foul, good and evil, which are the subjects of our present consultation, ought we to follow the opinion of the many and to fear them; or the opinion of the one man who has understanding? Ought we not to fear and reverence him more than all the rest of the world, and if we desert him shall we not corrupt and outrage that principle in us which may be assumed to be improved by justice and deteriorated by injustice? There is such a principle?

CRITO: Certainly there is, Socrates.

SOCRATES: Take a parallel instance: if, acting against the advice of those who have understanding, we ruin that which is improved by health and is corrupted by disease, would life be worth having? And that which has been corrupted is – the body?

CRITO: Yes.

SOCRATES: Is our life worth living, with an evil and corrupted body?

CRITO: Certainly not.

SOCRATES: And will it be worth living, if that higher part of man be corrupted which is improved by justice and depraved by injustice? Do we suppose that principle, whatever it may be in man, which has to do with justice and injustice, to be inferior to the body?

CRITO: Certainly not.

SOCRATES: More honourable than the body?

CRITO: Far more.

SOCRATES: Then, my friend, we must not particularly regard what the many say of us: but what he, the one man who has understanding of just and unjust, will say, and what the truth will say. And therefore you begin in error when you advise that we should regard the opinion of the many about just and unjust, good and evil, honourable and dishonourable. 'Well,' someone will say, 'but the many can kill us.'

CRITO: That will clearly be the answer, Socrates; you are right there.

SOCRATES: But still, my excellent friend, I find that the old argument is unshaken as ever. And I should like to know whether I may say the same of another proposition – that not life, but a good life, is to be chiefly valued?

CRITO: Yes, that also remains unshaken.

SOCRATES: And a good life is equivalent to a just and honourable one – that holds also?

CRITO: Yes, it does.

SOCRATES: From these premisses I proceed to argue the question whether it is or is not right for me to try and escape without the consent of the Athenians: and if it is clearly right, then I will make the attempt; but if not, I will abstain. The other considerations which you mention, of money and loss of character and the duty of educating one's children, are, I fear, only the doctrines of the multitude, who would restore people to life, if they were able, as thoughtlessly as they put them to death – and with as little reason. But now, since the argument has carried us thus far, the only question which remains to be considered is, whether we shall do rightly, I by escaping and you by helping me, and by paying the agents of my escape in money and thanks; or whether in reality we shall not do rightly; and if the latter, then death or any other calamity which may ensue on my remaining quietly here must not be allowed to enter into the calculation.

CRITO: I think that you are right, Socrates; how then shall we proceed?

SOCRATES: Let us consider the matter together, and do you either refute me if you can, and I will be convinced; or else cease, my dear friend, from repeating to me that I ought to escape against the wishes of the Athenians: for I am very eager that what I do should be done with your approval. And now please to consider my first position, and try how you can best answer me.

CRITO: I will.

SOCRATES: Are we to say that we are never intentionally to do wrong, or that in one way we ought and in another way we ought not to do wrong, or is doing wrong always evil and dishonourable, as has already been often acknowledged by us? Are all the admissions we have made within these last few days to be thrown over? And have we, at our age, been earnestly discoursing with one another all our life long only to discover that we are no better than children? Or, in spite of the opinion of the many, and in spite of all consequences whether for the better or the worse, shall we insist on the truth of what was then said, that injustice is always an evil and dishonour to him who acts unjustly? Shall we say so or not?

CRITO: Yes.

SOCRATES: Then we must do no wrong?

CRITO: Certainly not.

SOCRATES: Nor when injured injure in return, as the many imagine; for we must injure no one at all?

CRITO: Clearly not.

SOCRATES: Again, Crito, may we do evil?

CRITO: Surely not, Socrates.

SOCRATES: And what of doing evil in return for evil, which is the morality of the many – is that just or not?

CRITO: Not just.

SOCRATES: For doing evil to another is the same as injuring him?

CRITO: Very true.

SOCRATES: Then we ought not to retaliate or render evil for evil to anyone, whatever evil we may have suffered from him. But I would have you consider, Crito, whether you really mean what you are saying. For this opinion has never been held, and never will be held, by any considerable number of persons; and those who are agreed and those who are not agreed upon this point have no common ground, and can only despise one another when they see how widely they differ. Tell me, then, whether you agree with and assent to my first principle, that neither injury nor retaliation nor warding off evil by evil is ever right. And shall that be the premiss of our argument? Or do you decline and dissent from this? For so I have ever thought, and continue to think; but, if you are of another opinion, let me hear what you have to say. If, however, you remain of the same mind as formerly, I will proceed to the next step.

CRITO: You may proceed, for I have not changed my mind.

SOCRATES: Then I will go on to the next point, which may be put in the form of a question: ought a man to do what he admits to be right, or ought he to betray the right?

CRITO: He ought to do what he thinks right.

SOCRATES: But if this is true, what is the application? In leaving the prison against the will of the Athenians, do I wrong any? Or rather do I not wrong those whom I ought least to wrong? Do I not desert the principles which were acknowledged by us to be just – what do you say?

CRITO: I cannot answer your question, Socrates; for I do not understand it.

SOCRATES: Then consider the matter in this way: imagine that I am about to run away (you may call the proceeding by any name which you like), and the laws and the state appear to me and interrogate me: 'Tell us, Socrates,' they say; 'what are you about? Are you not going by an act of yours to bring us to ruin – the laws, and the whole state, as far as in you lies? Do you imagine that a state can subsist and not be overthrown, in which the decisions of law have no power, but are set aside and trampled upon by individuals?'

What will be our answer, Crito, to these and the like words? Anyone, and especially a rhetorician, will have a good deal to say against the subversion of the law which requires a sentence to be carried out. Shall we reply, 'Yes; but the state has injured us and given an unjust sentence.' Suppose we say that?

CRITO: Very good, Socrates.

SOCRATES: 'And was that our agreement with you?' the law would answer; 'or were you to abide by the sentence of the state?' And if we were to express our astonishment at their words, the law would probably add: 'Answer, Socrates, instead of opening your eyes – you are in the habit of asking and answering questions. Tell us – what complaint have you to make against us which justifies you in attempting to ruin us and the state? In the first place did we not bring you into existence? Your father married your mother by our aid and begat you. Say whether you have any objection to urge against those of us who regulate marriage?' None, I should reply. 'Or against those of us who after birth regulate the nurture and education of children, in which you also were trained? Were not the laws, which have the charge of education, right in commanding your father to train you in music and gymnastic?' Right, I should reply. 'Well then, since you were brought into the world and nurtured and educated by us, can you deny in the first place that you are our child and slave, as your fathers were before you? And if this is true you cannot suppose that you are on equal terms with us in matters of right and wrong, or think that you have a right to do to us what we are doing to you. Would you have any right to strike or revile or do any other evil to your father or your master, if you had one, because you have been struck or reviled by him, or received some other evil at his hands? You would not say this. And because we think right to destroy you, do you think that you have any right to destroy us in return, and your country as far as in you lies? Will you, O professor of true virtue, pretend that you are justified in this? Has a philosopher like you failed to discover that our country is more precious and higher and holier far than mother or father or any ancestor, and more to be regarded in the eyes of the gods and of men of understanding? Also to be soothed, and gently and reverently entreated when angry, even more than a father, and either to be persuaded, or if not persuaded, to be obeyed? And when we are punished by her, whether with imprisonment or stripes, the punishment is to be endured in silence; and if she lead us to wounds or death in battle, thither we follow as is right; neither may anyone yield or retreat or leave his rank, but whether in battle or in a court of law, or in any other place, he must do what his city and his country order him; or he must change their view of what is just: and if he may do no violence to his father or mother, much less may he do violence to his country.' What answer shall we make to this, Crito? Do the laws speak truly, or do they not?

CRITO: I think that they do.

SOCRATES: Then the laws will say: 'Consider, Socrates, if we are speaking truly that in your present attempt you are going to do us a wrong. For, having brought you into the world, and nurtured and educated you, and given you and every other citizen a share in every good which we had to give, we further proclaim to any Athenian by the liberty which we allow him, that if he does not like us, the laws, when he has become of age and has seen the ways of the city, and made our acquaintance, he may go where he pleases and take his goods with him. None of us laws will forbid him or interfere with anyone who does not like us and the city, and who wants to emigrate to a colony or to any other city; he may go where he likes, with his property. But he who has experience of the manner in which we order justice and administer the state, and still remains, has by so doing entered into an implied contract that he will do as we command him. And he who disobeys us is, as we maintain, thrice wrong; first, because in disobeying us he is disobeying his parents; secondly, because we are the authors of his education; thirdly, because having made an agreement with us that he will duly obey our commands, he neither obeys them nor convinces us that our commands are unjust; although we do not roughly require unquestioning obedience, but give him the alternative of obeying or convincing us – that is what we offer, and he does neither.

'These are the sort of accusations to which, as we were saying, you, Socrates, will be exposed if you accomplish your intentions; you, above all other Athenians.' Suppose now I ask, why I rather than anybody else? No doubt they will justly retort upon me that I above all other Athenians have acknowledged the agreement. 'There is clear proof,' they will say, 'Socrates, that we and the city were not displeasing to you. Of all Athenians you have been the most constant resident in the city, which, as you never leave, you may be supposed to love. For you never went out of the city either to see the games, except once when you went to the Isthmus, or to any other place unless when you were on military service; nor did you travel as other men do. Nor had you any curiosity to know other states or their laws: your affections did not go beyond us and our state; we were your special favourites, and you acquiesced in our government of you; and here in this city you begat your children, which is a proof of your satisfaction. Moreover, you might in the course of the trial, if you had liked, have fixed the penalty at banishment; you might then have done with the state's assent what you are now setting out to do without it. But you pretended that you preferred death to exile, and that you were not unwilling to die. And now you have forgotten these fine sentiments, and pay no respect to us the laws, of whom you are the destroyer; and are doing what only a miserable slave would do, running away and turning your back upon the compacts and agreements of your citizenship which you made with us. And first of all answer this very question: are we right in saying that you agreed to live under our government in deed, and not in word only? Is that true or not?' How shall we answer, Crito? Must we not assent?

CRITO: We cannot help it, Socrates.

SOCRATES: Then will they not say: 'You, Socrates, are breaking the covenants and agreements which you made with us at your leisure, not under any compulsion or deception or in enforced haste, but after you have had seventy years to think of them, during which time you were at liberty to leave the city, if we were not to your mind or if our covenants appeared to you to be unfair. You had your choice, and might have gone either to Lacedaemon or Crete, both which states are often praised by you for their good government, or to some other Hellenic or foreign state. Whereas you, above all other Athenians, seemed to be so fond of the state, and obviously therefore of us her laws (for who would care about a state without its laws?) that you never stirred out of her; the halt, the blind, the maimed were not more stationary in her than you were. And now you refuse to abide by your agreements. Not so, Socrates, if you will take our advice; do not make yourself ridiculous by leaving the city.

'For just consider, if you transgress and err in this sort of way, what good will you do either to yourself or to your friends? That your friends will be in danger of being driven into exile and deprived of citizenship, or of losing their property, is tolerably certain; and you yourself, if you fly to one of the neighbouring cities, as, for example, Thebes or Megara, both of which are well governed, will come to them as an enemy of their government and all patriotic citizens will look askance at you as a subverter of the laws, and you will confirm in the minds of the judges the justice of their own condemnation of you. For he who is a corrupter of the laws is more than likely to be a corrupter of the young and foolish portion of mankind. Will you then flee from well-ordered cities and virtuous men? And is existence worth having on these terms? Or will you go to them without shame, and talk to them, saying – what will you say to them? What you say here about virtue and justice and institutions and laws being the best things among men? Would that be decent of Socrates? Surely not. But if you go away from well-governed states to Crito's friends in Thessaly, where there is great disorder and licence, they will be charmed to hear the tale of your escape from prison, set off with ludicrous particulars of the manner in which you were wrapped in a goatskin or some other disguise, and metamorphosed as the manner is of runaways; but will there be no one to remind you that

in your old age, when little time was left to you, you
were not ashamed to violate the most sacred laws from
a greedy desire of life? Perhaps not, if you keep them in
a good temper; but if they are out of temper you will
hear many degrading things. You will live, but how?
Fawning upon all men, and the servant of all men; and
doing what? Faring sumptuously in Thessaly, having
gone abroad in order that you may get a dinner. And
where will be your fine sentiments about justice and
virtue? Say that you wish to live for the sake of your
children – you want to bring them up and educate
them – will you take them into Thessaly and deprive
them of Athenian citizenship? Is this the benefit which
you will confer upon them? Or are you under the
impression that they will be better cared for and
educated here if you are still alive, although absent
from them; for your friends will take care of them? Do
you fancy that if you have left Athens for Thessaly they
will take care of them, but if you have left it for the
other world that they will not take care of them? Nay;
but if they who call themselves friends are good for
anything, they will – to be sure they will.

'Listen, then, Socrates, to us who have brought you
up. Think not of life and children first, and of justice
afterwards, but of justice first, that you may so vindicate
yourself before the princes of the world below. For
neither will you nor any that belong to you be happier
or holier or juster in this life, or happier in another, if
you do as Crito bids. Now you depart, if it must be so,
in innocence, a sufferer and not a doer of evil; a victim,
not of the laws but of men. But if you leave the city,
basely returning evil for evil and injury for injury,
breaking the covenants and agreements which you have
made with us, and wronging those whom you ought

least of all to wrong, that is to say, yourself, your friends, your country, and us, we shall be angry with you while you live, and our brethren, the laws in the world below, will give you no friendly welcome; for they will know that you have done your best to destroy us. Listen, then, to us and not to Crito.'

This, dear Crito, is the voice which I seem to hear murmuring in my ears, like the sound of the flute in the ears of the mystic; that voice, I say, is humming in my ears, and prevents me from hearing any other. Be assured, then, that anything more which you may say to shake this my faith will be said in vain. Yet speak, if you have anything to say.

CRITO: I have nothing to say.

SOCRATES: It is enough then, Crito. Let us fulfil the will of god, and follow whither he leads.

PLATO
PHAEDO

PHAEDO

Persons of the dialogue
PHAEDO, *who is the narrator of the dialogue*
to Echecrates of Phlius
APOLLODORUS
SIMMIAS
CEBES
SOCRATES
CRITO
ATTENDANT OF THE PRISON

SCENE: *The Prison of Socrates*
PLACE OF THE NARRATION: *Phlius*

ECHECRATES: WERE you yourself, Phaedo, in the prison with Socrates on the day when he drank the poison?

PHAEDO: Yes, Echecrates, I was.

ECHECRATES: I should so like to know what he said during his last hours, and the manner of his death. No Phliasian goes much to Athens now, and it is a long time since any stranger has come from there who could give us a trustworthy account. We heard that he died by taking poison: but that was all.

PHAEDO: Did you not hear of the proceedings at the trial?

ECHECRATES: Yes; someone told us about the trial, and we could not understand why, having been condemned, he should have been put to death, not at the time, but long afterwards. What was the reason of this?

PHAEDO: An accident, Echecrates: the stern of the ship which the Athenians send to Delos happened to have been crowned on the day before he was tried.

ECHECRATES: What is this ship?

PHAEDO: It is the ship in which, according to Athenian tradition, Theseus went to Crete when he took with him 'the fourteen', and was the saviour of them and of himself. And they are said to have vowed to Apollo at the time, that if they were saved they would send a yearly mission to Delos. Well, the custom has continued without a break to this day, and the whole period of the voyage to and from Delos, beginning when the priest of Apollo crowns the stern of the ship, is a holy season, during which it is strictly forbidden to pollute the city by executions; and when the vessel is detained by contrary winds, the time spent in going and returning is very considerable. As I was saying, the ship was crowned on the day before the trial, and this was the reason why Socrates lay in prison and was not put to death until long after he was condemned.

ECHECRATES: What was the manner of his death, Phaedo? What was said or done? And which of his friends were with him? Or would the authorities forbid them to be present – so that he had no friends near him when he died?

PHAEDO: No; there were some with him, in fact a good many.

ECHECRATES: If you have nothing else to do, I wish that you would tell me what passed, as exactly as you can.

PHAEDO: I have nothing at all to do, and will try to give you the facts. To be reminded of Socrates is always the greatest delight to me, whether I speak myself or hear another speak of him.

ECHECRATES: You will have listeners who are of the

same mind with you; just try to relate everything as precisely as possible.

PHAEDO: I had a singular feeling at being in his company. For I could hardly believe that I was present at the death of a friend, and therefore I did not pity him, Echecrates; he died so fearlessly, and his words and bearing were so noble and gracious, that to me he appeared blessed. I realized that even in going to the other world he could not be without a divine call, and that he would be happy, if any man ever was, when he arrived there; and therefore no feeling of pity for him entered my mind, as might have seemed natural at such an hour. Nor on the other hand did I feel pleasure that we were occupied as usual with philosophy (that was the theme of our conversation). My state of mind was curious, a strange compound of pleasure and pain, as I reflected that he was soon to die; and this double feeling was shared by us all; we were laughing and weeping by turns, especially the excitable Apollodorus – you know what kind of man he is?

ECHECRATES: Yes.

PHAEDO: He was quite beside himself; and I and all of us were greatly moved.

ECHECRATES: Who were present?

PHAEDO: Of native Athenians there were, besides Apollodorus, Critobulus and his father, Hermogenes, Epigenes, Aeschines, Antisthenes; likewise Ctesippus of the deme of Paeania, Menexenus, and some others; Plato, if I am not mistaken, was ill.

ECHECRATES: Were there any strangers?

PHAEDO: Yes, there were; Simmias the Theban, and Cebes, and Phaedondes; Euclides and Terpsion, who came from Megara.

ECHECRATES: And was Aristippus there, and Cleombrotus?

PHAEDO: No, they were said to be in Aegina.

ECHECRATES: Anyone else?

PHAEDO: I feel fairly sure that these were all.

ECHECRATES: Well, and what did you talk about?

PHAEDO: I will begin at the beginning, and endeavour to repeat the entire conversation. During the whole time we had all been used to visit Socrates daily, assembling early in the morning at the court in which the trial took place as it was not far from the prison. There we would wait talking with one another until the opening of the doors (for they were not opened very early); then we went in and generally passed the day with Socrates. On the last morning we assembled sooner than usual, having heard on the day before when we quitted the prison in the evening that the sacred ship had come from Delos; and so we arranged to meet very early at the accustomed place. On our arrival the jailer who answered the door, instead of admitting us, came out and told us to wait until he called us. 'For the Eleven', he said, 'are now with Socrates; they are taking off his chains, and giving orders that he is to die today.' He soon returned and said that we might come in. On entering we found Socrates just released from chains, and Xanthippe, whom you know, sitting by him, and holding his child in her arms. When she saw us she uttered a cry and burst out in true feminine fashion: 'O Socrates, this is the last time that you will converse with your friends, and they with you.' Socrates turned to Crito and said: 'Crito, let someone take her home.' Some of Crito's people accordingly led her away, crying out and beating her breast. When she was gone, Socrates, sitting up on the couch, bent and rubbed his leg, saying, as he was rubbing: How singular is the thing mankind call pleasure, and how curiously related to pain, which might be thought to be the opposite of it; for they are never present to a man at the same instant, and yet he who pursues and gets either is generally compelled to get the other; their bodies are two, but they are joined by a single head. And I cannot help thinking that if Aesop had remembered them, he would have made a fable about god trying to reconcile their strife, and how, when he could not, he fastened their heads together; and this is the reason why when one comes the other follows: as I know by my own experience now, when after the pain in my leg which was caused by the chain pleasure, it seems, has succeeded.

Upon this Cebes said: I am glad, Socrates, that you have mentioned the name of Aesop. For it reminds me of a question which has been asked by many, and was asked of me only the day before yesterday by Evenus – he will be sure to ask it again, and therefore if you would like me to have an answer ready for him, you may as well tell me what I should say to him: he wanted to know for what conceivable reason you, who never before wrote a line of poetry, now that you are in prison are turning Aesop's fables into verse, and also composing that hymn in honour of Apollo.

Tell him, Cebes, he replied, what is the truth – that I had no idea of rivalling him or his poems; to do so, as I knew, would be no easy task. But I wanted to see whether I could satisfy my conscience on a scruple which I felt about the meaning of certain dreams. In the course of my life I have often had intimations in dreams 'that I should make music'. The same dream came to me sometimes in one form, and sometimes in another, but always saying the same or nearly the same words: 'Set to work and make music', said the dream. And hitherto I had imagined that this was only intended to exhort and encourage me in the study of philosophy, which has been the pursuit of my life, and is the noblest and best of music. The dream was bidding me do what I was already doing, in the same way that the competitor in a race is bidden by the spectators to run when he is already running. But I was not certain of this; for the dream might have meant music in the popular sense of the word, and being under sentence of death, and the festival giving me a respite, I thought that it would be safer for me to satisfy the scruple, and, in obedience to the dream, to compose a few verses before I departed. And first I made a hymn in honour of the god of the festival, and then considering that a poet, if he is really to be a poet, should not only put together words, but should invent stories, and that I have no invention, I took some fables of Aesop, which I had ready at hand and knew by heart – the first that occurred to me – and turned them into verse. Tell this to Evenus, Cebes, and bid him farewell from me; say that I would have him come after me if he be a wise man, and not tarry; and that today I am likely to be going, for the Athenians say that I must.

Simmias said: What a message for such a man! Having been a frequent companion of his I should say that, as far as I know him, he will never take your advice unless he is obliged.

Why, said Socrates – is not Evenus a philosopher?

I think that he is, said Simmias.

Then he, or any man who has the spirit of philosophy, will be willing to die; but he will not take his own life, I conceive, for that is held to be unlawful.

Here he changed his position, and put his legs off the couch on to the ground, and during the rest of the conversation he remained sitting.

Why do you say, inquired Cebes, that a man ought not to take his own life, but that the philosopher will be ready to follow one who is dying?

Socrates replied: And have you, Cebes and Simmias, who are the disciples of Philolaus, never heard him speak of this?

Yes, but his language was indefinite, Socrates.

My words, too, are only an echo; but there is no reason why I should hesitate to repeat what I have heard: and indeed, when a man is going to the other world, it seems highly proper for him to reason and speculate about the nature of our sojourn there. What could one do better in the interval between this and the setting of the sun?

Then tell me, Socrates, why is suicide held to be unlawful? As I have certainly heard Philolaus, about whom you were just now asking, affirm when he was staying with us at Thebes; and there are others who say the same, although I have never heard anybody give a definite reason.

Do not lose heart, replied Socrates, and the day may come when you will hear one. I suppose that you wonder why, when other things which are evil may be good at certain times and to certain persons, death is to be the only exception, and why, when a man is better dead, he is not permitted to be his own benefactor, but must wait for the kindness of another.

Fery true, said Cebes, laughing gently and speaking in his native Boeotian.

I admit the appearance of inconsistency in what I am saying; but there may not be any real inconsistency after all. There is a doctrine whispered in secret that man is a prisoner who has no right to open the door and run away; this is a great mystery, not to be easily apprehended. Yet I too believe that the gods are our guardians, and that we men are a chattel of theirs. Do you not agree?

Yes, I quite agree, said Cebes.

And if one of your own chattels, an ox or an ass, for example, took the liberty of putting itself out of the way when you had given no intimation of your wish that it should die, would you not be angry with it, and would you not punish it if you could?

Certainly, replied Cebes.

Then, if we look at the matter thus, there may be reason in saying that a man should wait, and not take his own life unless god sends some constraint such as that which has now come upon me.

Yes, Socrates, said Cebes, there seems to be truth in what you say. And yet how can you reconcile this seemingly true belief that god is our guardian and we his chattels, with the uncomplaining willingness to die which you were just now attributing to the philosopher? That the wisest of men should leave without reluctance a service in which they are ruled by the gods, who are the best of rulers, is not reasonable; for surely no wise man thinks that when set at liberty he will be able to take better care of himself. A fool may perhaps think so – he may argue that he had better run away from his master, not considering that he ought not to run away from the good but to cling to it, and that there would therefore be no sense in his running away. The wise man will want to be ever with him who is better than himself. Now this, Socrates, looks like the reverse of what was just now said; upon this view the wise man should sorrow and the fool rejoice at passing out of life.

The earnestness of Cebes seemed to please Socrates. Here, said he, turning to us, is a man who is always inquiring, and is not so easily convinced by the first thing which he hears.

And to me too, added Simmias, the objection which he is now making does appear to have some force. For what can be the meaning of a truly wise man wanting to fly away and lightly leave a master who is better than himself? And I rather imagine that Cebes is referring to you; he thinks that you are too ready to leave us, and too ready to leave the gods whom you acknowledge to be our good masters.

Yes, replied Socrates; there is justice in what you say. And so you think that I ought to answer your indictment as if I were in a court?

We should like you to do so, said Simmias.

Then I must try to make a more successful defence before you than I did before the judges. For I am quite ready to admit, Simmias and Cebes, that in meeting death without resentment I should be doing wrong, if I were not persuaded in the first place that I am going to other gods who are wise and good (of which I am as certain as I can be of any such matters), and secondly (though I am not so sure of this last) to men departed, better than those whom I leave behind; and therefore I do not resent it as I might have done, for I have good hope that there is yet something remaining for the dead, and as has been said of old, some far better thing for the good than for the evil.

But do you mean to take away your thoughts with

you, Socrates? said Simmias. Will you not impart them to us? For they are a benefit in which we too are entitled to share. Moreover, if you succeed in convincing us, that will be the answer to the charge against yourself.

I will do my best, replied Socrates. But you must first let me hear what Crito wants; he has long been wishing to say something to me.

Only this, Socrates, replied Crito: The attendant who is to give you the poison has been telling me, and he wants me to tell you, that you are not to talk much; talking, he says, increases heat, and this is apt to interfere with the action of the poison; persons who excite themselves are sometimes obliged to take a second or even a third dose.

Never mind him, said Socrates, let him be prepared to give the poison twice or even thrice if necessary; that is all.

I knew quite well what you would say, replied Crito; but he has been worrying me about it for some time.

Never mind him, he repeated; and went on. Now, O my judges, I desire to prove to you that the real philosopher has reason to be of good cheer when he is about to die, and that after death he may hope to obtain the greatest good in the other world. And how this may be, Simmias and Cebes, I will endeavour to explain. For I deem that the true votary of philosophy is likely to be misunderstood by other men; they do not perceive that of his own accord he is always engaged in the pursuit of dying and death; and if this be so, and he has had the desire of death all his life long, why when his time comes should he repine at that which he has been always pursuing and desiring?

Simmias said laughingly: Though I am not altogether

in a laughing humour, you have made me laugh,
Socrates; for I cannot help thinking that the many
when they hear your words will say how truly you have
described philosophers, and our people at home will
likewise say that philosophers are in reality moribund,
and that they have found them out to be deserving of
the death which they desire.

And they are right, Simmias, in thinking so, with the
exception of the words 'they have found them out'; for
they have not found out either in what sense the true
philosopher is moribund and deserves death, or what
manner of death he deserves. But enough of them – let
us discuss the matter among ourselves. Do we attach a
definite meaning to the word 'death'?

To be sure, replied Simmias.

Is it not just the separation of soul and body? And to
be dead is the completion of this; when the soul exists
by herself and is released from the body, and the body
is released from the soul. This, I presume, is what is
meant by death?

Just so, he replied.

There is another question, which will probably
throw light on our present inquiry if you and I can
agree about it: ought the philosopher to care about
such pleasures – if they are to be called pleasures – as
those of eating and drinking?

Certainly not, answered Simmias.

And what about the pleasures of love – should he
care for them?

By no means.

And will he think much of the other ways of
indulging the body, for example, the acquisition of
costly raiment or sandals, or other adornments of the
body? Instead of caring about them, does he not rather

despise anything more than nature needs? What do you say?

I should say that the true philosopher would despise them.

Would you not say that he is entirely concerned with the soul and not with the body? He would like, as far as he can, to get away from the body and to turn to the soul.

Quite true.

First, therefore, in matters of this sort philosophers, above all other men, may be observed in every sort of way to dissever the soul from the communion of the body.

Very true.

Whereas, Simmias, the rest of the world are of opinion that to him who has no taste for bodily pleasures and no part in them, life is not worth having; and that he who is indifferent about them is as good as dead.

Perfectly true.

What again shall we say of the actual acquirement of knowledge? Is the body, if invited to share in the inquiry, a hindrance or a help? I mean to say, have sight and hearing, as found in man, any truth in them? Are they not, as the poets are always repeating, inaccurate witnesses? And yet, if even they are inaccurate and indistinct, what is to be said of the other senses? For you will allow that they are the best of them?

Certainly, he replied.

Then when does the soul attain truth? For in attempting to consider anything in company with the body she is obviously deceived by it.

True.

Then must not true reality be revealed to her in thought, if at all?

Yes.

And thought is best when the mind is gathered into herself and none of these things trouble her – neither sounds nor sights nor pain, nor again any pleasure – when she takes leave of the body, and has as little as possible to do with it, when she has no bodily sense or desire, but is aspiring after true being?

Certainly.

And here again it is characteristic of the philosopher to despise the body; his soul runs away from his body and desires to be alone and by herself?

That is true.

Well, but there is another thing, Simmias: is there or is there not an absolute justice?

Assuredly there is.

And an absolute beauty and absolute good?

Of course.

But did you ever behold any of them with your eyes?

Certainly not.

Or did you ever reach them with any other bodily sense? And I speak not of these alone, but of absolute greatness, and health, and strength, and, in short, of the reality or true nature of everything. Is the truth of them ever perceived through the bodily organs? Or rather, is not the nearest approach to the knowledge of their several natures made by him who so orders his intellectual vision as to have the most exact conception of the essence of each thing which he considers?

Certainly.

And he attains to the purest knowledge of them who goes to each with the intellect alone, not introducing or intruding in the act of thought sight or any other sense together with reason, but with the intellect in its own purity searches into the truth of each thing in its

277

purity; he who has got rid, as far as he can, of eyes and ears and, so to speak, of the whole body, these being in his opinion distracting elements which when they associate with the soul hinder her from acquiring truth and knowledge – who, if not he, is likely to attain to the knowledge of true being?

What you say has a wonderful truth in it, Socrates, replied Simmias.

And when real philosophers consider all these things, will they not be led to make a reflection which they will express in words something like the following? 'Have we not found,' they will say, 'a path of thought which seems to bring us and our argument to the conclusion that while we are in the body, and while the soul is mixed with the evils of the body, our desire will not be satisfied? And our desire is of the truth. For the body is a source of countless distractions by reason of the mere requirement of food, and is liable also to diseases which overtake and impede us in the pursuit of truth: it fills us full of loves, and lusts, and fears, and fancies of all kinds, and endless foolery, and in very truth, as men say, takes away from us the power of thinking at all. Whence come wars, and fightings, and factions? Whence but from the body and the lusts of the body? All wars are occasioned by the love of money, and money has to be acquired for the sake of the body and in slavish ministration to it; and by reason of all these impediments we have no time to give to philosophy; and, last and worst of all, even if the body allows us leisure and we betake ourselves to some speculation, it is always breaking in upon us, causing turmoil and confusion in our inquiries, and so amazing us that we are prevented from seeing the truth. It has been proved to us by experience that if we would have pure knowledge of anything we must be quit of the body – the soul by herself must behold things by themselves: and then we shall attain that which we desire, and of which we say that we are lovers – wisdom; not while we live, but, as the argument shows, only after death; for if while in company with the body the soul cannot have pure knowledge, one of two things follows – either knowledge is not to be attained at all, or, if at all, after death. For then, and not till then, the soul will be parted from the body and exist by herself alone. In this present life, we think that we make the nearest approach to knowledge when we have the least possible intercourse or communion with the body, and do not suffer the contagion of the bodily nature, but keep ourselves pure until the hour when god himself is pleased to release us. And thus getting rid of the foolishness of the body we may expect to be pure and hold converse with the pure, and to know of ourselves all that exists in perfection unalloyed, which, I take it, is no other than the truth. For the impure are not permitted to lay hold of the pure.' These are the sort of words, Simmias, which the true lovers of knowledge cannot help saying to one another, and thinking. You would agree; would you not?

Undoubtedly, Socrates.

But, O my friend, if this be true, there is great reason to hope that, going whither I go, when I have come to the end of my journey I shall fully attain that which has been the pursuit of our lives. And therefore I accept with good hope this change of abode which is now enjoined upon me, and not I only, but every other man who believes that his mind has been made ready and that he is in a manner purified.

Certainly, replied Simmias.

And does it not follow that purification is nothing but that separation of the soul from the body, which has for some time been the subject of our argument; the habit of the soul gathering and collecting herself into herself from all sides out of the body; the dwelling in her own place alone, as in another life, so also in this, as far as she can – the release of the soul from the chains of the body?

Very true, he said.

And this separation and release of the soul from the body is termed death?

To be sure, he said.

And the true philosophers, and they only, are ever seeking to release the soul. Is not the separation and release of the soul from the body their especial study?

That is true.

And, as I was saying at first, there would be a ridiculous contradiction in men studying to live as nearly as they can in a state like that of death, and yet repining when death comes upon them.

Clearly.

In fact, the true philosophers, Simmias, are always occupied in the practice of dying, wherefore also to them least of all men is death terrible. Look at the matter thus: if they have been in every way estranged from the body, and are wanting to be alone with the soul, when this desire of theirs is being granted, how inconsistent would they be if they trembled and repined, instead of rejoicing at their departure to that place where, when they arrive, they hope to gain that which in life they desired – and their desire was for wisdom – and at the same time to be rid of the company of their enemy. Many a man who has lost by death an earthly love, or wife, or son, has been willing to go in

quest of them to the world below, animated by the hope
of seeing them there and of being with those for whom
he yearned. And will he who is a true lover of wisdom,
and is strongly persuaded in like manner that only in
the world below he can worthily enjoy her, still repine at
death? Will he not depart with joy? Surely he will, O my
friend, if he be a true philosopher. For he will have a
firm conviction that there, and there only, he can find
wisdom in her purity. And if this be true, he would be
very absurd, as I was saying, if he were afraid of death.

He would indeed, replied Simmias.

And when you see a man who is repining at the
approach of death, is not his reluctance a sufficient
proof that after all he is not a lover of wisdom, but a
lover of the body, and probably at the same time a
lover of either money or power, or both?

Quite so, he replied.

And then, Simmias, is not the quality we term
courage most characteristic of the philosopher?

Certainly.

There is temperance again – I mean the quality
which the vulgar also call by that name, the calm
disdain and control of the passions – is not temperance
a virtue belonging to those only who disdain the body,
and who pass their lives in philosophy?

Most assuredly.

For the courage and temperance of other men, if
you care to consider them, are really a paradox.

How so?

Well, he said, you are aware that death is regarded
by men in general as a great evil.

Very true, he said.

And do not courageous men face death because
they are afraid of yet greater evils?

That is quite true.

Then all but the philosophers are courageous only from fear, and because they are afraid; and yet that a man should be courageous from fear, and because he is a coward, is surely a strange thing.

Very true.

And are not the self-restrained exactly in the same case? They are temperate because in a sense they are intemperate – which might seem to be impossible, but is nevertheless the sort of thing which happens with this fatuous temperance. For there are pleasures which they are afraid of losing; and in their desire to keep them, they abstain from some pleasures because they are overcome by others; and although to be conquered by pleasure is called by men intemperance, to them the conquest of pleasure consists in being conquered by pleasure. And that is what I mean by saying that, in a sense, they are made temperate through intemperance.

Such appears to be the case.

Yet perhaps the exchange of one fear or pleasure or pain for another fear or pleasure or pain, of the greater for the less as if they were coins, is not the right exchange by the standard of virtue. O my dear Simmias, is there not one true coin for which all these ought to be exchanged – and that is wisdom – and only in company with this do we attain real courage or temperance or justice? In a word, is not all true virtue the companion of wisdom, no matter what fears or pleasures or other similar goods or evils may or may not attend her? But the virtue which is made up of these goods, when they are severed from wisdom and exchanged with one another, is perhaps a mere façade of virtue, a slavish quality, wholly false and unsound;

the truth is far different – temperance and justice and courage are in reality a purging away of all these things, and wisdom herself may be a kind of baptism into that purity. The founders of the mysteries would appear to have had a real meaning, and were not devoid of sense when they intimated in a figure long ago that he who passes unsanctified and uninitiated into the world below will lie in a slough, but that he who arrives there after initiation and purification will dwell with the gods. For 'many', as they say in the mysteries, 'are the thyrsus-bearers, but few are the mystics' – meaning, as I interpret the words, 'the true philosophers'. In the number of whom, during my whole life, I have been seeking, according to my ability, to find a place; whether I have sought in a right way or not, and whether we have succeeded, we shall know for certain in a little while, if god will, when we arrive in the other world – such is my belief. And therefore I answer that I am right, Simmias and Cebes, in not grieving or repining at parting from you and my masters in this world, for I believe that I shall equally find good masters and friends in another world. If now I succeed in convincing you by my defence better than I did the Athenian judges, it will be well.

When Socrates had finished, Cebes began to speak: I agree, Socrates, in the greater part of what you say. But in what concerns the soul, men are apt to be incredulous; they fear that when she has left the body her place may be nowhere, and that on the very day of death she may perish and come to an end immediately on her release from the body, issuing forth like smoke or breath, dispersing and vanishing away into nothingness in her flight. If she could only be collected into herself after she has obtained release from the evils of which you were speaking, there would be much reason for the goodly hope, Socrates, that what you say is true. But surely it requires a great deal of persuasion and proof to show that when the man is dead his soul yet exists, and has any force or intelligence.

True, Cebes, said Socrates; and shall I suggest that we speculate a little together concerning the probabilities of these things?

For my part, said Cebes, I should greatly like to know your opinion about them.

I reckon, said Socrates, that no one who heard me now, not even if he were one of my old enemies, the comic poets, could accuse me of idle talking about matters in which I have no concern. If you please, then, we will proceed with the inquiry.

Suppose we consider the question whether the souls of men after death are or are not in the world below. There comes into my mind an ancient doctrine which affirms that they are there after they leave our world, and returning hither, are born again from the dead. Now if it be true that the living come from the dead, then our souls must exist in the other world, for if not, how could they have been born again? And this would be conclusive, if it were established that the living are born from the dead and have no other origin; but if this is not so, then other arguments will have to be adduced.

Very true, replied Cebes.

Then let us consider the whole question, not in relation to man only, but in relation to animals generally, and to plants, and to everything of which there is generation, and the proof will be easier. Are not all things which have opposites generated out of their opposites? I mean such things as the beautiful and the ugly, the just and the unjust – and there are innumerable other cases. Let us consider therefore whether it is necessary that a thing should come to be from its own opposite, if it has one, and from no other source: for example, anything which becomes greater must become greater after being less?

True.

And that which becomes less must have been once greater and then have become less?

Yes.

And the weaker is generated from the stronger, and the swifter from the slower?

Very true.

And the worse is from the better, and the more just is from the more unjust?

Of course.

And is this true of all opposites? And are we convinced that all of them are generated out of opposites?

Yes.

And in this universal opposition of all things, are there not also two intermediate processes which are ever going on, from one to the other opposite, and back again; for example, where there is a greater and a less there is also the intermediate process of increase and diminution, and so a thing is said to increase or to diminish?

Yes, he said.

And there are many other processes, such as analysis and combination, cooling and heating, which equally involve a passage into and out of one another. And this necessarily holds of all opposites, even though not always expressed in words – they are really generated out of one another, and there is a passing or process from one to the other of them?

Very true, he replied.

Well, and is there not an opposite of being alive, as sleep is the opposite of being awake?

True, he said.

And what is it?

Being dead, he answered.

And these, if they are opposites, are generated the one from the other, and have their two intermediate processes also?

Of course.

Now, said Socrates, I will analyse one of the two pairs of opposites which I have mentioned to you, and also its intermediate processes, and you shall analyse the other to me. The two members of the first pair are sleep and waking. The state of sleep is opposed to the state of waking, and out of sleeping waking is generated, and out of waking, sleeping; and the process of generation is in the one case falling asleep, and in the other waking up. Do you agree?

I entirely agree.

Then, suppose that you analyse life and death to me in the same manner. Is not the state of death opposed to that of life?

Yes.

And they are generated one from the other?

Yes.

What is generated from the living?

The dead.

And what from the dead?

I can only say in answer – the living.

Then the living, whether things or persons, Cebes, are generated from the dead?

So it would seem, he replied.

Then the inference is that our souls exist in the world below?

It appears so.

And one of the two processes or generations is visible – for surely the act of dying is visible?

Surely, he said.

What then is to be the result? Shall we exclude the opposite process? And shall we suppose nature to be lame in this respect? Must we not rather assign to the act of dying some corresponding process of generation?

Certainly, he replied.

And what is that?

Return to life.

And return to life, if there be such a thing, is the birth of the dead into the number of the living?

Quite true.

Then here is a new way by which we arrive at the conclusion that the living come from the dead, just as the dead come from the living; and we agreed that this, if true, would be adequate proof that the souls of the dead must exist in some place out of which they come again.

Yes, Socrates, he said; the conclusion seems to flow necessarily out of our previous admissions.

And that these admissions were not wrong, Cebes, he said, may be shown, I think, as follows: if generation were in a straight line only, and there were no compensation or circle in nature, no turn or return of elements into their opposites, then you know that all things would at last have the same form and suffer the same fate, and there would be no more generation of them.

287

What do you mean? he said.

A simple thing enough, which I will illustrate by the case of sleep, he replied. You know that if there were no alternation of sleeping and waking, the tale of the sleeping Endymion would in the end have no point, because all other things would be asleep too, and he would not be distinguishable from the rest. Or if there were combination only, and no analysis of substances, then we should soon have the chaos of Anaxagoras where 'all things were together'. And in like manner, my dear Cebes, if all things which partook of life were to die, and after they were dead remained in the form of death, and did not come to life again, all would at last be dead, and nothing would be alive – what other result could there be? For if living things had some other origin, and living things died, must not all things at last be swallowed up in death?

There is no escape, Socrates, said Cebes; and to me your argument seems to be absolutely true.

Yes, he said, Cebes, it is and must be so, in my opinion, and we have not been deluded in making these admissions; but I am confident that there truly is such a thing as living again, and that the living spring from the dead, and that the souls of the dead are in existence.

Yes, said Cebes interposing, your favourite doctrine, Socrates, that our learning is simply recollection, if true, also necessarily implies a previous time in which we have learned that which we now recollect. But this would be impossible unless our soul had been some-where before existing in this form of man; here then is another proof of the soul's immortality.

But tell me, Cebes, interrupted Simmias, what arguments are urged in favour of this doctrine of recollection. I am not very sure at the moment that I remember them.

One excellent proof, said Cebes, is afforded by questions. If you put a question to a person properly, he will give a true answer of himself, but how could he do this unless there were knowledge and a right account of the matter already in him? Again, this is most clearly shown when he is taken to a diagram or to anything of that sort.

But if, said Socrates, you are still incredulous, Simmias, I would ask you whether you may not agree with me when you look at the matter in another way – I mean, if you are still incredulous as to whether what is called learning is recollection?

Incredulous I am not, said Simmias; but I want to have this doctrine of recollection brought to my own recollection, and, from what Cebes has started to say, I am beginning to recollect and be convinced: but I should still like to hear you develop your own argument.

This is what I would say, he replied: We should agree, if I am not mistaken, that what a man is to recollect he must have known at some previous time.

Very true.

And do we also agree that knowledge obtained in the way I am about to describe is recollection? I mean to ask, whether a person who, having seen or heard or in any way perceived anything, knows not only that, but also thinks of something else which is the subject not of the same but of some other kind of knowledge, may not be fairly said to recollect that of which he thinks?

How do you mean?

I mean what I may illustrate by the following

instance: the knowledge of a lyre is not the same as the knowledge of a man?

Of course not.

And yet what is the feeling of lovers when they recognize a lyre, or a cloak, or anything else which the beloved has been in the habit of using? Do not they, from knowing the lyre, form in the mind's eye an image of the youth to whom the lyre belongs? And this is recollection. In like manner anyone who sees Simmias may often remember Cebes; and there are endless examples of the same thing.

Endless, indeed, replied Simmias.

And is not this sort of thing a kind of recollection – though the word is most commonly applied to a process of recovering that which has been already forgotten through time and inattention?

Very true, he said.

Well; and may you not also from seeing the picture of a horse or a lyre recollect a man? And from the picture of Simmias, you may be led to recollect Cebes?

True.

Or you may also be led to the recollection of Simmias himself?

Quite so.

And in all these cases, the recollection may be derived from things either like or unlike?

It may be.

And when the recollection is derived from like things, then another consideration is sure to arise, which is – whether the likeness in any degree falls short or not of that which is recollected?

Certainly, he said.

Now consider this question. We affirm, do we not, that there is such a thing as equality, not of one piece of wood or stone or similar material thing with another, but that, over and above this, there is absolute equality? Shall we say so?

Say so, yes, replied Simmias, and swear to it, with all the confidence in life.

And do we know the nature of this absolute existence?

To be sure, he said.

And whence did we obtain our knowledge? Did we not see equalities of material things, such as pieces of wood and stones, and conceive from them the idea of an equality which is different from them? For you will acknowledge that there is a difference? Or look at the matter in another way: do not the same pieces of wood or stone appear to one man equal, and to another unequal?

That is certain.

But did pure equals ever appear to you unequal? Or equality the same as inequality?

Never, Socrates.

Then these equal objects are not the same with the idea of equality?

I should say, clearly not, Socrates.

And yet from these equals, although differing from the idea of equality, you obtained the knowledge of that idea?

Very true, he said.

Which might be like, or might be unlike them?

Yes.

But that makes no difference: so long as from seeing one thing you conceive another, whether like or unlike, there must surely have been an act of recollection?

Very true.

But what would you say of equal portions of wood or other material equals? and what is the impression produced by them? Are they equals in the same sense in which absolute equality is equal? Or do they fall short of this perfect equality in a measure?

Yes, he said, in a very great measure too.

And must we not allow, that when a man, looking at any object, reflects 'the thing which I see aims at being like some other thing, but falls short of and cannot be like that other thing, and is inferior', he who so reflects must have had a previous knowledge of that to which the other, although similar, was inferior?

Certainly.

And has not this been our own case in the matter of equals and of absolute equality?

Precisely.

Then we must have known equality previously to the time when we first saw the material equals, and reflected that they all strive to attain absolute equality, but fall short of it?

Very true.

And we recognize also that we have only derived this conception of absolute equality, and can only derive it, from sight or touch, or from some other of the senses, which are all alike in this respect?

Yes, Socrates, for the purposes of the present argument, one of them is the same as the other.

From the senses then is derived the conception that all sensible equals aim at an absolute equality of which they fall short?

Yes.

Then before we began to see or hear or perceive in any way, we must have had a knowledge of absolute equality, or we could not have referred to that standard the equals which are derived from the senses? For to that they all aspire, and of that they fall short.

No other inference can be drawn from the previous statements.

And did we not begin to see and hear and have the use of our other senses as soon as we were born?

Certainly.

Then we must have acquired the knowledge of equality at some previous time?

Yes.

That is to say, before we were born, I suppose?

It seems so.

And if we acquired this knowledge before we were born, and were born having the use of it, then we also knew before we were born and at the instant of birth not only the equal or the greater or the less, but all other such ideas; for we are not speaking only of equality, but of beauty, goodness, justice, holiness, and of all which we stamp with the name of absolute being in the dialectical process, both when we ask and when we answer questions. Of all this we affirm with certainty that we acquired the knowledge before birth?

We do.

But if, after having acquired, we have not on each occasion forgotten what we acquired, then we must always come into life having this knowledge, and shall have it always as long as life lasts – for knowing is the acquiring and retaining knowledge and not losing it. Is not the loss of knowledge, Simmias, just what we call forgetting?

Quite true, Socrates.

But if this knowledge which we acquired before birth was lost by us at birth, and if afterwards by the use of the senses we recovered what we previously knew, will not the process which we call learning be a recovering of knowledge which is natural to us, and may not this be rightly termed recollection?

Very true.

So much is clear – that when we perceive something, either by the help of sight, or hearing, or some other sense, that perception can lead us to think of some other thing like or unlike which is associated with it but has been forgotten. Whence, as I was saying, one of two alternatives follows: either we all have this knowledge at birth, and continue to know through life; or, after birth, those who are said to learn only recollect, and learning is simply recollection.

Yes, that is quite true, Socrates.

And which alternative, Simmias, do you prefer? Have we the knowledge at our birth, or do we recollect afterwards things which we knew previously to our birth?

I cannot decide at the moment.

At any rate you can decide whether he who has knowledge will or will not be able to render an account of his knowledge? What do you say?

Certainly, he will.

But do you think that every man is able to give an account of the matters about which we were speaking a moment ago?

Would that they could, Socrates, but I much rather fear that tomorrow, at this time, there will no longer be anyone alive who is able to give an account of them such as ought to be given.

Then you are not of opinion, Simmias, that all men know these things?

Certainly not.

They are in process of recollecting that which they learned before?

Certainly.

But when did our souls acquire this knowledge – clearly not since we were born as men?

Certainly not.

And therefore, previously?

Yes.

Then, Simmias, our souls must also have existed without bodies before they were in the form of man, and must have had intelligence.

Unless indeed you suppose, Socrates, that all such knowledge is given us at the very moment of birth; for this is the only time which remains.

Yes, my friend, but if so, when, pray, do we lose it? for it is not in us when we are born – that is admitted. Do we lose it at the moment of receiving it, or if not at what other time?

No, Socrates, I perceive that I was unconsciously talking nonsense.

Then may we not say, Simmias, that if there do exist these things of which we are always talking, absolute beauty and goodness, and all that class of realities; and if to this we refer all our sensations and with this compare them, finding the realities to be pre-existent and our own possession – then just as surely as these exist, so surely must our souls have existed before our birth? Otherwise our whole argument would be worthless. By an equal compulsion we must believe both that these realities exist, and that our souls existed before our birth; and if not the realities, then not the souls.

Yes, Socrates; I am convinced that there is precisely the same necessity for the one as for the other; and the argument finds a safe refuge in the position that the existence of the soul before birth cannot be separated from the existence of the reality of which you speak. For there is nothing which to my mind is so patent as that beauty, goodness, and the other realities of which you were just now speaking, exist in the fullest possible measure; and I am satisfied with the proof.

Well, but is Cebes satisfied? For I must convince him too.

I think, said Simmias, that Cebes is satisfied: although he is the most incredulous of mortals, yet I believe that he is sufficiently convinced of the existence of the soul before birth. But that after death the soul will continue to exist is not yet proven even to my own satisfaction. I cannot get rid of the objection to which Cebes was referring – the common fear that at the moment when the man dies the soul is dispersed, and that this may be the end of her. For admitting that she may have come into being and been framed out of some unknown other elements, and was in existence before entering the human body, why after having entered in and gone out again may she not herself be destroyed and come to an end?

Very true, Simmias, said Cebes; it appears that about half of what was required has been proven; to wit, that our souls existed before we were born; that the soul will exist after death as well as before birth is the other half of which the proof is still wanting, and has to be supplied; when that is given the demonstration will be complete.

But that proof, Simmias and Cebes, has been already given, said Socrates, if you put the two arguments together – I mean this and the former one, in which we agreed that everything living is born of the dead. For if the soul exists before birth, and in coming to life and being born can be born only from death and the state of death, must she not after death continue to exist, since she has to be born again? Surely the proof which you desire has been already furnished. Still I suspect that you and Simmias would be glad to probe the argument further. Like children, you are haunted with a fear that when the soul leaves the body, the wind may really blow her away and scatter her; especially if a man should happen to die in a great storm and not when the weather is calm.

Cebes answered with a smile: Then, Socrates, you must argue us out of our fears – and yet, strictly speaking, they are not our fears, but perhaps even in us men there is a child to whom death is a sort of hobgoblin: him too we must persuade not to be afraid.

Socrates said: Let the voice of the charmer be applied daily until you have charmed away the fear.

And where shall we find a good charmer of our fears, Socrates, now that you are abandoning us?

Hellas, he replied, is a large place, Cebes, and has good men, and there are barbarous races not a few: seek for him among them all, far and wide, sparing neither pains nor money; for there is no better way of spending your money. And you must seek yourselves too, along with one another; for perhaps you will not easily find others better able to do it.

The search, replied Cebes, shall certainly be made. And now, if you please, let us return to the point of the argument at which we digressed.

By all means, replied Socrates; what else should I please?

Very good.

Must we not, said Socrates, ask ourselves what kind of thing that is which is liable to be scattered, and for what kind of thing we ought to fear that fate? and what is that for which we need have no fear? And then we may proceed further to inquire to which of the two classes soul belongs – our hopes and fears as to our own souls will turn upon the answers to these questions.

Very true, he said.

Now that which is compounded and is by nature composite may be supposed to be therefore capable, as of being compounded, so also of being dissolved; but that which is not composite, and that only, must be, if anything is, indissoluble.

Yes; I should imagine so, said Cebes.

And the non-composite may be assumed to be the same and unchanging, whereas the composite is always changing and never the same.

I agree, he said.

Then now let us return to the previous discussion. Is that reality of whose being we give account in the dialectical process – whether equality, beauty, or anything else – are these realities, I say, liable at times to some degree of change? Or are they each of them always what they are, having the same uniform self-existent and unchanging natures, not admitting of variation at all, or in any way, or at any time?

They must be always the same, Socrates, replied Cebes.

And what would you say of the many beautiful, for instance, men or horses or garments or any other such things, or of the many equal, or generally of all the things which are named by the same names as the realities – are they the same always? May they not rather be described in exactly opposite terms, as almost always changing and hardly ever the same either with themselves or with one another?

The latter, replied Cebes; they are always in a state of change.

And these you can touch and see and perceive with the senses, but the unchanging things you can only grasp with the mind – they are invisible and are not seen?

That is very true, he said.

Well then, added Socrates, let us suppose that there are two sorts of existences – one seen, the other unseen.

Let us suppose them.

The seen is the changing, and the unseen is the unchanging?

That may be also supposed.

And, further, of ourselves is not one part body, another part soul?

To be sure.

And to which class is the body more alike and akin?

Clearly to the seen – no one can doubt that.

And is the soul seen or not seen?

Not by man, Socrates.

And what we mean by 'seen' and 'not seen' is that which is or is not visible to the eye of man?

Yes, to the eye of man.

And is the soul seen or not seen?

Not seen.

Unseen then?

Yes.

Then the soul is more like to the unseen, and the body to the seen?

That follows necessarily, Socrates.

And were we not saying some time ago that the soul when using the body as an instrument of perception, that is to say, when using the sense of sight or hearing or some other sense (for the meaning of perceiving through the body is perceiving through the senses) — were we not saying that the soul too is then dragged by the body into the region of the changeable, and wanders and is confused; the world spins round her, and she is like a drunkard, when she touches change?

Very true.

But when returning into herself she reflects, then she passes into the other world, the region of purity, and eternity, and immortality, and unchangeableness, which are her kindred, and with them she ever lives, when she is by herself and is not let or hindered; then she ceases from her wandering, and being in contact with things unchanging is unchanging in relation to them. And this state of the soul is called wisdom?

That is well and truly said, Socrates, he replied.

And to which class is the soul more nearly alike and akin, as far as may be inferred from this argument, as well as from the preceding one?

I think, Socrates, that, in the opinion of everyone who follows the argument, the soul will be infinitely more like the unchangeable — even the most stupid person will not deny that.

And the body is more like the changing?

Yes.

Yet once more consider the matter in another light: When the soul and the body are united, then nature orders the soul to rule and govern, and the body to obey and serve. Now which of these two functions is like to the divine, and which to the mortal? Does not the divine appear to you to be that which is formed to govern and command, and the mortal to be that which is by its nature subject and servant?

True.

And which does the soul resemble?

The soul resembles the divine, and the body the mortal – there can be no doubt of that, Socrates.

Then reflect, Cebes: of all which has been said is not this the conclusion – that the soul is in the very likeness of the divine, and immortal, and rational, and uniform, and indissoluble, and unchangeable? And that the body is in the very likeness of the human, and mortal, and irrational, and multiform, and dissoluble, and changeable? Can we, my dear Cebes, find any possible ground for rejecting this conclusion?

We cannot.

But if it be true, then is not the body liable to speedy dissolution? And is not the soul almost or altogether indissoluble?

Certainly.

And do you further observe, that after a man is dead, the body, or visible part of him, which is lying in the visible world, and is called a corpse, and would naturally be dissolved and decomposed and dissipated, is not dissolved or decomposed at once, but may remain for some time, nay even for a long time, if the constitution be sound at the time of death, and the season of the year favourable? For the body when shrunk and embalmed, as the manner is in Egypt, may remain almost entire for a prodigious time; and even in decay, there are still some portions, such as the bones and ligaments, which are practically indestructible. Do you agree?

Yes.

And is it likely that the soul, which is invisible, in

passing to the place of the true Hades, which like her is invisible, and pure, and noble, and on her way to the good and wise god, whither, if god will, my soul is also soon to go – that the soul, I repeat, if this be her nature, is blown away and destroyed immediately on quitting the body, as the many say? That can never be, my dear Simmias and Cebes. The truth rather is that the soul which is pure at departing and draws after her no bodily taint, having never voluntarily during life had connexion with the body, which she is ever avoiding, herself gathered into herself, and making such abstraction her perpetual study – all this means that she has been a true disciple of philosophy; and therefore has in fact been always practising how to die without complaint. For is not such a life the practice of death?

Certainly.

That soul, I say, herself invisible, departs to the invisible world – to the divine and immortal and rational: thither arriving, she is secure of bliss and is released from the error and folly of men, their fears and wild passions and all other human ills, and for ever dwells, as they say of the initiated, in company with the gods. Is not this true, Cebes?

Yes, said Cebes, beyond a doubt.

But the soul which has been polluted, and is impure at the time of her departure, and is the companion and servant of the body always, and is in love with and bewitched by the body and by the desires and pleasures of the body, until she is led to believe that the truth only exists in a bodily form, which a man may touch and see, and drink and eat, and use for the purposes of his lusts – the soul, I mean, accustomed to hate and fear and avoid that which to the bodily eye is

PLATO: PHAEDO

dark and invisible, but is the object of mind and can be
attained by philosophy – do you suppose that such a
soul will depart pure and unalloyed?

Impossible, he replied.

She is intermixed with the corporeal, which the
continual association and constant care of the body
have wrought into her nature.

Very true.

And this corporeal element, my friend, is burden-
some and weighty and earthy, and is visible; a soul
thus hampered is depressed and dragged down again
into the visible world, because she is afraid of the
invisible and of the other world – prowling about
tombs and sepulchres, near which, as they tell us, are
seen certain ghostly apparitions of souls, spectres
emanating from souls which have not departed pure,
but still retain something of the visible element: which
is why they can be seen.

That is very likely. Socrates.

Yes, that is very likely, Cebes; and these must be the
souls, not of the good, but of the evil, which are
compelled to wander about such places in payment
of the penalty of their former evil way of life; and
they continue to wander until through the craving
after their constant associate, the corporeal, they are
imprisoned finally in another body. And they may
be supposed to find their prisons in natures of the
same character as they have cultivated in their former
lives.

What natures do you mean, Socrates?

What I mean is that men who have followed after
gluttony, and wantonness, and drunkenness, and have
had no thought of avoiding them, would pass into
asses and animals of that sort. What do you think?

303

I think such an opinion to be exceedingly probable.

And those who have chosen the portion of injustice, and tyranny, and violence, will pass into wolves, or into hawks and kites – whither else can we suppose them to go?

Yes, said Cebes; into such creatures, beyond question.

And there is no difficulty, he said, in assigning to each class of them places answering to their several natures and propensities?

There is not, he said.

Even among these, some are happier than others; and the happiest both in themselves and in the place to which they go are those who have practised the virtues of the populace, the social virtues which are called by them temperance and justice, and are acquired by habit and practice without philosophy and mind.

Why are they the happiest?

Because they may be expected to pass into some gentle and social kind which is like their own, such as bees or wasps or ants, or back again into the form of man, and worthy men may be supposed to spring from them.

Very likely.

But to the company of the gods no one who has not studied philosophy and who is not entirely pure at the time of his departure is admitted, save only the lover of knowledge. And this is the reason, Simmias and Cebes, why the true votaries of philosophy abstain from all fleshly lusts, and hold out against them and refuse to give themselves up to them – not because they fear poverty or the ruin of their families, like the lovers of money, and the world in general; nor like the lovers of power and honour, because they dread the dishonour or disgrace of evil deeds.

No, Socrates, that would not become them, said Cebes.

No indeed, he replied; and therefore they who have any care of their own souls, and do not merely live for the body and its fashioning, say farewell to all this; they will not walk in the ways of the blind: and when philosophy offers them purification and release from evil, they feel that they ought not to resist her influence, and whither she leads they turn and follow.

What do you mean, Socrates?

I will tell you, he said. The lovers of knowledge are conscious that the soul was simply fastened and glued to the body – until philosophy took her in hand, she could only view real existence through the bars of a prison, not in and through herself, and she was wallowing in the mire of every sort of ignorance. This was her original state; and then, as I was saying, and as the lovers of knowledge are well aware, philosophy saw the ingenuity of her prison – a prison built by lust so that a captive might be the principal accomplice in his own captivity – and took her in hand, and gently comforted her and sought to release her, pointing out that the eye and the ear and the other senses are full of deception, and persuading her to retire from them, and abstain from all but the necessary use of them, and be gathered up and collected into herself, bidding her trust only in herself and her own pure apprehension of pure existence, and to mistrust whatever comes to her through other channels and is subject to variation; for such things are sensible and visible, but what she sees in her own nature is of the mind and invisible. And the soul of the true philosopher thinks that she ought not to resist this deliverance, and therefore abstains from pleasures and desires and pains, as far as she is able;

reflecting that when a man has great joys or fears or desires, he suffers from them not merely the sort of evil which might be anticipated – as for example, the loss of his health or property which he has sacrificed to his lusts – but an evil greater far, which is the greatest and worst of all evils, and one of which he never thinks.

What is it, Socrates? said Cebes.

The evil is that when the feeling of pleasure or pain is most intense, every soul of man imagines the objects of this intense feeling to be then plainest and truest, though they are not so. And the things of sight are the chief of these objects, are they not?

Yes.

And is not this the state in which the soul becomes most firmly gripped by the body?

How so?

Why, because each pleasure and pain is a sort of nail which nails and rivets the soul to the body, until she becomes like the body, and believes that to be true which the body affirms to be true; and from agreeing with the body and having the same delights she is obliged to have the same habits and haunts, and is not likely ever to be pure at her departure to the world below, but is always infected by the body; and so she sinks into another body and there germinates and grows, and has therefore no part in the communion of the divine and pure and simple.

Most true, Socrates, answered Cebes.

And this, Cebes, is the reason why the true lovers of knowledge are temperate and brave; and not for the reason which the world gives.

Certainly not.

Certainly not! The soul of a philosopher will reason in quite another way; she will not ask philosophy to release her in order that in the very process of release she may deliver herself up again to the thraldom of pleasures and pains, doing a work only to be undone again, weaving and in turn unweaving her Penelope's web. But she will calm passion, and follow reason, and dwell always with her, contemplating the true and the divine and that which is beyond appearance and opinion, and thence deriving nourishment. Thus she seeks to live while she lives, and after death she hopes to go to her own kindred and to that which is like her, and to be freed from human ills. Thus nurtured, Simmias and Cebes, a soul will never fear that at her departure from the body she will be scattered and blown away by the winds and be nowhere and nothing.

When Socrates had done speaking, for a considerable time there was silence; he himself appeared to be meditating, as most of us were, on what had been said; only Cebes and Simmias spoke a few words to one another. And Socrates observing them asked what they thought of the argument, and whether there was anything wanting? For, said he, there are many points still open to suspicion and attack, if anyone were disposed to sift the matter thoroughly. Should you be considering some other matter I say no more, but if you feel any doubt on the present subject do not hesitate either to give us your own thoughts if you have any improvement to suggest, or, if you think that you will make more progress with my assistance, allow me to help you.

Simmias said: I must confess, Socrates, that doubts do arise in our minds, and each of us has for some time been urging and inciting the other to put the question which we wanted to have answered but which neither of us liked to ask, fearing that our importunity might be troublesome at such a time.

Socrates replied with a smile: O Simmias, what are you saying? I am not very likely to persuade other men that I do not regard my present situation as a misfortune if I cannot even persuade you, and find you afraid that I may be more irritable than I used to be. Will you not allow that I have as much of the spirit of prophecy in me as the swans? For they, when they perceive that they must die, having sung at times during their life, do then sing a longer and lovelier song than ever, rejoicing in the thought that they are about to go away to the god whose ministers they are. But men, because they are themselves afraid of death, slanderously affirm of the swans that they sing a lament at the last, a cry of woe, not considering that no bird sings when cold, or hungry, or in pain, not even the nightingale, nor the swallow, nor yet the hoopoe; which are said indeed to tune a woeful lay, although I do not believe this to be true of them any more than of the swans. But because they are sacred to Apollo, they have the gift of prophecy, and anticipate the good things of another world; wherefore they sing and rejoice in that day more than ever they did before. And I too, believing myself to be the consecrated servant of the same god, and the fellow servant of the swans, and thinking that I have received from my master gifts of prophecy which are not inferior to theirs, would not go out of life less merrily than the swans. Never mind then, if this be your only objection, but speak and ask anything which you like, while the eleven magistrates of Athens allow.

Very good, Socrates, said Simmias; then I will tell you my difficulty, and Cebes will tell you his. I feel myself (and I dare say that you have the same feeling) that it is impossible or at least very hard to attain any certainty about questions such as these in the present life. And yet I should deem him a coward who did not prove what is said about them to the uttermost, not desisting until he had examined them on every side. For he should persevere until he has achieved one of these things: either he should discover, or be taught the truth about them; or, if this be impossible, I would have him take the best and most irrefragable of human theories, and let this be the raft upon which he sails through life – not without risk, as I admit, if he cannot find some word of god which will more surely and safely carry him. And now, as you bid me, I will venture to question you, and then I shall not have to reproach myself hereafter with not having said at the time what I think. For when I consider the matter, either alone or with Cebes, the argument does certainly appear to me, Socrates, to be not sufficient.

Socrates answered: I dare say, my friend, that you may be right, but I should like to know in what respect the argument is insufficient.

In this respect, replied Simmias. Suppose a person to use the same argument about harmony and the lyre – might he not say that harmony is a thing invisible, incorporeal, perfect, divine, existing in the lyre which is harmonized, but that the lyre and the strings are matter and material, composite, earthy, and akin to mortality? And when someone breaks the lyre, or cuts and rends the strings, then he who takes this view would argue as you do, and on the same analogy, that the harmony survives, and has not perished – you cannot imagine, he would say, that the lyre without the strings, and the broken strings them-selves which are mortal remain, and yet that the harmony, which is of heavenly and immortal nature and kindred, has perished – perished before the mortal. The harmony must still be somewhere, and the wood and strings will decay before anything can happen to that. The thought, Socrates, must have occurred to your own mind that such is our conception of the soul; and that when the body is in a manner strung and held together by the elements of hot and cold, wet and dry, then the soul is the harmony or due proportionate admixture of them. But if so, whenever the strings of the body are unduly loosened or overstrained through disease or other injury, then the soul, though most divine, like other harmonies of music or of works of art, of course perishes at once, although the material remains of the body may last for a considerable time, until they are either decayed or burnt. And if any one maintains that the soul, being an admixture of the elements of the body, is first to perish in that which is called death, how shall we answer him?

Socrates looked fixedly at us as his manner was, and said with a smile: Simmias has reason on his side; and why does not some one of you who is better able than myself answer him? For there is force in his line of argument. But perhaps, before we answer him, we had better also hear what Cebes has to say that we may gain time for reflection, and when they have both spoken, we may either assent to them, if there is truth in their concord, or if not, then we must fight our case. Please to tell me then, Cebes, he said, what was the difficulty which troubled you?

Cebes said: I will tell you. My feeling is that the argument is where it was, and open to the same objections which were urged before; for I am ready to admit that the existence of the soul before entering into the bodily form has been very ingeniously, and, if I may say so, quite sufficiently proven; but the existence of the soul after death is in my judgment unproven. Now in spite of Simmias' objections I am not disposed to deny that the soul is stronger and more lasting than the body, being of opinion that in all such respects the soul very far excels the body. Well then, says the argument to me, why do you remain unconvinced? When you see that the weaker continues in existence after the man is dead, will you not admit that the more lasting must also survive during the same period of time? Now I will ask you to consider whether the objection, which I think I must, like Simmias, express in a figure, is of any weight. The analogy which I will adduce is that of an old weaver, who dies, and after his death somebody says: 'He is not dead, he must be alive somewhere – see, there is the coat which he himself wove and wore, surviving whole and unruined, And then he proceeds to ask of someone who is incredulous, whether a man lasts longer, or the coat which is in use and wear; and when he is answered that a man lasts far longer, thinks that he has thus certainly demonstrated the survival of the man, inasmuch as the less lasting has not perished. But that, Simmias, as I would beg you to remark, is a mistake; anyone would retort that he who talks thus is talking nonsense. For the truth is that the weaver aforesaid, having woven and worn many such coats, outlived several of them, but was outlived by the last; yet a man is not therefore proved to be slighter and weaker than a coat. Now the relation of the body to the soul may be expressed in a similar figure; and anyone may very fairly say in like manner that the soul is lasting, and the body weak and shortlived in comparison. He may argue that every soul wears out

ON SOCRATES

many bodies, especially if a man live many years. While he is alive the body deliquesces and decays, and the soul always weaves another garment and repairs the waste. But of course, whenever the soul perishes, she must have on her last garment, and this will survive her; and then at length, when the soul is dead, the body will show its native weakness, and quickly decompose and pass away. I would therefore rather not rely on the argument from superior strength to prove the continued existence of the soul after death. For granting even more than you affirm to be possible, and acknowledging not only that the soul existed before birth, but also that the souls of some exist and will continue to exist after death, and will be born and die again and again, and that there is a natural strength in the soul by which she will hold out and be born many times – nevertheless, we may be still inclined to think that she will weary in the labours of successive births, and may at last succumb in one of her deaths and utterly perish; and this death and dissolution of the body which brings destruction to the soul may be unknown to any of us, for no one of us can have had any experience of it: and if so, then I maintain that he who is confident about death can have but a foolish confidence, unless he is able to prove that the soul is altogether immortal and imperishable. But if he cannot prove the soul's immortality, he who is about to die will always have reason to fear that when the body is disunited, the soul also may utterly perish.

All of us, as we afterwards remarked to one another, had an unpleasant feeling at hearing what they said. When we had been so firmly convinced before, now to have our faith shaken seemed to introduce a confusion and uncertainty, not only into the previous argument,

312

but into any future one; either we were but poor judges, or the subject itself might prove to be such that certainty was impossible.

ECHECRATES: There I feel with you – by heaven I do, Phaedo, and when you were speaking, I was moved to ask myself the same question: what argument can I ever trust again? For what could be more convincing than the argument of Socrates, which has now fallen into discredit? That the soul is a kind of harmony is a doctrine which has always had a wonderful hold upon me, and, when mentioned, came back to me at once, as my own original conviction. And now I must begin again and find another argument which will assure me that when the man is dead the soul survives. Tell me, I implore you, how did Socrates pursue the argument? Did he appear to share the unpleasant feeling which you mention? Or did he calmly meet the attack? And did he succeed in meeting it, or fail? Narrate what passed as exactly as you can.

PHAEDO: Often, Echecrates, I have wondered at Socrates, but never more than on that occasion. That he should be able to answer was perhaps nothing, but what astonished me was, first, the gentle and pleasant and approving manner in which he received the words of the young men, and then his quick sense of the wound which had been inflicted on us by the argument, and the readiness with which he healed it. He might be compared to a general rallying his defeated and broken army, urging them to follow his lead and return to the field.

ECHECRATES: What followed?

PHAEDO: You shall hear, for I was close to him on his right hand, seated on a sort of stool, and he on a couch which was a good deal higher. He stroked my head, and pressed the hair upon my neck – he had a way of teasing me about my hair; and then he said: Tomorrow, Phaedo, I suppose that these fair locks of yours will be severed.

Yes, Socrates, I suppose that they will, I replied.

Not so, if you will take my advice.

What shall I do with them? I said.

Today, he replied, and not tomorrow, if this argument dies and we cannot bring it to life again, you and I will both cut off our hair: and if I were you, and the argument got away from me, and I could not hold my ground against Simmias and Cebes, I would myself take an oath, like the Argives, not to let my hair grow any more until I had renewed the conflict and defeated them.

Yes, I said; but Heracles himself is said not to be a match for two.

Summon me then, he said, and I will be your Iolaus until the sun goes down.

I summon you rather, I rejoined, not as Heracles summoning Iolaus, but as Iolaus might summon Heracles.

That will do as well, he said. But first let us take care that we avoid a danger.

Of what nature? I said.

Lest we become misologists, he replied: no worse thing can happen to a man than this. For as there are misanthropists or haters of mankind, there are also misologists or haters of argument, and both spring from the same cause, which is ignorance of the world. Misanthropy arises out of the too great confidence of inexperience – you trust a man and think him altogether true and sound and faithful, and then in a little while he turns out to be false and knavish; and then another and another, and when this has happened several times to a man, especially when it happens among those whom he deems to be his own most trusted and familiar friends, after many disappointments he at last hates all men, and believes that no one has any good in him at all. You must have observed this process?

I have.

And is it not discreditable? Is it not obvious that such a one was attempting to deal with other men before he had acquired the art of human relationships? This art would have taught him the true state of the case, that few are the good and few the evil, and that the great majority are in the interval between them.

What do you mean? I said.

I mean, he replied, as you might say of the very large and very small – that nothing is more uncommon than a very large or very small man; and this applies generally to all extremes, whether of great and small, or swift and slow, or fair and foul, or black and white: and whether the instances you select be men or dogs or anything else, very few are the extremes, but in the mean between them there is a countless multitude. Did you never observe this?

Yes, I said, I have.

And do you not imagine, he said, that if there were a competition in evil, even there the pre-eminent would be found to be very few?

That is very likely, I said.

Yes, that is very likely, he replied; although in this respect arguments are unlike men – there I was led on by you to say more than I had intended. The point of comparison was, that when a simple man who has no skill in dialectics believes an argument to be true which

315

he afterwards imagines to be false, whether really false or not, and then another and another – and those especially who have devoted themselves to the study of antinomies come, as you know, to think at last that they have grown to be the wisest of mankind, and that they alone perceive how unsound and unstable are things themselves and all our arguments about them, and how all existence, like the currents in the Euripus, hurries up and down in never-ceasing ebb and flow.

That is quite true, I said.

Yes, Phaedo, he replied, and if there be such a thing as truth or certainty or possibility of knowledge, how melancholy that a man should have lighted upon some argument or other which at first seemed true and then turned out to be false, and instead of blaming himself and his own want of wit, should at last out of sheer annoyance be only too glad to transfer the blame from himself to arguments in general: and for ever afterwards should hate and revile them, and lose truth and the knowledge of realities.

Yes, indeed, I said; that would be most melancholy.

Let us then, in the first place, he said, be careful of allowing or of admitting into our souls the notion that there may be no health or soundness in any arguments at all. Rather say that we have not yet attained to soundness in ourselves, and that we must struggle manfully and do our best to gain it – you and all other men having regard to the whole of your future life, and I myself in the prospect of death. For at this moment I fear that I have not the temper of a philosopher; like the vulgar, I am only a partisan. Now the partisan, when he is engaged in a dispute, cares nothing about the rights of the question, but is anxious only to convince his hearers of his own assertions. And the difference between him and me at the present moment is merely this – that whereas he seeks to convince his hearers that what he says is true, I am rather seeking to convince myself; to convince my hearers is a secondary matter with me. And do but see how I stand to gain either way by the argument. For if what I say is true, then I do well to be persuaded of the truth; but if there be nothing after death, still, during the short time that remains, I shall not distress my friends with lamentations, and my folly will not last, but will die very soon, and therefore no harm will be done. This is the state of mind, Simmias and Cebes, in which I approach the argument. And I would ask you to be thinking of the truth and not of Socrates: agree with me, if I seem to you to be speaking the truth; or if not, withstand me might and main, that I may not deceive you as well as myself in my enthusiasm, and like the bee leave my sting in you before I die.

And now let us proceed, he said. And first of all let me be sure that I have in my mind what you were saying. Simmias, if I remember rightly, has fears and misgivings whether the soul, although a fairer and diviner thing than the body, being as she is in the form of harmony may not perish first. On the other hand, Cebes appeared to grant that the soul was more lasting than the body, but he said that no one could know whether the soul, after having worn out many bodies, might not perish herself and leave her last body behind her; and that this might be death, the destruction not of the body but of the soul, for in the body the work of destruction is ever going on. Are not these, Simmias and Cebes, the points which we have to consider?

They both agreed to this statement of them.

He proceeded: And did you deny the force of the whole preceding argument, or of a part only?

Of a part only, they replied.

And what did you think, he said, of that part of the argument in which we said that learning was recollection, and hence inferred that the soul must have previously existed somewhere else before she was imprisoned in the body?

Cebes said that he had been wonderfully impressed by that part of the argument, and that his conviction remained absolutely unshaken. Simmias agreed, and added that he himself could hardly imagine the possibility of his ever thinking differently.

But, rejoined Socrates, you will have to think differently, my Theban friend, if you still maintain that harmony is a composite thing, and that the soul is a harmony which is made out of strings set in the frame of the body; for you will surely never allow yourself to say that a harmony is composed and exists prior to the elements necessary to its composition.

Never, Socrates.

But do you not see that this is what you imply when you say both that the soul existed before she took the form and body of man, and that she was made up of elements which as yet had no existence? For harmony is not like that to which you are comparing it; but first the lyre, and the strings, and the sounds exist in a state of discord, and then harmony is made last of all, and perishes first. And how can such an account of the soul as this be in concord with your former statement?

Not at all, replied Simmias.

And yet, he said, there surely ought to be harmony in a discourse of which harmony is the theme?

There ought, replied Simmias.

But there is no harmony, he said, in the two propositions that learning is recollection, and that the soul is a harmony. Which of them will you retain?

I think, he replied, that I have a much stronger faith, Socrates, in the first of the two; of the latter I have had no demonstration at all, but derived it only from a specious analogy, which has commended it to most of its adherents. I know too well that these arguments from analogies are impostors, and unless great caution is observed in the use of them, they are very deceptive – in geometry, and in other things too. But the doctrine of learning and recollection derives its proof from a satisfactory postulate: and the proof was that the soul must have existed before she came into the body, because to her belongs the reality of which the very name signifies existence. Having, as I am convinced, rightly accepted this postulate, and on sufficient grounds, I must, as I suppose, cease to argue or allow others to argue that the soul is a harmony.

Let me put the matter, Simmias, he said, in another point of view: do you imagine that a harmony or any other composition can be in a state other than that of the elements out of which it is compounded?

Certainly not.

Or do or suffer anything other than they do or suffer?

He agreed.

Then a harmony does not, properly speaking, lead the parts or elements which make up the harmony, but only follows them.

He assented.

So it is far from being possible that a harmony can

have any motion, or sound, or other quality which is opposed to that of its parts.

Far indeed, he replied.

And does not the nature of every harmony depend upon the manner in which the elements are harmonized?

I do not understand you, he said.

I mean to say that a harmony is more of a harmony, and more completely a harmony, when more truly and fully harmonized, supposing such a thing is possible; and less of a harmony, and less completely a harmony, when less truly and fully harmonized.

True.

Now does the soul admit of degrees? Or is one soul in the very least degree more or less, or more or less completely, a soul than another?

Not in the least.

Yet surely of two souls, one is said to have intelligence and virtue, and to be good, and the other to have folly and vice, and to be an evil soul: and this is said truly?

Yes, truly.

But what will those who maintain the soul to be a harmony say of this presence of virtue and vice in the soul? Will they say that here is another harmony, and another discord, and that the virtuous soul is harmonized, and herself being a harmony has another harmony within her, and that the vicious soul is both herself inharmonical and has no other harmony within her?

I cannot tell, replied Simmias; but clearly something of the sort would be asserted by those who say that the soul is a harmony.

And we have already admitted that no soul is more

a soul than another; which means admitting that one harmony is not more or less harmony, or more or less completely a harmony, than another?

Quite true.

And that which is not more or less a harmony is not more or less harmonized?

True.

And that which is not more or less harmonized cannot have more or less of harmony, but only an equal harmony?

Yes, an equal harmony.

Then one soul not being more or less completely a soul than another, is not more or less harmonized?

Exactly.

And therefore has neither more nor less of discord, nor yet of harmony?

She has not.

And having neither more nor less of harmony or of discord, one soul has no more vice or virtue than another, if vice be discord and virtue harmony?

Not at all more.

Or speaking more correctly, Simmias, the soul, if she is a harmony, will never have any vice; because a harmony, being entirely harmony, can have no part in the inharmonical.

No.

Nor, I presume, could a soul, being entirely soul, have any part in vice?

How can she have, if the previous argument holds?

Then, if all souls are equally by their nature souls, all souls of all living creatures will be equally good?

I agree with you, Socrates, he said.

Well, can all this be true, think you? he said; and would such consequences have followed if the assumption that the soul is a harmony were correct?

It cannot be true.

Once more, he said, what ruler is there of the elements of human nature other than the soul, and especially the wise soul? Do you know of any?

Indeed, I do not.

And is the soul in agreement with the affections of the body? Or is she at variance with them? For example, when the body is hot and thirsty, does not the soul pull us away from drinking? And when the body is hungry, away from eating? And this is only one instance out of ten thousand of the opposition of the soul to the things of the body.

Very true.

But we have already acknowledged that the soul, if she were a harmony, could never utter a note at variance with the tensions and relaxations and percussions and other affections of the strings out of which she is composed; she could only follow, she could not lead them.

It must be so, he replied.

And yet do we not now discover the soul to be doing the exact opposite – leading the elements of which she is believed to be composed; almost always opposing and coercing them in all sorts of ways throughout life, sometimes more violently with the pains of medicine and gymnastic; then again more gently; now threatening, now admonishing the desires, passions, fears, as if talking to a thing which is not herself, as Homer in the Odyssey represents Odysseus doing in the words –

He beat his breast, and thus reproached his heart:

Endure, my heart; far worse hast thou endured!

Do you think that Homer wrote this under the idea that the soul is a harmony destined to be led by the affections of the body, and not rather of a nature which should lead and master them – herself far too divine a thing to be compared with any harmony?

Yes, Socrates, I quite think so.

Then, my friend, we can never be right in saying that the soul is a kind of harmony, for we should apparently contradict the divine Homer, and contradict ourselves.

True, he said.

Thus much, said Socrates, of Harmonia, your Theban goddess, who has graciously yielded to us; but what shall I say, Cebes, to her husband Cadmus, and how shall I make peace with him?

I think that you will discover a way of propitiating him, said Cebes; I am sure that you have put the argument with Harmonia in a manner that I could never have expected. For when Simmias was mentioning his difficulty, I quite imagined that no answer could be given to him, and therefore I was surprised at finding that his argument could not sustain the first onset of yours, and not impossibly the other, whom you call Cadmus, may share a similar fate.

Nay, my good friend, said Socrates, do not boast, lest some evil eye should blight the growing argument. That, however, may be left in the hands of those above, while we draw near the foe in Homeric fashion, and try the mettle of your words. Here lies the point: you want to have it proven to you that the soul is imperishable and immortal, for otherwise the philosopher, who meets death confidently in the belief that he will fare better in the world below than if he had led another sort of life, must be the dupe of a vain and foolish confidence: and you say that the demonstration of the strength and divinity of the soul, and of her existence prior to our becoming men, does not necessarily imply her immortality, but only that she is long-lived, and has known and done much in a former state of immense duration. Still she is not on that account immortal; and her entrance into the human form may itself be a sort of disease which is the beginning of dissolution, and she may be sorely vexed during her earthly life, and sooner or later perish in that which is called death. And whether the soul enters into the body once only or many times, does not, so you say, make any difference in the fears of individuals. For any man who is not devoid of sense must fear, if he has no knowledge and can give no account of the soul's immortality. This, or something like this, I suspect to be your view, Cebes; and I have designedly repeated it more than once in order that nothing may escape us, and that you may, if you wish, add or subtract anything.

But, said Cebes, as far as I see at present, I have nothing to add or subtract; I mean what you say that I mean.

Socrates paused for a long while, and seemed to be absorbed in reflection. At length he said: You are raising a tremendous question, Cebes, involving the whole nature and cause of coming into being and ceasing to be, about which, if you like, I will give you my own experience; and if anything which I say seems helpful to you, you may use it to overcome your difficulty.

I should very much like, said Cebes, to hear what you have to say.

Then I will tell you, said Socrates. When I was young, Cebes, I had a prodigious desire to know that department of philosophy which is called the investi-

gation of nature; to know the causes of things, and why
a thing is and is created or destroyed, appeared to me
to be a lofty profession; and I was always agitating
myself with the consideration of questions such as
these: is the growth of animals the result of some
putrefaction which the hot and the cold principle
suffer, as some have said? Is the blood the element
with which we think, or the air, or the fire? Or perhaps
nothing of the kind – but the brain may be the
originating power of the perceptions of hearing and
sight and smell, and memory and opinion may come
from them, and knowledge from memory and opinion
when they have attained fixity. And then I went on to
examine the corruptions of them, and then to the
things of heaven and earth, and at last I concluded
myself to be utterly and absolutely incapable of these
inquiries, as I will satisfactorily prove to you. For I was
fascinated by them to such a degree that my eyes grew
blind to things which I had seemed to myself, and also
to others, to know quite well; I unlearned what I had
before thought self-evident truths; e.g. such a fact as
that the growth of man is the result of eating and
drinking; for when by the digestion of food flesh is
added to flesh and bone to bone, and when by the
same process each tissue has received its appropriate
accretion, then the lesser bulk becomes larger and so
the small man becomes big. Was not that a reasonable
notion?

Yes, said Cebes, I think so.

Well; but let me tell you something more. There was
a time when I thought that I understood the meaning
of greater and less pretty well; and when I saw a big
man standing by a little one, I fancied that one was
taller than the other just by the head, and similarly

with horses: and still more clearly did I seem to perceive that ten is more than eight because it has two additional units, and that two cubits are more than one because it is larger by a half of itself.

And what is now your notion of such matters? said Cebes.

I should be far enough from imagining, he replied, that I knew the cause of any of them, by heaven I should; for I cannot satisfy myself that, when one is added to one, either the one to which the addition is made or the one which is added becomes two, or that the two units added together make two by reason of the addition. I cannot understand how, when separated from the other, each of them was one and not two, and now, when they are brought together, the mere juxtaposition or meeting of them should be the cause of their becoming two. Neither can I believe that the division of one is the way to make two; for then an opposite cause would produce the same effect – as in the former instance the addition and juxtaposition of one to one was the cause of two, in this the separation and subtraction of one from the other would be the cause. Nor am I any longer satisfied that I understand how the unit comes into being at all, or in short how anything else is either generated or destroyed or exists, so long as this is the method of approach; but I have in my mind some confused notion of a new method, and can never admit the other.

Then I heard someone reading, as he said, from a book of Anaxagoras, that mind was the disposer and cause of all, and I was delighted at this notion, which appeared quite admirable, and I said to myself: if mind is the disposer, mind will dispose all for the best, and put each particular in the best place; and I argued that if anyone desired to find out the cause of the generation or destruction or existence of anything, he must find out what state of being or doing or suffering was best for that thing, and therefore a man had only to consider what was best and most desirable both for the thing itself and for other things, and then he must necessarily also know the worse, since the same science comprehended both. Arguing in this way, I rejoiced to think that I had found in Anaxagoras a teacher of the causes of existence such as I desired, and I imagined that he would tell me first whether the earth is flat or round; and after telling me this, he would proceed to explain the cause and the necessity of this being so, starting from the greater good, and demonstrating that it is better for the earth to be such as it is; and if he said that the earth was in the centre, he would further explain that this position was the better, and I should be satisfied with the explanation given, and not want any other sort of cause. And I thought that I would then go on and ask him about the sun and moon and stars, and that he would explain to me their comparative swiftness, and their returnings and various states, active and passive, and in what way all of them were for the best. For I could not imagine that when he spoke of mind as the disposer of them, he would give any other account of their being as they are, except that this was best; and I thought that while explaining to me in detail the cause of each and the cause of all, he would also explain to me what was best for each and what was good for all. These hopes I would not have sold for a large sum of money, and I seized the books and started to read them as fast as I could in my eagerness to know the best and the worse.

How high were my hopes, and how quickly were they

lost to me! As I proceeded, I found my philosopher altogether forsaking mind and making no appeal to any other principle of order, but having recourse to air, and ether, and water, and many other eccentricities. I might compare him to a person who began by maintaining generally that mind is the cause of the actions of Socrates, but who, when he endeavoured to explain the causes of my several actions in detail, went on to show that I sit here because my body is made up of bones and muscles; and the bones, as he would say, are hard and have joints which divide them, and the muscles are elastic, and they cover the bones, which have also a covering or environment of flesh and skin which contains them; and as the bones swing in their sockets, through the contraction or relaxation of the muscles I am able to bend my limbs, and this is why I am sitting here in a curved posture – that is what he would say; and he would have a similar explanation of my talking to you, which he would attribute to sound, and air, and hearing, and he would assign ten thousand other causes of the same sort, forgetting to mention the true cause, which is, that the Athenians have thought it better to condemn me, and accordingly I have thought it better and more right to remain here and undergo my sentence; for I strongly suspect that these muscles and bones of mine would long ago have been in Megara or Boeotia, borne there by their own idea of what was best, if I did not think it more right and honourable to endure any penalty ordered by the state, instead of running away into exile. There is surely a strange confusion of causes and conditions in all this. It may be said, indeed, that without bones and muscles and the other parts of the body I cannot execute my purposes. But to say at the same time that

I act from mind, and that I do as I do because of them and not from the choice of the best, is a very careless and idle mode of speaking. I wonder that they cannot distinguish the cause from the condition without which the cause would never be the cause; it is the latter, I think, which the many, feeling about in the dark, are always mistaking and misnaming 'cause'. And thus one man sets the earth within a cosmic whirling, and steadies it by the heaven; another gives the air as a support to the earth, which is a sort of broad trough. They never look for the power which in arranging them as they are arranges them for the best; and instead of ascribing to it any superhuman strength, they rather expect to discover another Atlas who is stronger and more everlasting than this earthly Atlas, and better able to hold all things together. That it is really the good and the right which holds and binds things together, they never reflect. Such then is the principle of causation which I would fain learn if anyone would teach me. But as I have failed either to discover it myself, or to learn it of anyone else, I will exhibit to you, if you like, the method I have followed as the second best mode of inquiring into the cause.

I should very much like to hear, he replied.

Socrates proceeded: I thought that as I had failed in the study of material things, I ought to be careful that I did not lose the eye of my soul, as people may injure their bodily eye by observing and gazing on the sun during an eclipse, unless they take the precaution of only looking at the image reflected in the water, or in some similar medium. So in my own case, I was afraid that my soul might be blinded altogether if I looked at things with my eyes or tried to apprehend them by the help of particular senses. And I thought that I had better retreat to the domain of reasoning and seek there the truth of existence. I dare say that the simile is not perfect – for I do not quite agree that he who contemplates things through the medium of thought, sees them only 'through a glass darkly', more so than he who considers them in their material existence. However, this was the method which I adopted: I first assumed some proposition, which I judged to be the strongest, and then I affirmed as true whatever seemed to agree with this, whether relating to causation or to anything else; and that which disagreed I regarded as untrue. But I should like to explain my meaning more clearly, as I do not think that you as yet understand me.

No indeed, replied Cebes, not very well.

There is nothing new, he said, in what I am about to tell you; but only what I have been always and everywhere repeating in the previous discussion and on other occasions: I shall try to show you the sort of causation which has occupied my thoughts. I shall have to go back to those familiar theories which are in the mouth of everyone, and first of all assume that there is an absolute beauty and goodness and greatness, and the like; grant me these and admit that they exist, and I hope to be able to show you the nature of cause, and to prove the immortality of the soul.

Cebes said: You may proceed at once with the proof, for I grant you this.

Well, he said, then I should like to know whether you agree with me in the next step; for I cannot help thinking that if there be anything beautiful other than absolute beauty it is beautiful only in so far as it partakes of absolute beauty – and I should say the same of everything. Do you agree in this notion of the cause?

Yes, he said, I agree.

He proceeded: I no longer look for, nor can I understand, those other ingenious causes which are alleged; and if a person says to me that the bloom of colour, or form, or any such thing is a source of beauty, I dismiss all that, which is only confusing to me, and simply and singly, and perhaps foolishly, hold and am assured in my own mind that nothing makes a thing beautiful but the presence or participation of beauty in whatever way or manner obtained; for as to the manner I am uncertain, but I stoutly contend that by beauty all beautiful things become beautiful. This appears to me to be the safest answer which I can give, either to myself or to another, and to this I cling, in the persuasion that this principle will never be overthrown, and that to myself or to anyone who asks the question, I may safely reply, that by beauty beautiful things become beautiful. Do you not agree with me?

I do.

And that by greatness great things become great and greater greater, and by smallness the less become less?

True.

Then if a person were to remark that A is taller by a head than B, and B less by a head than A, you would refuse to admit his statement, and would stoutly contend that what you mean is only that the greater is greater by, and by reason of, greatness, and the less is less only by, and by reason of, smallness. I imagine you would be afraid of a counter-argument that if the greater is greater and the less less by the head, then, first, the greater is greater and the less less by the same thing; and, secondly, the greater man is greater by the head which is itself small, and so you get the monstrous absurdity that a man is great by something small. You would be afraid of this, would you not?

Indeed I should, said Cebes, laughing.

In like manner you would think it dangerous to say that ten exceeded eight by, and by reason of, two; but would say by, and by reason of, number; or you would say that two cubits exceed one cubit not by a half, but by magnitude? For there is the same danger in all these cases.

Very true, he said.

Again, would you not be cautious of affirming that the addition of one to one, or the division of one, is the cause of two? And you would loudly asseverate that you know of no way in which anything comes into existence except by participation in the distinctive reality of that in which it participates, and consequently, as far as you know, the only cause of two is the participation in duality – this is the way to make two, and the participation in unity is the way to make one. You would say: 'I will let alone all subtleties like these of division and addition – wiser heads than mine may answer them; inexperienced as I am, and ready to start, as the proverb says, at my own shadow, I cannot afford to give up the sure ground of the original postulate.' And if anyone fastens on you there, you would not mind him, or answer him until you could see whether the consequences which follow agree with one another or not, and when you are further required to give an account of this postulate, you would give it in the same way, assuming some higher postulate which seemed to you to be the best founded, until you arrived at a satisfactory resting-place; but you would not jumble together the fundamental principle and the consequences in your reasoning, like the eristics – at least if you wanted to discover real existence. Not that this confusion signifies to them, who probably never care or think about the matter at all, for they have the wit to be well pleased with themselves however thorough may be the muddle of their ideas. But you, if you are a philosopher, will certainly do as I say.

What you say is most true, said Simmias and Cebes, both speaking at once.

ECHECRATES: Yes, Phaedo; and I do not wonder at their assenting. Anyone who has the least sense will acknowledge the wonderful clearness of Socrates' reasoning.

PHAEDO: Certainly, Echecrates; and such was the feeling of the whole company at the time.

ECHECRATES: Yes, and equally of ourselves, who were not of the company, and are now listening to your recital. But what followed?

PHAEDO: After all this had been admitted, and they had agreed that the forms exist individually, and that other things participate in them and derive their names from them, Socrates, if I remember rightly, said: This is your way of speaking; and yet when you say that Simmias is greater than Socrates and less than Phaedo, do you not predicate of Simmias both greatness and smallness?

Yes, I do.

But still, he continued, you allow that Simmias does not in fact exceed Socrates, as the words may seem to imply, essentially because he is Simmias, but by reason of the size which he happens to have; exactly as on the other hand he does not exceed Socrates because Socrates is Socrates, but because Socrates has smallness when compared with the greatness of Simmias?

True.

And if Phaedo exceeds him in size, this is not because Phaedo is Phaedo, but because Phaedo has greatness relatively to Simmias, who is comparatively smaller?

That is true.

And therefore Simmias is said to be small, and is also said to be great, because he is in a mean between them, submitting his smallness to be exceeded by the greatness of the one, and presenting his greatness to the other to exceed that other's smallness. He added, laughing, I am speaking like a book, but I believe that what I am saying is true.

Simmias assented.

I speak as I do because I want you to agree with me in thinking, not only that absolute greatness will never be simultaneously great and small, but also that the greatness in us will never admit the small or consent to be exceeded; instead of this, one of two things will happen, either it will fly and retire before its opposite, the small, or at the approach of its opposite it has already ceased to exist; but it refuses to become other than what it was by staying and receiving smallness. For instance, I having received and admitted smallness remain as I was, and am the same person and small: but greatness has not condescended to become small. In like manner the smallness in us refuses to be or become great; nor can any other opposite which remains the same ever be or become its own opposite, but either goes away or perishes in the change.

That, replied Cebes, is quite my notion.

Hereupon one of the company, though I do not exactly remember which of them, said: In heaven's name, is not this the direct contrary of what was admitted before – that out of the greater came the less and out of the less the greater, and that opposites were simply generated from opposites; but now this principle seems to be utterly denied.

Socrates turned his head to the speaker and listened. I like your courage, he said, in reminding us of this. But you do not observe that there is a difference in the two cases. For then we were saying that an opposite thing comes into being from its opposite; now, however, speaking of bare opposites, and taking them either as they are realized in us or as they exist in themselves, we say that one of them can never become the other: then, my friend, we were speaking of things in which opposites are inherent and which are called after them, but now about the opposites which are inherent in them and which give their name to them; and these essential opposites will never, as we maintain, admit of generation into or out of one another. At the same time, turning to Cebes, he said: Are you at all disconcerted, Cebes, at our friend's objection?

No, not by this one, said Cebes; and yet I cannot deny that I am often disturbed by objections.

Then we are agreed after all, said Socrates, that the opposite will never in any case be opposed to itself?

To that we are quite agreed, he replied.

Yet once more let me ask you to consider the question from another point of view, and see whether you agree with me: there is a thing which you term heat, and another thing which you term cold?

Certainly.

But are they the same as fire and snow?

Most assuredly not.

Heat is a thing different from fire, and cold is not the same with snow?

Yes.

And yet I fancy you agree that when snow receives heat (to use our previous phraseology), they will not remain snow and heat; but at the advance of the heat, the snow will either retire or perish?

Very true, he replied.

And the fire too at the advance of the cold will either retire or perish; but it will never receive the cold, and yet insist upon remaining what it was, and so be at once fire and cold.

That is true, he said.

And in some cases the name of the form is attached not only to the form in an eternal connexion; but something else which, not being the form, yet never exists without it, is also entitled to be called by that name. I will try to make this clearer by an example: the odd number is always called by the name of odd?

Very true.

But is this the only thing which is called odd? Here is my point. Are there not other things which have their own name, and yet must be called odd, because, although not the same as oddness, they are essentially never without oddness? I mean such a case as that of the number three, and there are many other examples. Take that case. Would you not say that three may be called by its proper name, and also be called odd, which is not the same with three? And this may be said not only of three but also of five, and of every alternate number – each of them without being oddness is odd; and in the same way two and four, and the other series of alternate numbers, has every number even, without being evenness. Do you agree?

Of course.

Then now mark the point at which I am aiming: –

not only do essential opposites seem to exclude one
another, but also concrete things, which, although
not in themselves opposed, contain opposites; these,
I say, likewise reject the form opposed to that which is
contained in them, and when it approaches them
they either perish or withdraw. For example, will not
the number three endure annihilation or anything
sooner than be converted into an even number, while
remaining three?

Very true, said Cebes.

And yet, he said, the number two is certainly not
opposed to the number three?

It is not.

Then not only do opposite forms repel the advance
of one another, but also there are other things which
withdraw before the approach of opposites.

Very true, he said.

Suppose, he said, that we endeavour, if possible, to
determine what these are.

By all means.

Are they not, Cebes, such as compel anything of
which they have possession, not only to take their own
form, but also the form of an opposite?

What do you mean?

I mean, as I was just now saying, and as I am sure
that you know, that those things which are possessed
by the form of the number three must not only be three
in number, but must also be odd.

Quite true.

And such things will never suffer the intrusion of the
form opposite to that which gives this impress?

No.

And this impress was given by the form of the odd?

Yes.

And to the odd is opposed the even?

True.

Then the form of the even number will never intrude on three?

No.

Then three has no part in the even?

None.

Then the triad or number three is uneven?

Very true.

To return then to my definition of things which are not opposite to one of a pair of opposites, and yet do not admit that opposite – as, in the instance given, three, although not opposed to the even, does not any the more admit of the even, but always brings the opposite into play on the other side; or as two does not receive the odd, or fire the cold – from these examples (and there are many more of them) perhaps you may be able to arrive at the general conclusion, that not only opposites will not receive opposites, but also that nothing which brings an opposite will admit the opposite of that which it brings, in that to which it is brought. And here let me recapitulate – for there is no harm in repetition. The number five will not admit the form of the even, any more than ten, which is the double of five, will admit the form of the odd. The double has itself a different opposite, but never-theless rejects the odd altogether. Nor similarly will parts in the ratio 3:2 admit the form of the whole, nor will the half or the one-third, or any such fraction: You will agree?

Yes, he said, I entirely agree and go along with you in that.

And now, he said, let us begin again; and do not you answer my question in the words in which I ask it, but follow my example: let me have not the old safe answer of which I spoke at first, but another equally safe, of which the truth will be inferred by you from what has been just said. If you ask me 'what that is, of which the inherence makes the body hot', I shall reply not heat (this is what I call the safe and stupid answer), but fire, a far superior answer, which we are now in a condition to give. Or if you ask me 'why a body is diseased', I shall not say from disease, but from fever; and instead of saying that oddness is the cause of odd numbers, I shall say that the monad is the cause of them: and so of things in general, as I dare say that you will understand sufficiently without my adducing any further examples.

Yes, he said, I quite understand you.

Tell me, then, what is that of which the inherence will render the body alive?

The soul, he replied.

And is this always the case?

Yes, he said, of course.

Then whatever the soul occupies, to that she comes bearing life?

Yes, certainly.

And is there any opposite to life?

There is, he said.

And what is that?

Death.

Then from our previous conclusion it follows that the soul will never admit the opposite of what she always brings.

Impossible, replied Cebes.

And now, he said, what did we just now call that which does not admit the form of the even?

Uneven.

And that which does not admit the musical or the just?

The unmusical, he said, and the unjust.

And what do we call that which does not admit death?

The immortal, he said.

And does the soul admit of death?

No.

Then the soul is immortal?

Yes, he said.

And may we say that this has been proven?

Yes, abundantly proven, Socrates, he replied.

Supposing that the odd were necessarily imperishable, must not three be imperishable?

Of course.

And if that which is cold were necessarily imperishable, when heat came attacking the snow, must not the snow have retired whole and unmelted – for it could never have perished, nor again could it have remained and admitted the heat?

True, he said.

Again, if that which cannot be cooled were imperishable, the fire when assailed by cold would not have perished or have been extinguished, but would have gone away unaffected?

Certainly, he said.

And the same may be said of the immortal: if the immortal is also imperishable, the soul when attacked by death cannot perish; for the preceding argument shows that the soul will not admit death, or exist as dead, any more than three or the odd number will exist as even, or fire, or the heat in the fire, will be cold. Yet a person may say: 'But although the odd will not become even at the approach of the even, why may not the odd perish and the even take the place of the odd?' Now to him who makes this objection, we cannot answer that the odd is imperishable; for this is not the fact. If we had accepted it as a fact, there would have been no difficulty in contending that at the approach of the even the odd and the number three took their departure; and the same argument would have held good of fire and heat and any other thing.

Very true.

And the same may be said of the immortal: if we agree that the immortal is also imperishable, then the soul will be imperishable as well as immortal; but if not, some other proof of her imperishableness will have to be given.

No other proof is needed, he said; for if the immortal, being eternal, is liable to perish, then nothing is imperishable.

Yes, replied Socrates, and all men, I think, will agree that god, and the essential form of life, and the immortal in general, will never perish.

Yes, all men, he said – that is true; and what is more, gods, if I am not mistaken, as well as men.

Seeing then that the immortal is indestructible, must not the soul, if she is immortal, be also imperishable?

Most certainly.

Then when death attacks a man, the mortal portion of him may be supposed to die, but the immortal retires at the approach of death and is preserved safe and indestructible?

Yes.

Then, Cebes, beyond question, the soul is immortal and imperishable, and our souls will truly exist in another world!

I am convinced, Socrates, said Cebes, and have nothing more to object; but if my friend Simmias, or anyone else, has any further objection to make, he had better speak out, and not keep silence, since I do not know to what other season he can defer the discussion if there is anything which he wants to say or to have said.

But I too, replied Simmias, can give no reason for doubting the result of the argument. It is when I think of the greatness of the subject and the feebleness of man that I still feel and cannot help feeling uncertain in my own mind.

Yes, Simmias, replied Socrates, that is well said: and I may add that our first principles, even if they appear to you certain, should be closely examined; and when they are satisfactorily analysed, then you will, I imagine, follow up the argument as far as is humanly possible; and if you make sure you have done so, there will be no need for any further inquiry.

Very true.

But then, O my friends, he said, if the soul is really immortal, what care should be taken of her, not only in respect of the portion of time allowed to what is called life, but of eternity! And the danger of neglecting her from this point of view does indeed now appear to be awful. If death had only been the end of all, dying would have been a godsend to the wicked, for they would have been happily quit not only of their body, but of their own evil together with their souls. But now, inasmuch as the soul is manifestly immortal, there is for her no release or salvation from evil except the attainment of the highest virtue and wisdom. For the soul when on her progress to the world below takes nothing with her but nurture and education;

and these are said greatly to benefit or greatly to injure the departed, at the very beginning of his journey thither.

For after death, as they say, each individual is led by the genius to whom he had been allotted in life to a certain place in which the dead are gathered together, whence after submitting to judgment they pass into the world below, following the guide who is appointed to conduct them from this world to the other: and when they have received their due and remained their time, another guide brings them back again after many revolutions of ages. Now this way to the other world is not, as Aeschylus says in the *Telephus*, a single and straight path – if that were so no guide would be needed, for no one could miss it; but there are many partings of the road, and windings, as I infer from the rites and sacrifices which are offered to the gods below in places where three ways meet on earth. The wise and orderly soul follows her appointed guide and knows her surroundings; but the soul which desires the body, and which, as I was relating before, has long been fluttering about the lifeless frame and the world of sight, is after many struggles and many sufferings hardly and with violence carried away by her attendant genius; and when she arrives at the place where the other souls are gathered, if she be impure and have done impure deeds, whether foul murders or other crimes which are the brothers of these, and the works of brothers in crime – from that soul everyone flees and turns away; no one will be her companion, no one her guide, but alone she wanders in extremity of distress until certain times are fulfilled, and when they are fulfilled, she is borne irresistibly to her own fitting habitation; as every pure and just soul which has passed through life in the company and under the guidance of the gods has also her own proper home.

Now the earth has divers wonderful regions, and is indeed in nature and extent very unlike the notions of geographers, as I believe on the authority of one who shall be nameless.

What do you mean, Socrates? said Simmias. I have myself heard many descriptions of the earth, but I do not know, and I should very much like to hear the account in which you put faith.

Well, Simmias, replied Socrates, it scarcely needs the art of Glaucus to give you a description; although I know not that the art of Glaucus could prove the truth of my tale, which I myself should perhaps never be able to prove, and even if I could, I fear, Simmias, that my life would come to an end before the argument was completed. I may describe to you, however, the form and regions of the earth according to my conception of them.

That, said Simmias, will be enough.

Well then, he said, my conviction is, that the earth is a round body in the centre of the heavens, and therefore has no need of air or of any similar force to be a support, but is kept there and hindered from falling or inclining any way by the equability of the surrounding heaven and by her own equipoise. For that which, being in equipoise, is in the centre of that which is equably diffused, will not incline any way in any degree, but being similarly related to every extreme will remain unmoving, and not deviate. And this is my first belief.

Which is surely a correct one, said Simmias.

Also I believe that the earth is very vast, and that we who dwell in the region extending from the River Phasis to the Pillars of Heracles inhabit a small portion only about the sea, like ants and frogs about a marsh, and that there are many other inhabitants of many other like places; for everywhere on the surface of the earth there are hollows of various forms and sizes, into which the water and the mist and the lower air have collected. But the true earth is pure and situated in the pure heaven – there are the stars also; and it is the heaven which is commonly spoken of by most authorities as the ether, and of which those other things are the sediment gathering in the hollows beneath. We who live in these hollows are deceived into the notion that we are dwelling above on the surface of the earth; which is just as if a creature who lived at the bottom of the sea were to fancy that he was living on the surface of the water, and that the sea was the heaven through which he saw the sun and the other stars, he having never come to the surface by reason of his feebleness and sluggishness, and having never lifted up his head and seen, nor ever heard from one who had seen, how much purer and fairer the world above is than his own. And such is exactly our case. We are dwelling in a hollow of the earth, and fancy that we are on the surface; and the air we call the heaven, in which we imagine that the stars move. But the fact is that owing to our feebleness and sluggishness we are prevented from reaching the surface of the air: for if any man could arrive at the exterior limit, or take the wings of a bird and come to the top, then, like a fish who puts his head out of the water and sees this world, he would see a world beyond; and, if the nature of man could sustain the sight, he would acknowledge that this other world was the place of the true heaven and the true light and the true earth. For our earth, and the stones, and the entire region which surrounds us, are spoilt and corroded, as in the sea all things are corroded by the brine, neither has the sea any notable or perfect growth, but even where it meets earth it has only caverns, and sand, and an endless slough of mud – in no wise to be compared to the fairer sights of our world. And still less is this our world to be compared with the other. If a myth is not to be despised, Simmias, I can tell you one that is well worth hearing about that upper earth which is under the heaven.

We shall be charmed, Socrates, replied Simmias, to listen to your myth.

The tale, my friend, he said, is as follows: in the first place, the true earth, when looked at from above, is in appearance like one of those balls which are made of twelve pieces of leather; it is variegated, a patchwork of different colours of which the colours used by painters on our earth are in a manner samples. But there the whole earth is made up of them, and they are brighter far and clearer than ours; there is a purple of wonderful lustre, also the radiance of gold, and the white which is in the earth is whiter than any chalk or snow. Of these and other colours the earth is made up, and they are more in number and fairer than the eye of man has ever seen; the very hollows (of which I was speaking) filled with air and water have a colour of their own, and are seen like light gleaming amid the diversity of the other colours, so that the whole presents a single and continuous appearance of variety in unity. And in this fair region all things which grow – trees, and flowers, and fruits – are in a like degree fairer than any here; and there are hills, having stones in them in a like degree smoother, and more transparent, and fairer in colour than our highly valued emeralds and cornelians and jaspers and other gems, which are but minute fragments of them: for there all the stones are like our precious stones, and fairer still. The reason is that they are pure, and not, like our precious stones, corroded or defiled by the confluence of corrupt briny elements which breed foulness and disease both in earth and stones, as well as in animals and plants. They are the jewels of the upper earth, which also shines with gold and silver and the like, and they are set in the light of day and are large and abundant and in all places, making the earth a sight to gladden the beholder's eye. And there are many animals and also men, some living inland, others dwelling about the air as we dwell about the sea; others in islands which the air flows round, near the mainland; and in a word, the air is used by them as the water and the sea are by us, and the ether is to them what the air is to us. Moreover, the temperament of their seasons is such that they have no disease, and live much longer than we do, and have sight and hearing and intelligence and all the other faculties in far greater perfection, in the same proportion that air is purer than water or the ether than air. Also they have temples and sacred places in which the gods really dwell, and they hear their voices and receive their answers, and are conscious of them and hold converse with them face to face; and they see the sun, moon, and stars as they truly are, and their other blessedness is of a piece with this.

Such is the nature of the whole earth, and of the things which are around the earth; and there are divers regions in the hollows on the face of the globe everywhere, some of them deeper and more extended than that which we inhabit, others deeper but narrower, and some are shallower and also wider. All have numerous perforations, and there are passages broad and narrow in the interior of the earth, connecting them with one another; and there flows out of and into them, as into basins, a vast tide of water, and huge subterranean streams of perennial rivers, and springs hot and cold, and a great fire, and great rivers of fire, and streams of liquid mud, thin or thick (like the rivers of mud in Sicily, and the lava streams which follow them), and the regions about which they happen to flow are filled up with them. And there is a swinging or see-saw in the interior of the earth which moves all this up and down, and is due to the following cause: there is a chasm which is the vastest of them all, and pierces right through the whole earth; this is that chasm which Homer describes in the words 'Far off, where is the inmost depth beneath the earth'; and which he in other places, and many other poets, have called Tartarus. And the see-saw is caused by the streams flowing into and out of this chasm, and they each have the nature of the soil through which they flow. And the reason why the streams are always flowing in and out, is that the watery element has no bed or bottom, but is swinging and surging up and down, and the surrounding wind and air do the same; they follow the water up and down, towards the further side of the earth and back again; and just as in the act of respiration the air is always in process of inhalation and exhalation, so the wind swinging with the water in and out produces fearful and irresistible blasts: when the waters retire into the regions below, as they are called, they flow into the streams on the further side of the earth, and fill them up like water raised by a pump, and then when they leave those regions and rush back hither, they again fill the streams here, and these being filled flow through subterranean channels and find their way to their appointed places, forming seas, and lakes, and rivers, and springs. Thence they again enter the earth, some of them making a long circuit into many lands, others going to a few places and not so distant; and again fall into Tartarus, some at a point a good deal lower than that at which they rose, and others not much lower, but all in some degree lower than the point from which they came; and some fall in on the opposite side, and some on the same side. Some wind round the earth with one or many folds like the coils of a serpent, and after descending as far as they can fall again into the chasm. The rivers flowing in either direction can descend only to the centre and no further, for on either side of it their course would be uphill.

Now these rivers are many, and mighty, and diverse, and there are four principal ones, of which the greatest and outermost is that called Oceanus, which flows round in a circle; and diametrically opposite to it is Acheron, which flows in the opposite direction and passes through desert places and under the earth into the Acherusian lake: this is the lake to the shores of which the souls of the many go when they are dead, and after waiting an appointed time, which is to some a longer and to some a shorter time, they are sent back to be born again as animals. The third river passes out between the two, and near the place of outlet pours into a vast region of fire, and forms a lake larger than the Mediterranean Sea, boiling with water and mud; and proceeding muddy and turbid, and coiling round inside the earth, comes, among other places, to the extremities of the Acherusian lake, but mingles not with the waters of the lake, and after making many coils about the earth plunges into Tartarus at a deeper level. This is that Pyriphlegethon, as the stream is called, which throws up jets of lava in different parts of the earth. The fourth river goes out on the opposite side, and falls first of all, it is said, into a savage and frightful region, which is all of a blue-grey colour, like lapis lazuli; and this is that region which is called the Stygian, and the lake which the river forms by its influx is called Styx. After falling into the lake and receiving strange powers in the waters, it passes under the earth, winding round in the opposite direction to Pyriphlegethon, and meets it at the Acherusian lake from the opposite side. And the water of this river too mingles with no other, but flows round in a circle and falls into Tartarus over against Pyriphlegethon; and the name of the river, as the poets say, is Cocytus.

Such is the nature of the other world; and when the dead arrive at the place to which the genius of each severally guides them, first of all, they submit themselves to judgment, as they have lived well and piously or not. And those who appear to have lived neither well nor ill, go to the river Acheron, and embarking in the vessels which we may imagine they find there, are carried in them to the lake, and there they dwell and are purified of their evil deeds, and having suffered the penalty of the wrongs which they have done to others, they are absolved, and receive the rewards of their good deeds, each of them according to his deserts. But those who appear to be incurable by reason of the greatness of their crimes – who have committed many and terrible deeds of sacrilege, many murders foul and violent, or the like – such are hurled into Tartarus which is their fitting destiny, and they never come out. Those again who have committed crimes which, although great, are not irremediable – who in a moment of

anger, for example, have done some violence to a
father or a mother, and have repented for the remainder of their lives, or who have taken the life of another
under the like extenuating circumstances – these are
plunged into Tartarus, the pains of which they are
compelled to undergo for a year, but at the end of the
year the wave casts them forth – mere homicides by
way of Cocytus, parricides and matricides by Pyriphlegethon – and they are borne to the Acherusian
lake, and there they lift up their voices and call upon
the victims whom they have slain or wronged, to have
pity on them, and to be kind to them, and let them
come out into the lake. And if they prevail, then they
come forth and cease from their troubles; but if not,
they are carried back again into Tartarus and from
thence into the rivers unceasingly, until they obtain
mercy from those whom they have wronged: for that is
the sentence inflicted upon them by their judges. But
those who have been pre-eminent for holiness of life
are released from this earthly prison, and go to their
pure home which is above, and dwell on the true earth;
and of these, such as have duly purified themselves
with philosophy live henceforth altogether without the
body, in mansions fairer still, which are not easily to be
described, and of which the time now fails me to tell.

Wherefore, Simmias, seeing all these things, what
ought not we to do that we may obtain virtue and
wisdom in this life? Fair is the prize, and the hope great!

A man of sense ought not to assert that the
description which I have given of the soul and her
mansions is exactly true. But I do say that, inasmuch
as the soul is shown to be immortal, he may venture
to think, not improperly or unworthily, that something of the kind is true. The venture is a glorious one,

and he ought to comfort himself with words of power like these, which is the reason why I lengthen out the tale. Wherefore, I say, let a man be of good cheer about his soul, who having cast away the pleasures and ornaments of the body as alien to him and working harm rather than good, has sought after the pleasures of knowledge; and has arrayed the soul, not in some foreign attire, but in her own proper jewels, temperance, and justice, and courage, and nobility, and truth – in these adorned she is ready to go on her journey to the world below. You, Simmias and Cebes, and you others, will depart at some time or other. Me already, as a tragic poet would say, the voice of fate calls. Soon I must drink the poison; and I think that I had better repair to the bath first, in order that the women may not have the trouble of washing my body after I am dead.

When he had done speaking, Crito said: And have you any commands for us, Socrates – anything to say about your children, or any other matter in which we can serve you?

Nothing particular, Crito, he replied: only, as I have always told you, take care of yourselves; that is a service which you may be ever rendering to me and mine and to yourselves, whether you promise to do so or not. But if you have no thought for yourselves, and care not to walk in the path of life which I have shown you, not now for the first time, then however much and however earnestly you may promise at the moment, it will be of no avail.

We will do our best, said Crito: And in what way shall we bury you?

In any way that you like; but you must first get hold of me, and take care that I do not run away from you.

Then he turned to us, and added with a smile: I cannot make Crito believe that I am the same Socrates who have been talking and conducting the argument; he fancies that I am the other Socrates whom he will soon see, a dead body – and indeed he asks, How shall he bury me? And though I have spoken many words in the endeavour to show that when I have drunk the poison I shall leave you and go to the joys of the blessed – these words of mine, with which I was comforting you and myself, have had, as I perceive, no effect upon Crito. And therefore I want you to be surety for me to him now, as at the trial he was surety to the judges for me: but let the promise be of another sort; for he was surety for me to the judges that I would remain, and you must be my surety to him that I shall not remain, but go away and depart; and then he will suffer less at my death, and not be grieved when he sees my body being burned or buried. I would not have him sorrow at my hard lot, or say at the burial, Thus we lay out Socrates, or, Thus we follow him to the grave or bury him; for be well assured, my dear Crito, that false words are not only evil in themselves, but they infect the soul with evil. Be of good cheer then and say that you are burying my body only, and do with that whatever is usual, and what you think best.

When he had spoken these words, he arose and went into a chamber to bathe; Crito followed him and told us to wait. So we remained behind, talking and thinking of the subject of discourse, and also of the greatness of our loss; he was like a father of whom we were being bereaved, and we were about to pass the rest of our lives as orphans. When he had taken the bath his children were brought to him – (he had two young sons and an elder one); and the women of his family also came, and he talked to them and gave them a few directions in the presence of Crito; then he dismissed them and returned to us.

Now the hour of sunset was near, for a good deal of time had passed while he was within. When he came out, he sat down with us again after his bath, but not much was said. Soon the jailer, who was the servant of the Eleven, entered and stood by him, saying: To you, Socrates, whom after your time here I know to be the noblest and gentlest and best of all who ever came to this place, I will not impute the angry feelings of other men, who rage and swear at me, when, in obedience to the authorities, I bid them drink the poison – indeed, I am sure that you are not angry with me; for others, as you are aware, and not I, are to blame. And so fare you well, and try to bear lightly what must needs be – you know my errand. Then bursting into tears he turned and started on his way out.

Socrates looked up at him and said: I return your good wishes, and will do as you bid. Then turning to us, he said, How charming the man is: since I have been in prison he has always been coming to see me, and at times he would talk to me, and was as good to me as could be, and now see how generously he sorrows on my account. We must do as he says, Crito; and therefore let the cup be brought, if the poison is prepared: if not, let the attendant prepare some.

But, said Crito, the sun is still upon the hill-tops, and is not yet set. I know that many a one takes the draught quite a long time after the announcement has been made to him, when he has eaten and drunk to his satisfaction and enjoyed the society of his chosen friends; do not hurry – there is time enough.

Socrates said: Yes, Crito, and therein they of whom you speak act logically, for they think that they will be gainers by the delay; but I likewise act logically in not following their example, for I do not think that I should gain anything by drinking the poison a little later; I should only be ridiculous in my own eyes for sparing and saving a life which is already down to its dregs. Please then to do as I say, and not to refuse me.

Crito made a sign to the servant, who was standing by; and he went out, and having been absent for some time, returned with the jailer carrying the cup of poison. Socrates said: You, my good friend, who are experienced in these matters, shall give me directions how I am to proceed. The man answered: You have only to walk about until your legs are heavy, and then to lie down, and the poison will act. At the same time he handed the cup to Socrates, who in the easiest and gentlest manner, without the least fear or change of colour or feature, and looking at the man sideways with that droll glance of his, took the cup and said: What do you say about making a libation out of this cup to any god? May I, or not? The man answered: We only prepare, Socrates, just so much as we deem enough. I understand, he said: but a prayer to the gods I may and must offer, that they will prosper my journey from this to the other world – even so – and so be it according to my prayer. Then he held his breath and drank off the poison quite readily and cheerfully. And hitherto most of us had been fairly able to control our sorrow; but now when we saw him drinking, and saw too that he had finished the draught, we could no longer forbear, and in spite of myself my own tears were flowing fast; so that I covered my face and wept, not indeed for him, but at the thought of my own calamity in having to part from such a friend. Nor was I the first; for Crito, when he found himself unable to restrain his tears, had got up, and I followed; and at that moment, Apollodorus, who had been weeping all the time, burst out in a loud and passionate cry which broke us all down. Socrates alone retained his calmness: What is this strange outcry? he said. I sent away the women mainly in order that they might not misbehave in this fashion, for I have been told that a man should die in peace. Be quiet then, and bear yourselves with fortitude. When we heard his words we were ashamed, and refrained our tears; and he walked about until, as he said, his legs began to fail, and then he lay on his back, according to the directions, and the man who gave him the poison now and then looked at his feet and legs; and after a while he pressed his foot hard, and asked him if he could feel; and he said, No; and then his leg, and so upwards and upwards, and showed us that he was becoming cold and stiff. And he felt them himself, and said: When the poison reaches the heart, that will be the end. He was beginning to grow cold about the groin, when he uncovered his face, for he had covered himself up, and said – they were his last words – he said: Crito, I owe a cock to Aesculapius; will you remember to pay the debt? The debt shall be paid, said Crito; is there anything else? There was no answer to this question; but in a minute or two a movement was heard, and the attendant uncovered him; his eyes were set, and Crito closed his eyes and mouth.

Such was the end, Echecrates, of our friend; concerning whom we may truly say that of all the men of his time whom we have known, he was the wisest and justest and best.

ARISTOPHANES
THE CLOUDS

THE CLOUDS

Characters in the play

STREPSIADES, *a countryman compelled by the war to live in Athens*

PHEIDIPPIDES, *his son*

SOCRATES, *the philosopher*

Students, trained by Socrates in the Phrontisterium

Chorus of Clouds

RIGHT LOGIC

WRONG LOGIC

PASIAS, *creditors of Strepsiades*

AMYNIAS

CHAEREPHON, *a disciple of Socrates, noted for his cadaverous appearance.*

Servant of Strepsiades

A Witness

SCENE: *In the background are two buildings: one the house of Strepsiades, the other the Phrontisterium of Socrates. The interior of the former house is exposed to view by the action of the Eccyclema; and* STREPSIADES *and his son* PHEIDIPPIDES *are discovered in bed. The son is fast asleep; the father is restless and disquieted, and presently breaks out into the following soliloquy.*

STREPSIADES

O dear! O dear!
O Lord! O Zeus! these nights, how long they are.
Will they ne'er pass? Will the day never come?
Surely I heard the cock crow, hours ago.

Yet still my servants snore. These are new customs.
O 'ware of war for many various reasons;
One fears in war even to flog one's servants.
And here's this hopeful son of mine wrapped up
Snoring and sweating under five thick blankets.
Come, we'll wrap up and snore in opposition.

[*tries to sleep*

But I can't sleep a wink, devoured and bitten
By ticks, and bugbears, duns, and race-horses,
All through this son of mine. *He* curls his hair,
And sports his thoroughbreds, and drives his tandem;
Even in dreams he rides: while I – I'm ruined
Now that the Moon has reached her twentieths,
And paying time comes on. Boy! Light a lamp,
And fetch my ledger: now I'll reckon up
Who are my creditors, and what I owe them.
Come, let me see then. Fifty pounds to Pasias!
Why fifty pounds to Pasias? What were they for?
O, for the hack from Corinth. O dear! O dear!
I wish my eye had been hacked out before –

PHEIDIPPIDES [*in his sleep*]

You are cheating, Philon; keep to your own side.

STREPSIADES

Ah! There it is! That's what has ruined me!
Even in his very sleep he thinks of horses.

PHEIDIPPIDES [*in his sleep*]

How many heats do the war-chariots run?

STREPSIADES

A pretty many heats you have run your father.
Now then, what debt assails me after Pasias?
A curricle and wheels. Twelve pounds. Amynias.

PHEIDIPPIDES [*in his sleep*]

Here, give the horse a roll, and take him home.

360

STREPSIADES

You have rolled me out of house and home, my boy,
Cast in some suits already, while some swear
They'll seize my goods for payment.

PHEIDIPPIDES   Good my father,

What makes you toss so restless all night long?

STREPSIADES

There's a bum-bailiff from the mattress bites me.

PHEIDIP Come now, I prithee, let me sleep in peace.

STREPSIADES

Well then, you sleep: only be sure of this,
These debts will fall on your own head at last.
Alas, alas! Forever cursed be that same matchmaker,
Who stirred me up to marry your poor mother.
Mine in the country was the pleasantest life,
Untidy, easy-going, unrestrained,
Brimming with olives, sheepfolds, honey-bees.
Ah! Then I married – I a rustic – her
A fine town-lady, niece of Megacles.
A regular, proud, luxurious Coesyra.
This wife I married, and we came together,
I rank with wine-lees, fig-boards, greasy woolpacks;
She all with scents, and saffron, and tongue-kissings,
Feasting, expense, and lordly modes of loving.
She was not idle though, she was too fast.
I used to tell her, holding out my cloak,
Threadbare and worn; wife, you're too fast by half.

SERVANT

Here's no more oil remaining in the lamp.

STREPSIADES

O me! What made you light the tippling lamp?
Come and be whipp'd.

SERVANT   Why, what would you whip me for?

STREPSIADES

Why did you put one of those thick wicks in?
Well, when at last to me and my good woman
This hopeful son was born, our son and heir,
Why then we took to wrangle on the name.
She was for giving him some knightly name,
'Callippides', 'Xanthippus', or 'Charippus':
I wished 'Pheidonides', his grandsire's name.
Thus for some time we argued: till at last
We compromised it in Pheidippides.
This boy she took, and used to spoil him, saying,
Oh! when you are driving to the Acropolis, clad
Like Megacles, in your purple; whilst I said
Oh! When the goats you are driving from the fells,
Clad like your father, in your sheepskin coat.
Well, he cared nought for my advice, but soon
A galloping consumption caught my fortunes.
Now, cogitating all night long, I've found
One way, one marvellous transcendent way,
Which, if he'll follow, we may yet be saved.
So – but, however, I must rouse him first;
But how to rouse him kindliest? That's the rub.
Pheidippides, my sweet one.

PHEIDIPPIDES   Well, my father.

STREPSIADES

Shake hands, Pheidippides, shake hands and kiss me.

PHEIDIPPIDES

There; what's the matter?

STREPSIADES   Dost thou love me, boy?

PHEIDIPPIDES

Ay! By Poseidon there, the god of horses.

STREPSIADES

No, no, not that: miss out the god of horses,
That god's the origin of all my evils.

But if you love me from your heart and soul,
My son, obey me.

PHEIDIPPIDES   Very well: what in?

STREPSIADES

Strip with all speed, strip off your present habits,
And go and learn what I'll advise you to.

[*they come out into the open.*

PHEIDIPPIDES

Name your commands.

STREPSIADES   Will you obey?

PHEIDIPPIDES   I will,

By Dionysus!

STREPSIADES   Well, then, look this way.

See you that wicket and the lodge beyond?

PHEIDIPPIDES

I see: and prithee what is that, my father?

STREPSIADES

That is the thinking-house of sapient souls.
There dwell the men who teach – aye, who

persuade us,

That Heaven is one vast fire-extinguisher
Placed round about us, and that we're the cinders.
Aye, and they'll teach (only they'll want some money)
How one may speak and conquer, right or wrong.

PHEIDIPPIDES

Come, tell their names.

STREPSIADES   Well, I can't quite remember,

But they're deep thinkers, and true gentlemen.

PHEIDIPPIDES

Out on the rogues! I know them. Those rank pedants,
Those pale-faced, barefoot vagabonds you mean:
That Socrates, poor wretch, and Chaerephon.

STREPSIADES

Oh! Oh! Hush! Hush! don't use those foolish words;

But if the sorrows of my barley touch you,
Enter their Schools and cut the Turf for ever.

PHEIDIPPIDES

I wouldn't go, so help me Dionysus,
For all Leogoras' breed of Phasians!

STREPSIADES

Go, I beseech you, dearest, dearest son,
Go and be taught,

PHEIDIPPIDES   And what would you have me learn?

STREPSIADES

'Tis known that in their Schools they keep
                                        two Logics,
The Worse, Zeus save the mark, the Worse and Better.
This Second Logic then, I mean the Worse one,
They teach to talk unjustly and – prevail.
Think then, you only learn that Unjust Logic,
And all the debts, which I have incurred
                                        through you –
I'll never pay, no, not one farthing of them.

PHEIDIPPIDES

I will not go. How could I face the knights
With all my colour worn and torn away!

STREPSIADES: O! Then, by Earth, you have eat
                                        your last of mine,
You, and your coach-horse, and your sigma-brand:
Out with you! Go to the crows, for all I care.

PHEIDIPPIDES: But uncle Megacles won't leave me long
Without a horse: I'll go to him: good-bye.

                                                    [exit

STREPSIADES: I'm thrown, by Zeus, but I won't
                                        long lie prostrate.
I'll pray the gods and send myself to school:
I'll go at once and try their thinking-house.
Stay: how can I, forgetful, slow, old fool,

364

Learn the nice hair-splittings of subtle Logic?
Well, go I must. 'Twont do to linger here.
Come on, I'll knock the door. Boy! Ho, there! Boy!

STUDENT [*within*]

O, hang it all! Who's knocking at the door?

STREPSIADES

Me! Pheidon's son: Strepsiades of Cicynna.

STUDENT

Why, what a clown you are! To kick our door
In such a thoughtless inconsiderate way!
You've made my cogitation to miscarry.

STREPSIADES

Forgive me: I'm an awkward country fool.
But tell me, what was that I made miscarry?

STUDENT

'Tis not allowed: students alone may hear.

STREPSIADES

O that's all right: you may tell *me*: I'm come
To be a student in your thinking-house.

STUDENT

Come then. But they're high mysteries, remember.
'Twas Socrates was asking Chaerephon,
How many feet of its own a flea could jump.
For one first bit the brow of Chaerephon,
Then bounded off to Socrates's head.

STREPSIADES

How did he measure this?

STUDENT   Most cleverly.
He warmed some wax, and then he caught the flea,
And dipped its feet into the wax he'd melted:
Then let it cool, and there were Persian slippers!
These he took off, and so he found the distance.

STREPSIADES

O Zeus and king, what subtle intellects!

STUDENT

What would you say then if you heard another,
Our Master's own?

STREPSIADES   O come, do tell me that.

STUDENT

Why, Chaerephon was asking him in turn,
Which theory did he sanction; that the gnats
Hummed through their mouth, or backwards,
                                   through the tail?

STREPSIADES

Aye, and what said your Master of the gnat?

STUDENT

He answered thus: the entrail of the gnat
Is small: and through this narrow pipe the wind
Rushes with violence straight towards the tail;
There, close against the pipe, the hollow rump
Receives the wind, and whistles to the blast.

STREPSIADES

So then the rump is trumpet to the gnats!
O happy, happy in your entrail-learning!
Full surely need he fear nor debts, nor duns,
Who knows about the entrails of the gnats.

STUDENT

And yet, last night a mighty thought we lost
Through a green lizard.

STREPSIADES   Tell me, how was that?

STUDENT

Why, as Himself, with eyes and mouth wide open,
Mused on the moon, her paths and revolutions,
A lizard from the roof squirted full on him.

STREPSIADES

He, he, he, he. I like the lizard's spattering Socrates.

STUDENT

Then yesterday, poor we, we'd got no dinner.

366

STREPSIADES

Hah! What did he devise to do for barley?

STUDENT

He sprinkled on the table – some fine ash –
He bent a spit – he grasped it compass-wise –
And – filched a mantle from the wrestling school.

STREPSIADES

Good heavens! Why, Thales was a fool to this!
O open, open wide the study door,
And show me, show me, show me Socrates.
I die to be a student. Open, open!

> *Here, by means of the Eccyclema, the entire front
> of the Phrontisterium revolves, and the interior
> becomes visible.*

O Heracles, what kind of beasts are these!

STUDENT

Why, what's the matter? What do you think
                                        they're like?

STREPSIADES

Like? Why, those Spartans whom we brought
                                        from Pylus:
What makes them fix their eyes so on the ground?

STUDENT

They seek things underground.

STREPSIADES   O! To be sure,

Truffles! You there, don't trouble about that!
I'll tell you where the best and finest grow.
Look! Why do those stoop down so very much?

STUDENT

They're diving deep into the deepest secrets.

STREPSIADES

Then why's their rump turned up towards the sky?

STUDENT

It's taking private lessons on the stars.
[*to the other students*] Come, come: get in: We'll
catch us presently.

STREPSIADES

Not yet! Not yet! Just let them stop one moment,
While I impart a little matter to them.

STUDENT

No, no: they must go in: 'twould never do
To expose themselves too long to the open air.

STREPSIADES.

O! By the gods, now, what are these? Do tell me.

STUDENT.

This is Astronomy.

STREPSIADES   And what is this?

STUDENT

Geometry.

STREPSIADES   Well, what's the use of that?

STUDENT

To mete out lands.

STREPSIADES   What, for allotment grounds?

STUDENT

No, but all lands.

STREPSIADES   A choice idea, truly.

Then every man may take his choice, you mean.

STUDENT

Look; here's a chart of the whole world. Do you see?
This city's Athens.

STREPSIADES   Athens? I like that.

I see no dicasts sitting. That's not Athens.

STUDENT

In very truth, this is the Attic ground.

STREPSIADES

And where then are my townsmen of Cicynna?

STUDENT

Why, thereabouts; and here, you see, Euboea:
Here, reaching out a long way by the shore.

STREPSIADES

Yes, overreached by us and Pericles.
But now, where's Sparta?

STUDENT   Let me see: O, here.

STREPSIADES

Heavens! How near us. O do please manage this
To shove her off from us, a long way further.

STUDENT

We can't do that, by Zeus.

STREPSIADES   The worse for you.
Hallo! Who's that? That fellow in the basket?

STUDENT

That's He.

STREPSIADES Who's He?

STUDENT   Socrates!

STREPSIADES   Socrates!

You, sir, call out to him as loud as you can.

STUDENT

Call him yourself: I have not leisure now.

STREPSIADES

Socrates! Socrates!
Sweet Socrates!

SOCRATES   Mortal! why call'st thou me?

STREPSIADES.

O, first of all, please tell me what you are doing.

SOCRATES

I walk on air, and contemplate the Sun.

STREPSIADES

O then from a basket you contemn the gods,
And not from the earth, at any rate?

SOCRATES   Most true.

369

I could not have searched out celestial matters
Without suspending judgment, and infusing
My subtle spirit with the kindred air.
If from the ground I were to seek these things,
I could not find: so surely doth the earth
Draw to herself the essence of our thought.
The same too is the case with water-cress.

STREPSIADES

Hello! What's that?
Thought draws the essence into water-cress?
Come down, sweet Socrates, more near my level,
And teach the lessons which I come to learn.

[*Socrates comes to the ground*

SOCRATES.

And wherefore are thou come?

STREPSIADES   To learn to speak.
For, owing to my horrid debts and duns,
My goods are seized, I'm robbed, and mobbed,
                                   and plundered.

SOCRATES.

How did you get involved with your eyes open?

STREPSIADES

A galloping consumption seized my money.
Come now: do let me learn the unjust Logic
That can shirk debts: now do just let me learn it.
Name your own price, by all the gods I'll pay it.

SOCRATES.

The gods! Why you must know the gods with us
Don't pass for current coin.

STREPSIADES   Eh? What do you use then?
Have you got iron, as the Byzantines have?

SOCRATES.

Come, would you like to learn celestial matters,

370

How their truth stands?

STREPSIADES. Yes, if there's any truth.

SOCRATES.

And to hold intercourse with yon bright Clouds,
Our virgin goddesses?

STREPSIADES Yes, that I should.

SOCRATES.

Then sit you down upon that sacred bed.

STREPSIADES.

Well, I am sitting.

SOCRATES Here then, take this chaplet.

STREPSIADES.

Chaplet? Why? Why? Now, never, Socrates:
Don't sacrifice poor me, like Athamas.

SOCRATES.

Fear not: our entrance-services require
All to do this.

STREPSIADES But what am I to gain?

SOCRATES [*sprinkling grain on his head*]

You'll be the flower of talkers, prattlers, gossips:
Only keep quiet.

STREPSIADES Zeus! Your words come true!
I shall be flour indeed with all this peppering.

SOCRATES.

Old man, sit you still, and attend to my will,
        and hearken in peace to my prayer,
O Master and King, holding earth in your swing,
        O measureless infinite Air;
And thou glowing Ether,
        and Clouds who enwreathe her
        with thunder, and lightning, and storms,
Arise ye and shine, bright Ladies Divine,
        to your student in bodily forms.

STREPSIADES

No, but stay, no, but stay, just one moment I pray,
        while my cloak round my temples I wrap.
To think that I've come, stupid fool, from my home,
        with never a waterproof cap!

SOCRATES

Come forth, come forth, dread Clouds, and to earth
        your glorious majesty show;
Whether lightly ye rest on the time-honoured crest
        of Olympus environed in snow,
Or tread the soft dance 'mid the stately expanse
        of Ocean, the nymphs to beguile,
Or stoop to enfold with your pitchers of gold
        the mystical waves of the Nile,
Or around the white foam of Maeotis ye roam,
        or Mimas all wintry and bare,
O! Hear while we pray, and turn not away
        from the rites which your servants prepare.

CHORUS

[*preparing to ascend from the sea to the mountain tops*]
Clouds of all hue,
Rise we aloft with our garments of dew.
Come from old Ocean's unchangeable bed,
Come, till the mountain's green summits we tread,
Come to the peaks with their landscapes untold,
Gaze on the Earth with her harvests of gold,
Gaze on the rivers in majesty streaming,
Gaze on the lordly, invincible Sea,
Come, for the Eye of the Ether is beaming,
Come, for all Nature is flashing and free.
Let us shake off this close-clinging dew
From our members eternally new,
And sail upwards the wide world to view.
Come away! Come away!

SOCRATES

O goddesses mine, great Clouds and divine,
    ye have heeded and answered my prayer.
Heard ye their sound, and the thunder around,
    as it thrilled through the tremulous air?

STREPSIADES

Yes, by Zeus, and I shake, and I'm all of a quake,
    and I fear I must sound a reply,
Their thunders have made my soul so afraid,
    and those terrible voices so nigh:
So if lawful or not, I must run to a pot,
    by Zeus, if I stop I shall die.

SOCRATES

Don't act in our schools like those Comedy-fools
    with their scurrilous scandalous ways.
Deep silence be thine: while this Cluster divine
    their soul-stirring melody raise.

CHORUS

[*preparing to visit Attica*]

Come then with me,
Daughters of Mist, to the land of the free.
Come to the people whom Pallas hath blest,
Come to the soil where the Mysteries rest;
Come, where the glorified Temple invites
The pure to partake of its mystical rites:
Holy the gifts that are brought to the gods,
Shrines with festoons and with garlands are crowned,
Pilgrims resort to the sacred abodes,
Gorgeous the festivals all the year round.
And the Bromian rejoicings in Spring,
When the flutes with their deep music ring,
And the sweetly-toned Choruses sing
Come away! Come away!

STREPSIADES

   O Socrates pray, by all the gods, say,
                for I earnestly long to be told,
  Who are these that recite
               with such grandeur and might?
                    Are they glorified mortals of old?

SOCRATES

   No mortals are there, but Clouds of the air,
              great gods who the indolent fill:
  These grant us discourse, and logical force,
             and the art of persuasion instil,
  And periphrasis strange, and a power to arrange,
            and a marvellous judgment and skill.

STREPSIADES

   So then when I heard their omnipotent word,
            my spirit felt all of a flutter,
  And it yearns to begin subtle cobwebs to spin
           and about metaphysics to stutter,
  And together to glue an idea or two,
            and battle away in replies:
  So if it's not wrong, I earnestly long
           to behold them myself with my eyes.

SOCRATES

   Look up in the air, towards Parnes out there,
            for I see they will pitch before long
  These regions about.

STREPSIADES   Where? Point me them out.

SOCRATES   They are drifting, an infinite throng,
  And their long shadows quake over valley
              and brake.

STREPSIADES   Why, whatever's the matter today?
  I can't see, I declare.

SOCRATES   By the Entrance; look there!

STREPSIADES   Ah, I just got a glimpse, by the way.

[the Chorus enter the Orchestra

SOCRATES

There, now you must see how resplendent they
   be, or your eyes must be pumpkins, I vow.

STREPSIADES

Ah! I see them proceed; I should think so indeed:
   great powers! They fill everything now.

SOCRATES

So then till this day that celestials were they,
   you never imagined or knew?

STREPSIADES

Why, no, on my word, for I always had heard
   they were nothing but vapour and dew.

SOCRATES

O, then I declare, you can't be aware
   that 'tis these who the sophists protect,
Prophets sent beyond sea, quacks of every degree,
   fops signet-and-jewel-bedecked,
Astrological knaves, and fools who their staves
   of dithyrambs proudly rehearse –
'Tis the Clouds who all these support at their ease,
   because they exalt them in verse.

STREPSIADES

'Tis for this then they write
   of 'the on-rushin' might
    o' the light-stappin' rain-drappin' Cloud',
And the 'thousand black curls
   whilk the Tempest-lord whirls',
    and the 'thunder-blast stormy an' loud',
And 'birds o' the sky floating upwards on high',
   and 'air-water leddies' which 'drown
Wi' their saft falling dew the gran' Ether sae blue',
   and then in return they gulp down

Huge gobbets o' fishes an' bountifu' dishes
            o' mavises prime in their season.

SOCRATES

And is it not right such praise to requite?

STREPSIADES Ah, but tell me then what is the reason
    That if, as you say, they are Clouds, they today
                   as women appear to our view?
    For the ones in the air are not women, I swear.

SOCRATES   Why, what do they seem then to you?

STREPSIADES

I can't say very well, but they straggle and swell
               like fleeces spread out in the air;
Not like women they flit, no, by Zeus, not a bit,
               but these have got noses to wear.

SOCRATES

Well, now then, attend to this question, my friend.

STREPSIADES   Look sharp, and propound it to me.

SOCRATES

Didst thou never espy a Cloud in the sky,
          which a centaur or leopard might be,
Or a wolf, or a cow?

STREPSIADES   Very often, I vow:
         and show me the cause, I entreat.

SOCRATES

Why, I tell you that these
          become just what they please,
            and whenever they happen to meet
One shaggy and wild, like the tangle-haired child
            of old Xenophantes, their rule
Is at once to appear like Centaurs, to jeer
          the ridiculous look of the fool.

STREPSIADES

What then do they do if Simon they view,
          that fraudulent harpy to shame?

SOCRATES

Why, his nature to show to us mortals below,
             a wolfish appearance they frame.

STREPSIADES

O, they then I ween having yesterday seen
             Cleonymus quaking with fear
(Him who threw off his shield
        as he fled from the field),
             metamorphosed themselves into deer.

SOCRATES

Yes, and now they espy soft Cleisthenes nigh,
             and therefore as women appear.

STREPSIADES

O then without fail, All hail! and All hail!
             my welcome receive; and reply
With your voices so fine, so grand and divine,
             majestical Queens of the Sky!

CHORUS

Our welcome to thee, old man, who would see
             the marvels that science can show:
And thou, the high-priest of this subtlety feast,
             say what you would have us bestow?
Since there is not a sage for whom we'd engage
             our wonders more freely to do,
Except, it may be, for Prodicus: he for his knowledge
             may claim them, but you
For that sideways you throw your eyes as you go,
             and are all affectation and fuss;
No shoes will you wear, but assume the grand air
             on the strength of your dealings with us.

STREPSIADES

Oh Earth! What a sound, how august and profound!
        It fills me with wonder and awe.

SOCRATES
These, these then alone, for true Deities own,
                the rest are all godships of straw.

STREPSIADES
Let Zeus be left out: he's a god beyond doubt:
                come, that you can scarcely deny.

SOCRATES
Zeus, indeed! There's no Zeus:
                don't you be so obtuse.

STREPSIADES   No Zeus up aloft in the sky!
Then, you first must explain, who it is sends the rain;
                or I really must think you are wrong.

SOCRATES
Well then, be it known, these send it alone:
                I can prove it by arguments strong.
Was there ever a shower seen to fall in an hour
                when the sky was all cloudless and blue?
Yet on a fine day, when the Clouds are away,
                he might send one, according to you.

STREPSIADES
Well, it must be confessed,
            that chimes in with the rest:
                your words I am forced to believe.
Yet before, I had dreamed
            that the rain-water streamed
                from Zeus and his chamber-pot sieve.
But whence then, my friend,
            does the thunder descend,
                that does make me quake with affright?

SOCRATES
Why 'tis they, I declare, as they roll through the air.

STREPSIADES What, the Clouds? Did I hear you
                          aright?

SOCRATES

Ay: for when to the brim filled with water they swim,
  by necessity carried along,
They are hung up on high in the vault of the sky,
  and so by Necessity strong
In the midst of their course,
  they clash with great force,
  and thunder away without end.

STREPSIADES

But is it not he who compels this to be?
  Does not Zeus this necessity send?

SOCRATES

No Zeus have we there, but a Vortex of air.

STREPSIADES What! Vortex? That's something, I own.
I knew not before, that Zeus was no more,
  but Vortex was placed on his throne!
But I have not yet heard to what cause you referred
  the thunder's majestical roar.

SOCRATES

Yes, 'tis they, when on high full of water they fly,
  and then, as I told you before,
By Compression impelled,
  as they clash, are compelled
  a terrible clatter to make.

STREPSIADES

Come, how can that be? I really don't see.

SOCRATES   Yourself as my proof I will take.
Have you never then eat the broth-puddings you get
  when the Panathenaea comes round,
And felt with what might your bowels all night
  in turbulent tumult resound?

STREPSIADES

By Apollo, 'tis true, there's a mighty to-do,
  and my belly keeps rumbling about;

And the puddings begin to clatter within
           and kick up a wonderful rout:
Quite gently at first, papapax, papapax,
           but soon pappapappax away
Till at last, I'll be bound, I can thunder as loud,
           papapappappapappax, as They.

SOCRATES

Shalt thou then a sound so loud and profound
           from thy belly diminutive send,
And shall not the high and the infinite Sky
           go thundering on without end?
For both, you will find, on an impulse of wind
           and similar causes depend.

STREPSIADES

Well, but tell me from whom
    comes the bolt through the gloom,
           with its awful and terrible flashes;
And wherever it turns, some it singes and burns,
           and some it reduces to ashes!
For this 'tis quite plain, let who will send the rain,
           that Zeus against perjurers dashes.

SOCRATES

And how, you old fool of a dark-ages school,
           and an antediluvian wit,
If the perjured they strike, and not all men alike,
           have they never Cleonymus hit?
Then of Simon again, and Theorus explain:
           known perjurers, yet they escape.
But he smites his own shrine with his arrows divine,
           and 'Sunium, Attica's cape',
And the ancient gnarled oaks:
        now what prompted those strokes?
           They never forswore I should say.

STREPSIADES

Can't say that they do: your words appear true.
                    Whence comes then the thunderbolt, pray?

SOCRATES

When a wind that is dry, being lifted on high,
                    is suddenly pent into these,
It swells up their skin, like a bladder, within,
                    by Necessity's changeless decrees:
Till compressed very tight, it bursts them outright,
                    and away with an impulse so strong,
That at last by the force and the swing of its course
                    it takes fire as it whizzes along.

STREPSIADES

That's exactly the thing that I suffered one Spring,
                    at the great feast of Zeus, I admit:
I'd a paunch in the pot, but I wholly forgot
                    about making the safety-valve slit.
So it spluttered and swelled,
                    while the saucepan I held,
                    till at last with a vengeance it flew:
Took me quite by surprise,
                    dung-bespattered my eyes,
                    and scalded my face black and blue!

CHORUS

O thou who wouldst fain great wisdom attain,
                    and comest to us in thy need,
All Hellas around shall thy glory resound,
                    such a prosperous life thou shalt lead:
So thou art but endued with a memory good,
                    and accustomed profoundly to think,
And thy soul wilt inure all wants to endure,
                    and from no undertaking to shrink,
And art hardy and bold, to bear up against cold,
                    and with patience a supper thou losest:

Nor too much dost incline to gymnastics and wine,
    but all lusts of the body refusest:
And esteemest it best, what is always the test
    of a truly intelligent brain,
To prevail and succeed whensoever you plead,
    and hosts of tongue-conquests to gain.

STREPSIADES

But as far as a sturdy soul is concerned
    and a horrible restless care,
And a belly that pines and wears away
    on the wretchedest, frugalest fare,
You may hammer and strike as long as you like;
    I am quite invincible there.

SOCRATES

Now then you agree in rejecting with me
    the gods you believed in when young,
And *my* creed you'll embrace
    'I believe in wide Space,
    in the Clouds, in the eloquent Tongue.'

STREPSIADES

If I happened to meet other gods in the street,
    I'd show the cold shoulder, I vow.
No libation I'll pour: not one victim more
    on their altars I'll sacrifice now.

CHORUS

Now be honest and true, and say what we shall do:
    since you never shall fail of our aid,
If you hold us most dear in devotion and fear,
    and will ply the philosopher's trade.

STREPSIADES

O Ladies Divine, small ambition is mine:
    I only most modestly seek,
Out and out for the rest of my life to be best
    of the children of Hellas to speak.

CHORUS

> Say no more of your care,
>> we have granted your prayer:
>>> and know from this moment, that none
> More acts shall pass through in the People than you:
>> such favour from us you have won.

STREPSIADES

> Not acts, if you please: I want nothing of these:
>> this gift you may quickly withdraw;
> But I wish to succeed, just enough for my need,
>> and to slip through the clutches of law.

CHORUS

> This then you shall do, for your wishes are few:
>> not many nor great your demands,
> So away with all care from henceforth, and prepare
>> to be placed in our votaries' hands.

STREPSIADES

> This then will I do, confiding in you,
>> for Necessity presses me sore,
> And so sad is my life, 'twixt my cobs and my wife,
>> that I cannot put up with it more.
> So now, at your word, I give and afford
> My body to these, to treat as they please,
> To have and to hold, in squalor, in cold,
> In hunger and thirst, yea by Zeus, at the worst,
> To be flayed out of shape from my heels to my nape
> So along with my hide from my duns I escape,
> And to men may appear without conscience or fear,
> Bold, hasty, and wise, a concocter of lies,
> A rattler to speak, a dodger, a sneak,
> A regular claw of the tables of law,
> A shuffler complete, well worn in deceit,
> A supple, unprincipled, troublesome cheat;
> A hang-dog accurst, a bore with the worst,

In the tricks of the jury-courts thoroughly versed.
If all that I meet this praise shall repeat,
Work away as you choose, I will nothing refuse,
Without any reserve, from my head to my shoes.
You shan't see me wince though my gutlets you mince,
And these entrails of mine for a sausage combine,
Served up for the gentlemen students to dine.

CHORUS

Here's a spirit bold and high
Ready-armed for any strife.
[to Strepsiades] If you learn what I can teach
Of the mysteries of speech,
Your glory soon shall reach
To the summit of the sky.

STREPSIADES

And what am I to gain?

CHORUS

With the Clouds you will obtain
The most happy, the most enviable life.

STREPSIADES

Is it possible for me
Such felicity to see?

CHORUS.

Yes, and men shall come and wait
In their thousands at your gate,
Desiring consultations and advice
On an action or a pleading
From the man of light and leading,
And you'll pocket many talents in a trice.
[to Socrates]
Here, take the old man, and do all that you can,
          your new-fashioned thoughts to instil,
And stir up his mind with your notions refined,
          and test him with judgment and skill.

SOCRATES

Come now, you tell me something of your habits :
For if I don't know them, I can't determine
What engines I must bring to bear upon you.

STREPSIADES

Eh! What? Not going to storm me, by the gods?

SOCRATES

No, no: I want to ask you a few questions.
First: is your memory good?

STREPSIADES   Two ways, by Zeus:
If I'm owed anything, I'm mindful, very:
But if I owe, (Oh, dear!) forgetful, very.

SOCRATES

Well then: have you the gift of speaking in you?

STREPSIADES

The gift of speaking, no: of cheating, yes.

SOCRATES

No? How then can you learn?

STREPSIADES   O, well enough.

SOCRATES

Then when I throw you out some clever notion
About the laws of nature, you must catch it.

STREPSIADES

What! Must I snap up sapience, in dog-fashion?

SOCRATES

O! Why the man's an ignorant old savage:
I fear, my friend, that you'll require the whip.
Come, if one strikes you, what do you do?

STREPSIADES   I'm struck:
Then in a little while I call my witness:
Then in another little while I summon him.

SOCRATES

Put off your cloak.

STREPSIADES   Why, what have I done wrong?

SOCRATES

O, nothing, nothing: all go in here naked.

STREPSIADES

Well, but I have not come with a search-warrant.

SOCRATES

Fool! Throw it off.

STREPSIADES Well, tell me this one thing;

If I'm extremely careful and attentive,

Which of your students shall I most resemble?

SOCRATES

Why Chaerephon. You'll be his very image.

STREPSIADES

What! I shall be half-dead! O luckless me!

SOCRATES

Don't chatter there, but come and follow me;

Make haste now, quicker, here.

STREPSIADES O, but do first

Give me a honied cake: Zeus! How I tremble,

To go down there, as if to see Trophonius.

SOCRATES

Go on! Why keep you pottering round the door.

The actors retire into the Phrontisterium.
The Chorus remain in the orchestra
and deliver the Parabasis.

CHORUS

Yes! Go, and farewell; as your courage is great,

So bright be your fate.

May all good fortune his steps pursue,

Who now, in his life's dim twilight haze,

Is game such venturesome things to do,

To steep his mind in discoveries new,

To walk, a novice, in wisdom's ways.

O Spectators, I will utter
    Honest truths with accents free,
Yea! by mighty Dionysus,
    Him who bred and nurtured me.
So may I be deemed a poet,
    And this day obtain the prize,
As till that unhappy blunder
    I had always held you wise,
And of all my plays esteeming
    This the wisest and the best,
Served it up for your enjoyment,
    Which had, more than all the rest,
Cost me thought, and time, and labour:
    Then most scandalously treated,
I retired in mighty dudgeon,
    By unworthy foes defeated.
This is why I blame your critics,
    For whose sake I framed the play:
Yet the clever ones amongst you
    Even now I won't betray.
No! For ever since from judges
    Unto whom 'tis joy to speak,
Brothers Profligate and Modest
    Gained the praise we fondly seek,
When, for I was yet a Virgin,
    And it was not right to bear,
I exposed it, and Another
    Did the foundling nurse with care,
But 'twas ye who nobly nurtured,
    Ye who brought it up with skill –
From that hour I proudly cherish
    Pledges of your sure good will.
Now then comes its sister hither,
    Like Electra in the Play,

Comes in earnest expectation
   Kindred minds to meet today;
She will recognize full surely,
   If she find, her brother's tress.
And observe how pure her morals:
   Who, to notice first her dress,
Enters not with filthy symbols
   On her modest garments hung,
Jeering bald-heads dancing ballets
   For the laughter of the young.
In this play no wretched greybeard
   With a staff his fellow pokes,
So obscuring from the audience
   All the poorness of his jokes.
No one rushes in with torches,
   No one groans, 'Oh, dear! Oh, dear!'
Trusting in its genuine merits
   Comes this play before you here.
Yet though such a hero-poet,
   I, the bald-head, do not grow
Curling ringlets: neither do I
   Twice or thrice my pieces show.
Always fresh ideas sparkle,
   Always novel jests delight,
Nothing like each other, save that
   All are most exceeding bright.
I am he who floored the giant,
   Cleon, in his hour of pride,
Yet, when down I scorned to strike him,
   And I left him when he died!
But the others, when a handle
   Once Hyperbolus did lend,
Trample down the wretched caitiff
   And his mother, without end.

In his *Maricas the Drunkard*,
  Eupolis the charge began,
Shamefully my *Knights* distorting,
  As he is a shameful man,
Tacking on the tipsy beldame,
  Just the ballet-dance to keep,
Phrynichus's prime invention,
  Eat by monsters of the deep.
Then Hermippus on the caitiff
  Opened all his little skill,
And the rest upon the caitiff
  Are their wit exhausting still;
And my simil to pilfer
  'Of the Eels' they all combine.
Whoso laughs at their productions,
  Let him not delight in mine.
But for you who praise my genius,
  You who think my writings clever,
Ye shall gain a name for wisdom,
  Yea! for ever and for ever.
O mighty god, O heavenly king,
First unto thee my prayer I bring,
O come, Lord Zeus, to my choral song –
And thou, dread power, whose resistless hand
Heaves up the sea and the trembling land,
Lord of the trident, stern and strong –
And thou who sustainest the life of us all,
Come, Ether, our parent, O come to my call –
And thou who floodest the world with light,
Guiding thy steeds through the glittering sky,
To men below and to gods on high
A potentate heavenly-bright!
O most sapient wise spectators,
  Hither turn attention due,

We complain of sad ill-treatment,
    We've a bone to pick with you:
We have ever helped your city,
    Helped with all our might and main;
Yet you pay us no devotion,
    That is why we now complain.
We who always watch around you.
    For if any project seems
Ill-concocted, then we thunder,
    Then the rain comes down in streams.
And, remember, very lately,
    How we knit our brows together,
'Thunders crashing, lightnings flashing',
    Never was such awful weather;
And the Moon in haste eclipsed her,
    And the Sun in anger swore
He would curl his wick within him
    And give light to you no more,
Should you choose that mischief-worker,
    Cleon, whom the gods abhor,
Tanner, Slave, and Paphlagonian,
    To lead out your hosts to war.
Yet you chose him! Yet you chose him!
    For they say that Folly grows
Best and finest in this city,
    But the gracious gods dispose
Always all things for the better,
    Causing errors to succeed:
And how this sad job may profit,
    Surely he who runs may read.
Let the Cormorant be conviced,
    In command, of bribes and theft,
Let us have him gagged and muzzled,
    In the pillory chained and left,

Then again, in ancient fashion,
   All that ye have erred of late,
Will turn out your own advantage,
   And a blessing to the State.
'Phoebus, my king, come to me still',
Thou who holdest the Cynthian hill,
The lofty peak of the Delian isle –
And thou, his sister, to whom each day
Lydian maidens devoutly pray
In thy stately gilded Ephesian pile –
And Athene, our lady, the queen of us all,
With the Aegis of god, O come to my call –
And thou whose dancing torches of pine
Flicker, Parnassian glades along,
Dionysus, star of thy maenad throng,
Come, reveller most divine!
We, when we had finished packing,
   And prepared our journey down,
Met the Lady Moon, who charged us
   With a message for your town.
First, All hail to noble Athens,
   And her faithful true Allies;
Then, she said, your shameful conduct
   Made her angry passions rise,
Treating her so ill who always
   Aids you, not in words, but clearly;
Saves you, first of all, in torchlight
   Every month a drachma nearly,
So that each one says, if business
   Calls him out from home by night,
'Buy no link, my boy, this evening,
   For the Moon will lend her light.'
Other blessings too she sends you,
   Yet you will not mark your days

As she bids you, but confuse them,
    Jumbling them all sorts of ways.
And, she says, the gods in chorus
    Shower reproaches on her head,
When in bitter disappointment,
    They go supperless to bed,
Not obtaining festal banquets,
    Duly on the festal day;
Ye are badgering in the law-courts
    When ye should arise and slay!
And full oft when we celestials
    Some strict fast are duly keeping,
For the fate of mighty Memnon
    Or divine Sarpedon weeping,
Then you feast and pour libations:
    And Hyperbolus of late
Lost the crown he wore so proudly
    As Recorder of the Gate,
Through the wrath of us immortals:
    So perchance he'll rather know
Always all his days in future
    By the Lady Moon to go.

*The progress of Strepsiades, during the delivery of the
Parabasis, has been most unsatisfacory, and* SOCRATES
now emerges in great wrath at the obtuseness of his pupil.

SOCRATES

Never by Chaos, Air, and Respiration,
Never, no never have I seen a clown
So helpless, and forgetful, and absurd!
Why if he learns a quirk or two he clean
Forgets them ere he has learnt them: all the same,
I'll call him out of doors here to the light.
Take up your bed, Strepsiades, and come!

STREPSIADES (*within*)

By Zeus, I can't: the bugs make such resistance.

SOCRATES

Make haste. There, throw it down, and listen.

STREPSIADES

Well!

SOCRATES Attend to me: what shall I teach you first
That you've not learnt before? Which will you have,
Measures or rhythms or the right use of words?

STREPSIADES

O! Measures to be sure: for very lately
A grocer swindled me of full three pints.

SOCRATES

I don't mean that: but which do you like the best
Of all the measures; six feet, or eight feet?

STREPSIADES

Well, I like nothing better than the yard.

SOCRATES

Fool! Don't talk nonsense.

STREPSIADES   What will you bet me now
That two yards don't exactly make six feet?

SOCRATES

Consume you! What an ignorant clown you are!
Still, perhaps you can learn tunes more easily.

STREPSIADES

But will tunes help me to repair my fortunes?

SOCRATES

They'll help you to behave in company:
If you can tell which kind of tune is best
For the sword-dance, and which for finger music.

STREPSIADES

For fingers! Aye, but I know that.

SOCRATES   Say on, then.

STREPSIADES

    What is it but this finger? Though before,

    Ere this was grown, I used to play with that.

SOCRATES

    Insufferable dolt!

STREPSIADES   Well but, you goose,

    I don't want to learn this.

SOCRATES   What *do* you want then?

STREPSIADES

    Teach me the Logic! Teach me the unjust Logic!

SOCRATES

    But you must learn some other matters first:

    As, what are males among the quadrupeds.

STREPSIADES

    I should be mad indeed not to know that.

    The ram, the bull, the goat, the dog, the fowl.

SOCRATES

    Ah! There you are! There's a mistake at once!

    You call the male and female fowl the same.

STREPSIADES

    How! Tell me how.

SOCRATES   Why fowl and fowl of course.

STREPSIADES

    That's true though! What then shall I say in future?

SOCRATES

    Call one a fowless and the other a fowl.

STREPSIADES

    A fowless? Good! Bravo! Bravo! by Air.

    Now for that one bright piece of information

    I'll give you a barley bumper in your trough.

SOCRATES

    Look there, a fresh mistake; you called it trough,

    Masculine, when it's feminine.

STREPSIADES   How, pray?

How did I make it masculine?

SOCRATES   Why 'trough',

Just like 'Cleonymus'.

STREPSIADES   I don't quite catch it.

SOCRATES

Why 'trough,' 'Cleonymus,' both masculine.

STREPSIADES

Ah, but Cleonymus has got no trough,
His bread is kneaded in a rounded mortar:
Still, what must I say in future?

SOCRATES   What! Why, call it

A 'troughess', female, just as one says 'an actress'.

STREPSIADES

A 'troughess', female?

SOCRATES   That's the way to call it.

STREPSIADES

O 'troughess' then and Miss Cleonymus.

SOCRATES

Still you must learn some more about these names;
Which are the names or men and which of women.

STREPSIADES

Oh, I know which are women.

SOCRATES   Well, repeat some.

STREPSIADES

Demetria, Cleitagora, Philinna.

SOCRATES

Now tell me some men's names.

STREPSIADES   O yes, ten thousand.

Philon, Melesias, Amynias.

SOCRATES

Hold! I said men's names: these are women's names.

STREPSIADES

No, no, they're men's.

SOCRATES   They are *not* men's, for how

Would you address Amynias if you met him?

STREPSIADES

How? Somehow thus: 'Here, here Amynia!'

SOCRATES

Amynia! A woman's name, you see.

STREPSIADES

And rightly too; a sneak who shirks all service!
But all know this: let's pass to something else.

SOCRATES

Well, then, you get into the bed.

STREPSIADES   And then?

SOCRATES

Excogitate about your own affairs.

STREPSIADES

Not there: I do beseech, not there: at least
Let me excogitate on the bare ground.

SOCRATES

There is no way but this.

STREPSIADES   O luckless me!
How I shall suffer from the bugs today.

SOCRATES

Now then survey in every way,
With airy judgment sharp and quick:
Wrapping thoughts around you thick:
And if so be in one you stick,
Never stop to toil and bother,
Lightly, lightly, lightly leap,
To another, to another;
Far away be balmy sleep.

STREPSIADES

Ugh! Ugh! Ugh! Ugh! Ugh!

CHORUS

What's the matter? Where's the pain?

STREPSIADES

Friends! I'm dying. From the bed
Out creep bugbears scantly fed,
And my ribs they bite in twain,
And my life-blood out they suck,
And my manhood off they pluck,
And my loins they dig and drain,
And I'm dying, once again.

CHORUS

O take not the smart so deeply to heart.

STREPSIADES

Why, what can I do?
Vanished my skin so ruddy of hue,
Vanished my life-blood, vanished my shoe,
Vanished my purse, and what is still worse
As I hummed an old tune till my watch should be past,
I had very near vanished myself at the last.

SOCRATES

Hallo there, are you pondering?

STREPSIADES   Eh? What? I?
Yes to be sure.

SOCRATES

And what have your ponderings come to?

STREPSIADES

Whether these bugs will leave a bit of me.

SOCRATES

Consume you, wretch!

STREPSIADES   'Faith, I'm consumed already.

SOCRATES

Come, come, don't flinch: pull up the clothes again:
Search out and catch some very subtle dodge
To fleece your creditors.

STREPSIADES   O me, how can I
Fleece any one with all these fleeces on me?

397

[*puts his head under the clothes*]

SOCRATES

Come, let me peep a moment what he's doing.
Hey! He's asleep!

STREPSIADES   No, no! No fear of that!

SOCRATES

Caught anything?

STREPSIADES   No, nothing.

SOCRATES   Surely, something.

STREPSIADES

Well, I had something in my hand, I'll own.

SOCRATES

Pull up the clothes again, and go on pondering.

STREPSIADES

On what? Now do please tell me, Socrates.

SOCRATES

What is it that you want? First tell me that.

STREPSIADES

You have heard a million times what 'tis I want:
My debts! My debts! I want to shirk my debts.

SOCRATES

Come, come, pull up the clothes: refine your thoughts
With subtle wit: look at the case on all sides:
Mind you divide correctly.

STREPSIADES   Ugh! O me.

SOCRATES

Hush: if you meet with any difficulty,
Leave it a moment: then return again
To the same thought: then lift and weigh it well.

STREPSIADES

O, here, dear Socrates!

SOCRATES   Well, my old friend.

STREPSIADES

I've found a notion how to shirk my debts.

398

SOCRATES
  Well then, propound it.

STREPSIADES   What do you think of this?
  Suppose I hire some grand Thessalian witch
  To conjure down the Moon, and then I take it
  And clap it into some round helmet-box,
  And keep it fast there, like a looking-glass –

SOCRATES
  But what's the use of that?

STREPSIADES   The use, quotha:
  Why if the Moon should never rise again,
  I'd never pay one farthing.

SOCRATES   No! Why not?

STREPSIADES
  Why, don't we pay our interest by the month?

SOCRATES
  Good! Now I'll proffer you another problem.
  Suppose an action: damages, five talents:
  Now tell me how you can evade that same.

STREPSIADES
  How! How! Can't say at all: but I'll go seek.

SOCRATES
  Don't wrap your mind for ever round yourself,
  But let your thoughts range freely through the air,
  Like chafers with a thread about their feet.

STREPSIADES
  I've found a bright evasion of the action:
  Confess yourself, 'tis glorious.

SOCRATES   But what is it?

STREPSIADES
  I say, haven't you seen in druggists' shops
  That stone, that splendidly transparent stone,
  By which they kindle fire?

SOCRATES   The burning glass?

STREPSIADES

    That's it: well then, I'd get me one of these,
    And as the clerk was entering down my case,
    I'd stand, like this, some distance towards the sun,
    And burn out every line.

SOCRATES   By my Three Graces,
    A clever dodge!

STREPSIADES   O me, how pleased I am
    To have a debt like that clean blotted out.

SOCRATES

    Come, now, make haste and snap up this.

STREPSIADES

    Well, what?

SOCRATES   How to prevent an adversary's suit
    Supposing you were sure to lose it; tell me.

STREPSIADES

    O, nothing easier.

SOCRATES   How, pray?

STREPSIADES   Why thus,
    While there was yet one trial intervening,
    Ere mine was cited, I'd go hang myself.

SOCRATES

    Absurd!

STREPSIADES No, by the gods, it isn't though:
    They could not prosecute me were I dead.

SOCRATES

    Nonsense! Be off: I'll try no more to teach you.

STREPSIADES

    Why not? Do, please: now, please do, Socrates.

SOCRATES

    Why, you forget all that you learn, directly.
    Come, say what you learnt first: there's a
                         chance for you.

STREPSIADES

    Ah! What was first? Dear me: whatever was it?
    Whatever's that we knead the barley in?
    Bless us, what was it?

SOCRATES   Be off, and feed the crows,
    You most forgetful, most absurd old dolt!

STREPSIADES

    O me! What will become of me, poor wretch!
    I'm clean undone: I haven't learnt to speak –
    O gracious Clouds, now do advise me something.

CHORUS

    Our counsel, ancient friend, is simply this,
    To send your son, if you have one at home,
    And let him learn this wisdom in your stead.

STREPSIADES

    Yes! I've a son, quite a fine gentleman:
    But he won't learn, so what am I to do?

CHORUS

    What! Is he master?

STREPSIADES   Well: he's strong and vigorous,
    And he's got some of the Coesyra blood within him:
    Still I'll go for him, and if he won't come
    By all the gods I'll turn him out of doors.
    Go in one moment, I'll be back directly.

                                [exit

CHORUS

    Dost thou not see
    How bounteous we
    Our favours free
    Will shower on you,
    Since whatsoe'er your will prepare
    This dupe will do.
    But now that you have dazzled and elated

                                so your man,

Make haste and seize whate'er you please
                              as quickly as you can,
For cases such as these, my friend,
Are very prone to change and bend.

     SOCRATES *goes into the Phrontisterium.*
     STREPSIADES *and* PHEIDIPPIDES
     re-enter from their house

STREPSIADES

Get out! You shan't stop here: so help me Mist!
Be off, and eat up Megacles's columns.

PHEIDIPPIDES

How now, my father? What's i' the wind today?
You're wandering; by Olympian Zeus, you are.

STREPSIADES

Look there! Olympian Zeus! You blockhead you,
Come to *your* age, and yet believe in Zeus!

PHEIDIPPIDES

Why prithee, what's the joke?

STREPSIADES
                    'Tis so preposterous
When babes like you hold antiquated notions.
But come and I'll impart a thing or two,
A wrinkle, making you a man indeed.
But, mind: don't whisper this to any one.

PHEIDIPPIDES.

Well, what's the matter?

STREPSIADES
            Didn't you swear by Zeus?

PHEIDIPPIDES

I did.

STREPSIADES See now, how good a thing is learning.
There is no Zeus, Pheidippides.

PHEIDIPPIDES
                  Who then?

STREPSIADES

Why Vortex reigns, and he has turned out Zeus.

PHEIDIPPIDES

  O me, what stuff.

STREPSIADES   Be sure that this is so.

PHEIDIPPIDES

  Who says so, pray?

STREPSIADES   The Melian – Socrates,

  And Chaerephon, who knows about the flea-tracks.

PHEIDIPPIDES.

  And are you come to such a pitch of madness

  As to put faith in brain-struck men?

STREPSIADES   O hush!

  And don't blaspheme such very dexterous men

  And sapient too: men of such frugal habits

  They never shave, nor use your precious ointment,

  Nor go to baths to clean themselves: but you

  Have taken *me* for a corpse and cleaned me out.

  Come, come, make haste, do come and learn for me.

PHEIDIPPIDES

  What can one learn from them that is worth knowing?

STREPSIADES

  Learn! Why, whatever's clever in the world:

  And you shall learn how gross and dense you are.

  But stop one moment: I'll be back directly.

PHEIDIPPIDES

  O me! What must I do with my mad father?

  Shall I indict him for his lunacy,

  Or tell the undertakers of his symptoms?

STREPSIADES

  Now then! You see this, don't you? What

                  do you call it?

PHEIDIPPIDES

  That? Why, a fowl.

STREPSIADES   Good! Now then, what is this?

PHEIDIPPIDES.

That's a fowl too.

STREPSIADES   What both! Ridiculous!

Never say that again, but mind you always
Call this a fowless and the other a fowl.

PHEIDIPPIDES

A fowless! These then are the mighty secrets
You have picked up amongst those earth-born fellows.

STREPSIADES

And lots besides: but everything I learn
I straight forget: I am so old and stupid.

PHEIDIPPIDES

And this is what you have lost your mantle for?

STREPSIADES

It's very absent sometimes: 'Tisn't lost.

PHEIDIPPIDES

And what have you done with your shoes,
                              you dotard you!

STREPSIADES

Like Pericles, all for the best, I've lost them.
Come, come; go with me: humour me in this,
And then do what you like. Ah! I remember
How I to humour you, a coaxing baby,
With the first obol which my judgeship fetched me
Bought you a go-cart at the great Diasia.

PHEIDIPPIDES.

The time will come when you'll repent of this.

STREPSIADES

Good boy to obey me. Hallo! Socrates.
Come here; come here; I've brought this son of mine,
Trouble enough, I'll warrant you.

        SOCRATES *comes out of the Phrontisterium.*

SOCRATES   Poor infant,

ARISTOPHANES: THE CLOUDS

Not yet aware of my suspension-wonders.

PHEIDIPPIDES

You'd make a wondrous piece of ware, suspended.

STREPSIADES

Hey! Hang the lad! Do you abuse the Master?

SOCRATES

And look, 'suthspended!' In what foolish fashion
He mouthed the word with pouting lips agape.
How can *he* learn evasion of a suit,
Timely citation, damaging replies?
Hyperbolus, though, learnt them for a talent.

STREPSIADES

O never fear! He's very sharp, by nature.
For when he was a little chap, *so* high,
He used to build small baby-houses, boats,
Go-carts of leather, darling little frogs
Carved from pomegranates, you can't think
how nicely!
So now, I prithee, teach him both your Logics,
The Better, as you call it, and the Worse
Which with the worse cause can defeat the Better;
Or if not both, at all events the Worse.

SOCRATES

Aye, with his own ears he shall hear them argue.
I shan't be there.

STREPSIADES   But please remember this,
Give him the knack of reasoning down all Justice.

[*Socrates and Strepsiades go out*

The two LOGICS *enter.*

RIGHT LOGIC

Come show yourself now with your confident brow.
To the stage, if you dare!

405

WRONG LOGIC
'Lead on where you please':
              I shall smash you with ease,
                        If an audience be there.

RIGHT LOGIC
You'll smash me, you say! And who are *you*, pray?

WRONG LOGIC
A Logic, like you.

RIGHT LOGIC   But the Worst of the two.

WRONG LOGIC
Yet you I can drub whom my Better they dub.

RIGHT LOGIC
By what artifice taught?

WRONG LOGIC   By original thought.

RIGHT LOGIC
Aye truly your trade so successful is made
By means of these noodles of ours, I'm afraid.

WRONG LOGIC
Not noodles, but wise.

RIGHT LOGIC   I'll smash you and your lies!

WRONG LOGIC
By what method, forsooth?

RIGHT LOGIC   By speaking the Truth.

WRONG LOGIC
Your words I will meet, and entirely defeat:
There never *was* Justice or Truth, I repeat.

RIGHT LOGIC
No Justice! you say?

WRONG LOGIC   Well, where does it stay?

RIGHT LOGIC
With the gods in the air.

WRONG LOGIC   If Justice be there,
How comes it that Zeus could his father reduce,
Yet live with their godships unpunished and loose?

RIGHT LOGIC
  Ugh! Ugh!
  These evils come thick, I feel awfully sick,
  A basin, quick, quick!

WRONG LOGIC
  You're a useless old drone with one foot in the grave!

RIGHT LOGIC
  You're a shameless, unprincipled, dissolute knave!

WRONG LOGIC
  Hey! a rosy festoon.

RIGHT LOGIC   And a vulgar buffoon!

WRONG LOGIC
  What! Lilies from *you*?

RIGHT LOGIC   And a parricide too!

WRONG LOGIC
  'Tis with gold (you don't know it)
                you sprinkle my head.

RIGHT LOGIC
  O gold it is now? But it used to be lead!

WRONG LOGIC
  But now it's a grace and a glory instead.

RIGHT LOGIC
  You're a little too bold.

WRONG LOGIC   You're a good deal too old.

RIGHT LOGIC
  'Tis through you I well know not a stripling will go
  To attend to the rules which are taught in the Schools;
  But Athens one day shall be up to the fools.

WRONG LOGIC
  How squalid your dress!

RIGHT LOGIC   Yours is fine, I confess,
  Yet of old, I declare, but a pauper you were;
  And passed yourself off, our compassion to draw
  As a Telephus (Euripidean),

Well pleased from a beggarly wallet to gnaw
At inanities Pandeletean.

WRONG LOGIC

O me! for the wisdom you've mentioned in jest!

RIGHT LOGIC

O me! for the folly of you, and the rest
Who you to destroy their children employ!

WRONG LOGIC

Him you never shall teach; you are quite out of date.

RIGHT LOGIC

If not, he'll be lost, as he'll find to his cost:
Taught nothing by you but to chatter and prate.

WRONG LOGIC

He raves, as you see: let him be, let him be.

RIGHT LOGIC

Touch him if you dare! I bid you beware.

CHORUS

Forbear, forbear to wrangle and scold!
Each of you show
You what you taught their fathers of old,
You let us know
Your system untried, that hearing each side
From the lips of the rivals the youth may decide
To which of your schools he will go.

RIGHT LOGIC

This then will I do.

WRONG LOGIC   And so will I too.

CHORUS

And who will put in his claim to begin?

WRONG LOGIC

If *he* wishes, he may: I kindly give way:
And out of his argument quickly will I
Draw facts and devices to fledge the reply

Wherewith I will shoot him and smite and refute him.
And at last if a word from his mouth shall be heard
My sayings like fierce savage hornets shall pierce
His forehead and eyes,
Till in fear and distraction he yields and he – dies!

CHORUS

With thoughts and words and maxims
                    pondered well
Now then in confidence let both begin:
Try which his rival can in speech excel,
Try which this perilous wordy war can win,
Which all my votaries' hopes are fondly centred in.
O Thou who wert born our sires to adorn
              with characters blameless and fair,
Say on what you please, say on and to these
              your glorious Nature declare.

RIGHT LOGIC

To hear then prepare of the Discipline rare
              which flourished in Athens of yore
When Honour and Truth
           were in fashion with youth
              and Sobriety bloomed on our shore;
First of all the old rule was preserved in our school
           that 'boys should be seen and not heard':
And then to the home of the Harpist would come
              decorous in action and word
All the lads of one town,
           though the snow peppered down,
              in spite of all wind and all weather:
And they sung an old song as they paced it along,
           not shambling with thighs glued together:
'O the dread shout of War how it peals from afar',
             or 'Pallas the Stormer adore',

To some manly old air all simple and bare
      which their fathers had chanted before.
And should anyone dare the tune to impair
      and with intricate twistings to fill,
Such as Phrynis is fain, and his long-winded train,
      perversely to quaver and trill,
Many stripes would he feel in return for his zeal,
      as to genuine Music a foe.
And every one's thigh was forward and high
      as they sat to be drilled in a row,
So that nothing the while indecent or vile
      the eye of a stranger might meet;
And then with their hand
   they would smooth down the sand
      whenever they rose from their seat,
To leave not a trace of themselves in the place
      for a vigilant lover to view.
They never would soil their persons with oil
      but were inartificial and true.
Nor tempered their throat to a soft mincing note
      and sighs to their lovers addressed:
Nor laid themselves out, as they strutted about,
      to the wanton desires of the rest:
Nor would anyone dare such stimulant fare
      as the head of the radish to wish:
Nor to make over bold with the food of the old,
      the anise, and parsley, and fish:
Nor dainties to quaff, nor giggle and laugh,
      nor foot within foot to enfold.

WRONG LOGIC

Faugh! This smells very strong of some musty old
      song, and Chirrupers mounted in gold;
And Slaughter of beasts, and old-fashioned feasts.

RIGHT LOGIC

Yet these are the precepts which taught
The heroes of old to be hardy and bold,
   and the men who at Marathon fought!
But now must the lad from his boyhood be clad
   in a man's all-enveloping cloak:
So that, oft as the Panathenaea returns,
   I feel myself ready to choke
When the dancers go by with their shields to their
   thigh, not caring for Pallas a jot.
You therefore young man,
   choose me while you can;
   cast in with my Method your lot;
And then you shall learn the forum to spurn,
   and from dissolute baths to abstain,
And fashions impure and shameful abjure,
   and scorners repel with disdain:
And rise from your chair if an elder be there,
   and respecfully give him your place,
And with love and with fear your parents revere,
   and shrink from the brand of disgrace,
And deep in your breast be the image imprest
   of Modesty, simple and true,
Nor resort any more to a dancing-girl's door,
   nor glance at the harlotry crew,
Lest at length by the blow of the apple they throw
   from the hopes of your manhood you fall.
Nor dare to reply when your father is nigh,
   nor 'musty old Japhet' to call
In your malice and rage that sacred old age
   which lovingly cherished your youth.

WRONG LOGIC

Yes, yes, my young friend, if to him you attend,
   by Bacchus I swear of a truth

You will scarce with the sty of Hippocrates vie,
      as a mammy-suck known even there!

RIGHT LOGIC

But then you'll excel in the games you love well,
      all blooming, athletic and fair:
Not learning to prate as your idlers debate
      with marvellous prickly dispute,
Nor dragged into court day by day to make sport
      in some small disagreeable suit:
But you will below to the Academe go,
      and under the olives contend
With your chaplet of reed, in a contest of speed
      with some excellent rival and friend:
All fragrant with woodbine and peaceful content,
      and the leaf which the lime blossoms fling,
When the plane whispers love to the elm in the
      grove in the beautiful season of Spring.
If then you'll obey and do what I say
And follow with me the more excellent way,
Your chest shall be white, your skin shall be bright,
Your arms shall be tight, your tongue shall be slight,
And everything else shall be proper and right.
But if you pursue what men nowadays do,
You will have, to begin, a cold pallid skin,
Arms small and chest weak, tongue practised
      to speak,
Special laws very long, and the symptoms all strong
Which show that your life is licentious and wrong.
And your mind he'll prepare so that foul to be fair
And fair to be foul you shall always declare;
And you'll find yourself soon, if you listen to him,
With the filth of Antimachus filled to the brim!

CHORUS

O glorious sage! With loveliest wisdom teeming!

Sweet on thy words does ancient virtue rest!
Thrice happy they who watched thy youth's
                              bright beaming!
Thou of the vaunted genius, do thy best;
This man has gained applause: his wisdom
                              stands confest,
And you with clever words and thoughts
    Must needs your case adorn,
Else he will surely win the day,
    And you retreat with scorn.

WRONG LOGIC

Aye, say you so? Why I have been
    Half-burst; I do so long
To overthrow his arguments
                with arguments more strong.
I am the Lesser Logic? True:
    These schoolmen call me so,
Simply because I was the first
    Of all mankind to show
How old established rules and laws
    Might contradicted be:
And this, as you may guess, is worth
    A thousand pounds to me,
To take the feebler cause, and yet
    To win the disputation.
And mark me now, how I'll confute
    His boasted education!
You said that always from warm baths
    The stripling must abstain:
Why must he? On what grounds do you
    Of these warm baths complain?

RIGHT LOGIC

Why, it's the worst thing possible,
    It quite unstrings a man.

413

WRONG LOGIC

    Hold there: I've got you round the waist:
        Escape me if you can.
    And first: of all the sons of Zeus
        Which think you was the best?
    Which was the manliest? Which endured
        More toils than all the rest?

RIGHT LOGIC

    Well, I suppose that Heracles
        Was bravest and most bold.

WRONG LOGIC

    And are the baths of Heracles
        So wonderfully cold?
    Aha! you blame warm baths, I think.

RIGHT LOGIC

      This, this is what they say:
    This is the stuff our precious youths
        Are chattering all the day!
    This is what makes them haunt the baths,
        And shun the manlier games!

WRONG LOGIC

    Well, then, we'll take the forum next:
        I praise it, and he blames.
    But if it *was* so bad, do you think
        Old Homer would have made
    Nestor and all his worthies ply
        A real forensic trade?
    Well: then he says a stripling's tongue
        Should always idle be:
    I say it should be used of course:
        So there we disagree.
    And next he says you must be chaste:
        A most preposterous plan!

Come, tell me did you ever know
    One single blessed man
Gain the least good by chastity?
    Come, prove I'm wrong: make haste.

RIGHT LOGIC

  Yes, many, many! Peleus gained
    A sword by being chaste.

WRONG LOGIC

  A sword indeed! A wondrous meed
    The unlucky fool obtained.
Hyperbolus the lamp-maker
    Hath many a talent gained
By knavish tricks which I have taught:
    But not a sword, no, no!

RIGHT LOGIC

  Then Peleus did to his chaste life
    The bed of Thetis owe.

WRONG LOGIC

  And then she cut and ran away!
    For nothing so engages
A woman's heart as forward warmth,
    Old shred of those dark ages!
For take this chastity, young man:
    Sift it inside and out:
Count all the pleasures, all the joys,
    It bids you live without:
No kind of dames, no kind of games,
    No laughing, feasting, drinking –
Why life itself is little worth
    Without these joys, I'm thinking.
Well I must notice now the wants
    By Nature's self implanted;
You love, seduce, you can't help that,
    You're caught, convicted. Granted.

You're done for, you can't say one word,
    While if you follow me,
Indulge your genius, laugh and quaff,
    Hold nothing base to be.
Why, if you're in adultery caught,
    Your pleas will still be ample:
You've done no wrong, you'll say, and then
    Bring Zeus as your example.
He fell before the wondrous powers
    By Love and Beauty wielded:
And how can you, the mortal, stand,
    Where he, the immortal, yielded?

RIGHT LOGIC

Aye, but suppose in spite of all,
    He must be wedged and sanded:
Won't he be probed, or else can you
    Prevent it? Now be candid.

WRONG LOGIC

And what's the damage if it should be so?

RIGHT LOGIC

What greater damage can the young man know?

WRONG LOGIC

What will you do, if this dispute I win?

RIGHT LOGIC

I'll be for ever silent.

WRONG LOGIC   Good, begin.

The Counsellor: from whence comes he?

RIGHT LOGIC

From probed adulterers.

WRONG LOGIC

I agree. The Tragic Poets: whence are they?

RIGHT LOGIC

From probed adulterers.

WRONG LOGIC   So I say.

The Orators: what class of men?

RIGHT LOGIC
All probed adulterers.

WRONG LOGIC   Right again.
You feel your error, I'll engage,
But look once more around the stage,
Survey the audience, which they be,
Probed or not probed.

RIGHT LOGIC   I see, I see.

WRONG LOGIC
Well, give your verdict.

RIGHT LOGIC   It must go
For probed adulterers: him I know,
And him, and him: the probed are most.

WRONG LOGIC
How stand we then?

RIGHT LOGIC   I own, I've lost.
O Cinaeds, Cinaeds, take my robe!
Your words have won, to you I run
To live and die with glorious probe!

> SOCRATES *reappears from the Phrontisterium*
> *and* STREPSIADES *from his own house to see*
> *how matters are progressing*

SOCRATES
Well, what do you want? To take away your son
At once, or shall I teach him how to speak?

STREPSIADES
Teach him, and flog him, and be sure you well
Sharpen his mother wit, grind the one edge
Fit for my little law-suits, and the other
Why make that serve for more important matters.

SOCRATES
O, never fear! He'll make a splendid sophist.

STREPSIADES

Well, well, I hope he'll be a poor pale rascal.

[exit Strepsiades; Socrates and Pheidippides
go into the Phrontisterium

CHORUS

Go: but in us the thought is strong,
 You will repent of this ere long.
Now we wish to tell the Judges
 All the blessings they shall gain
If, as Justice plainly warrants,
 We the worthy prize obtain.
First, whenever in the season
 Ye would fain your fields renew,
All the world shall wait expectant
 Till we've poured our rain on you:
Then of all your crops and vineyards
 We will take the utmost care
So that neither drought oppress them,
 Nor the heavy rain impair.
But if anyone amongst you
 Dare to treat our claims with scorn,
Mortal he, the Clouds immortal,
 Better had he ne'er been born!
He from his estates shall gather
 Neither corn, nor oil, nor wine,
For whenever blossoms sparkle
 On the olive or the vine
They shall all at once be blighted,
 We will ply our slings so true.
And if ever we behold him
 Building up his mansions new,
With our tight and nipping hailstones
 We will all his tiles destroy.
But if he, his friends or kinsfolk,

Would a marriage-feast enjoy,
All night long we'll pour in torrents:
    So perchance he'll rather pray
To endure the drought of Egypt,
    Than decide amiss today!

> STREPSIADES *now re-enters, bringing*
> *a large bag of corn.*

STREPSIADES

The fifth, the fourth, the third, and then the second,
And then that day which more than all the rest
I loathe and shrink from and abominate,
Then comes at once that hateful Old-and-New day.
And every single blessed dun has sworn
He'll stake his gage, and ruin and destroy me.
And when I make a modest small request,
'O my good friend, part don't exact at present,
And part defer, and part remit,' they swear
So they shall never touch it, and abuse me
As a rank swindler, threatening me with actions.
Now let them bring their actions! Who's afraid?
Not I, if these have taught my son to speak.
But here's the door: I'll knock and soon find out.
Boy! Ho there, boy!

> SOCRATES *comes out*

SOCRATES   I clasp Strepsiades.

STREPSIADES

And I clasp you: but take this meal-bag first.
'Tis meet and right to glorify one's tutors.
But tell me, tell me, has my son yet learnt
That Second Logic which he saw just now?

SOCRATES

He hath.

STREPSIADES   Hurrah! great Sovereign Knavery!

SOCRATES
    You may escape whatever suit you please.
STREPSIADES
    What, if I borrowed before witnesses?
SOCRATES
    Before a thousand, and the more the merrier.
STREPSIADES
    'Then shall my song be loud and deep.'
    Weep, obol-weighers, weep, weep, weep,
    Ye, and your principals, and compound interests,
    For ye shall never pester me again.
    Such a son have I bred,
    (He is within this door,)
    Born to inspire my foemen with dread,
    Born his old father's house to restore:
    Keen and polished of tongue is he,
    He my champion and guard shall be.
    He will set his old father free:
    Run you, and call him forth to me.
    'O my child! O my sweet! Come out I entreat;
    'Tis the voice of your sire.'
SOCRATES   Here's the man you require.
STREPSIADES
    Joy, joy of my heart!
SOCRATES   Take your son and depart.
STREPSIADES
    O come, O come, my son, my son,
    O dear! O dear!
    O joy, to see your beautiful complexion!
    Aye now you have an aspect negative
    And disputative, and our native query
    Shines forth there 'What d'ye say?' You've the true face
    Which rogues put on, of injured innocence.
    You have the regular Attic look about you.

So now, you save me, for 'twas you undid me.

PHEIDIPPIDES

What is it ails you?

STREPSIADES   Why the Old-and-New day.

PHEIDIPPIDES

And is there such a day as Old-and-New?

STREPSIADES

Yes: that's the day they mean to stake their gages.

PHEIDIPPIDES

They'll lose them if they stake them. What!

                                Do you think

That one day can be two days, both together?

STREPSIADES

Why, can't it be so?

PHEIDIPPIDES   Surely not; or else

A woman might at once be old and young.

STREPSIADES

Still, the law says so.

PHEIDIPPIDES   True: but I believe

They don't quite understand it.

STREPSIADES   You explain it.

PHEIDIPPIDES

Old Solon had a democratic turn.

STREPSIADES

Well, but that's nothing to the Old-and-New.

PHEIDIPPIDES

Hence then he fixed that summonses be issued
For these two days, the old one and the new one,
So that the gage be staked on the New-month.

STREPSIADES

What made him add 'the old' then?

PHEIDIPPIDES   I will tell you.

He wished the litigants to meet on *that* day
And compromise their quarrels: if they could not,

Then let them fight it out on the New-month.

STREPSIADES

Why then do magistrates receive the stakes
On the Old-and-New instead of the New-month?

PHEIDIPPIDES

Well, I believe they act like the foretasters.
They wish to bag the gage as soon as possible,
And thus they gain a whole day's foretaste of it.

STREPSIADES

Aha! Poor dupes, why sit ye mooning there
Game for us Artful Dodgers, you dull stones,
You ciphers, lambkins, butts piled up together!
O! My success inspires me, and I'll sing
Glad eulogies on me and thee, my son.
'Man, most blessed, most divine,
What a wondrous wit is thine,
What a son to grace thy line,'
Friends and neighbours day by day
Thus will say,
When with envious eyes my suits they see you win:
But first I'll feast you, so come in, my son, come in.

The father and son re-enter the house. PASIAS, *the first
creditor named in the father's opening soliloquy,
now enters with a witness who is to see that
the summons is duly served on the debtor.*

PASIAS

What! Must a man lose his own property!
No: never, never. Better have refused
With a bold face, than be so plagued as this.
See! To get paid my own just debts, I'm forced
To drag you to bear witness, and what's worse
I needs must quarrel with my townsman here.
Well, I won't shame my country, while I live,

I'll go to law, I'll summon him.

STREPSIADES   Hallo!

PASIAS

To the next Old-and-New.

STREPSIADES   Bear witness, all!

He named two days. You'll summon me; what for?

PASIAS

The fifty pounds I lent you when you bought

That iron-grey.

STREPSIADES   Just listen to the fellow!

The whole world knows that I detest all horses.

PASIAS

I swear you swore by all the gods to pay me.

STREPSIADES

Well, now I swear I won't: Pheidippides

Has learnt since then the unanswerable Logic.

PASIAS

And will you therefore shirk my just demand?

STREPSIADES

Of course I will: else why should he have learnt it?

PASIAS

And will you dare forswear it by the gods?

STREPSIADES

The gods indeed! What gods?

PASIAS

Poseidon, Hermes, Zeus.

STREPSIADES   By Zeus I would,

Though I gave two-pence half-penny for

                              the privilege.

PASIAS

O then confound you for a shameless rogue!

STREPSIADES

Hallo! This butt should be rubbed down with salt.

PASIAS

   Zounds! You deride me!

STREPSIADES   Why, 'twill hold four gallons.

PASIAS

   You 'scape me not, by mighty Zeus, and all
   The gods!

STREPSIADES   I wonderfully like the gods;

   An oath by Zeus is sport to knowing ones.

PASIAS

   Sooner or later you'll repent of this.
   Come, do you mean to pay your debts or don't you?
   Tell me, and I'll be off.

STREPSIADES   Now do have patience;

   I'll give you a clear answer in one moment.

PASIAS

   What do you think he'll do?

WITNESS   I think he'll pay you.

STREPSIADES

   Where is that horrid dun? O here: now tell me
   What you call this.

PASIAS   What I call that? A trough.

STREPSIADES

   Heavens! What a fool: and do *you* want your money?
   I'll never pay one penny to a fellow
   Who calls my troughess, trough. So there's
                    your answer.

PASIAS

   Then you won't pay me?

STREPSIADES   No, not if I know it.

   Come, put your best foot forward, and be off:
   March off, I say, this instant!

PASIAS   May I die

   If I don't go at once and stake my gage!

STREPSIADES

No don't: the fifty pounds are loss enough:
And really on my word I would not wish you
To lose this too just for one silly blunder.

        [Pasias goes away to bring his action

He is hardly out of sight when AMYNIAS, *the second
   creditor mentioned in the opening soliloquy, is
   heard without, bewailing the injury he has
   sustained in a carriage accident.*

AMYNIAS

Ah me! Oh! Oh! Oh!

STREPSIADES

Hallo! Who's that making that horrible noise?
Not one of Carcinus's snivelling gods?

AMYNIAS

Who cares to know what I am? What imports it?
An ill-starred man.

STREPSIADES   Then keep it to yourself.

AMYNIAS

'O heavy fate!' 'O Fortune, thou hast broken
My chariot wheels!' 'Thou hast undone me, Pallas!'

STREPSIADES

How! Has Tlepolemus been at you, man?

AMYNIAS

Jeer me not, friend, but tell your worthy son
To pay me back the money which I lent him:
I'm in a bad way and the times are pressing.

STREPSIADES

What money do you mean?

AMYNIAS   Why, what he borrowed.

STREPSIADES

You *are* in a bad way, I really think.

AMYNIAS

   Driving my four-wheel out I fell, by Zeus.

STREPSIADES

   You rave as if you'd fall'n times out-of-mind.

AMYNIAS

   I rave? How so? I only claim my own.

STREPSIADES

   You can't be quite right, surely.

AMYNIAS   Why, what mean you?

STREPSIADES

   I shrewdly guess your brain's received a shake.

AMYNIAS

   I shrewdly guess that you'll receive a summons
   If you don't pay my money.

STREPSIADES   Well then, tell me,
   Which theory do you side with, that the rain
   Falls fresh each time, or that the sun draws back
   The same old rain, and sends it down again?

AMYNIAS

   I'm very sure I neither know nor care.

STREPSIADES

   Not care! Good heavens! And do *you* claim
                           your money,
   So unenlightened in the Laws of Nature?

AMYNIAS

   If you're hard up then, pay me back the interest
   At least.

STREPSIADES Int–er–est? What kind of a beast is that?

AMYNIAS

   What else than day by day and month by month
   Larger and larger still the silver grows
   As time sweeps by.

STREPSIADES   Finely and nobly said.
   What then! Think you the sea is larger now

Than 'twas last year?

AMYNIAS No surely, 'tis no larger:
It is not right it should be.

STREPSIADES And do you then,
Insatiable grasper, when the sea,
Receiving all these rivers, grows no larger,
Do you desire your silver to grow larger?
Come now, you prosecute your journey off!
Here, fetch the whip.

AMYNIAS Bear witness, I appeal.

STREPSIADES
Be off! What, won't you? Gee up, sigma-brand!

AMYNIAS
I say! A clear assault!

STREPSIADES You won't be off?
I'll stimulate you; Zeus! I'll goad your haunches.
Aha! You run: I thought I'd stir you up
You and your phaetons, and wheels, and all!

[*Amynias goes off*

STREPSIADES *returns to the feast with*
which he is entertaining his son.

CHORUS
What a thing it is to long
For matters which are wrong!
For you see how this old man
Is seeking if he can
His creditors trepan:
And I confidently say
That he will this very day
Such a blow
Amid his prosperous cheats receive,
That he will deeply deeply grieve.
For I think that he has won
That he wanted for his son,

And the lad has learned the way
All justice to gainsay,
Be it what or where it may:
That he'll trump up any tale,
Right or wrong, and so prevail.
This I know.
Yea! And perchance the time will come
When he shall wish his son were dumb.

[*Strepsiades runs out of his house, shrieking,
closely followed by his son.*

STREPSIADES

Oh! Oh!
Help! Murder! Help! O neighbours, kinsfolk,
                      townsmen,
Help, one and all, against this base assault,
Ah! Ah! My cheek! My head! O luckless me!
Wretch! Do you strike your father?

PHEIDIPPIDES   Yes, papa.

STREPSIADES

See! See! He owns he struck me.

PHEIDIPPIDES   To be sure.

STREPSIADES

Scoundrel! and parricide! And house-breaker!

PHEIDIPPIDES

Thank you: go on, go on: do please go on.
I am quite delighted to be called such names!

STREPSIADES

O probed adulterer.

PHEIDIPPIDES   Roses from your lips.

STREPSIADES

Strike you your father?

PHEIDIPPIDES   O dear yes: what's more
I'll prove I struck you justly.

STREPSIADES   Struck me justly!

Villain! how can you strike a father justly?

PHEIDIPPIDES

Yes, and I'll demonstrate it, if you please.

STREPSIADES

Demonstrate this?

PHEIDIPPIDES   Oh yes, quite easily.

Come, take your choice, which Logic do you choose?

STREPSIADES

Which what?

PHEIDIPPIDES   Logic: the Better or the Worse?

STREPSIADES

Ah, then, in very truth I've had you taught
To reason down all Justice, if you think
You can prove this, that it is just and right
That fathers should be beaten by their sons!

PHEIDIPPIDES

Well, well, I think I'll prove it, if you'll listen,
So that even you won't have one word to answer.

STREPSIADES

Come, I should like to hear what you've to say.

CHORUS

'Tis yours, old man, some method to contrive
    This fight to win:
He would not without arms wherewith to strive
    So bold have been.
He knows, be sure, whereon to trust.
His eager bearing proves he must.
So come and tell us from what cause
    This sad dispute began;
Come, tell us how it first arose:
    Do tell us if you can.

STREPSIADES

Well from the very first I will
    The whole contention show:

429

'Twas when I went into the house
    To feast him, as you know,
I bade him bring his lyre and sing,
    The supper to adorn,
Some lay of old Simonides,
    As, how the Ram was shorn:
But he replied, to sing at meals
    Was coarse and obsolete;
Like some old beldame humming airs
    The while she grinds her wheat.

PHEIDIPPIDES

And should you not be thrashed who told
    Your son, from food abstaining,
To sing! As though you were, forsooth,
    Cicalas entertaining.

STREPSIADES

You hear him! So he said just now
    Or e'er high words began:
And next he called Simonides
    A very sorry man.
And when I heard him, I could scarce
    My rising wrath command;
Yet so I did, and him I bid
    Take myrtle in his hand
And chant some lines from Aeschylus,
    But he replied with ire,
'Believe me I'm not one of those
    Who Aeschylus admire,
That rough, unpolished, turgid bard,
    That mouther of bombast!'
When he said this, my heart began
    To heave extremely fast;
Yet still I kept my passion down,
    And said, 'Then prithee you,

Sing one of those new-fangled songs
 Which modern striplings do.'
And he began the shameful tale
 Euripides has told
How a brother and a sister lived
 Incestuous lives of old.
Then, then I could no more restrain,
 But first I must confess
With strong abuse I loaded him,
 And so, as you may guess,
We stormed and bandied threat for threat:
 Till out at last he flew,
And smashed and thrashed and thumped
       and bumped
 And bruised me black and blue.

PHEIDIPPIDES

And rightly too, who coolly dared
 Euripides to blame,
Most sapient bard.

STREPSIADES   Most sapient bard!
 You, what's your fitting name?
Ah! but he'll pummel me again.

PHEIDIPPIDES

He will: and justly too.

STREPSIADES

What? Justly, heartless villain,
 When 'twas I who nurtured you?
I knew your little lisping ways,
 How soon, you'd hardly think,
If you cried 'bree!' I guessed your wants,
 And used to give you drink:
If you said 'mamm!' I fetched you bread
 With fond discernment true,
And you could hardly say 'cacca!'

When through the door I flew
And held you out a full arm's length
　Your little needs to do:
But now when I was crying
That I with pain was dying,
You brute! You would not tarry
Me out of doors to carry,
But choking with despair
I've been and done it there.

CHORUS

Sure all young hearts are palpitating now
　To hear him plead,
Since if those lips with artful words avow
　The daring deed,
And once a favouring verdict win,
A fig for every old man's skin.
O thou, who rakest up new thoughts
　With daring hands profane,
Try all you can, ingenious man,
　That verdict to obtain.

PHEIDIPPIDES

How sweet it is these novel arts,
　These clever words, to know,
And have the power established rules
　And laws to overthrow.
Why, in old times when horses were
　My sole delight, 'twas wonder
If I could say a dozen words
　Without some awful blunder!
But now that he has made me quit
　That reckless mode of living,
And I have been to subtle thoughts
　My whole attention giving,

I hope to prove by logic strict
   'Tis right to beat my father.

STREPSIADES

O! Buy your horses back, by Zeus,
   Since I would ten times rather
Have to support a four-in-hand,
   So I be struck no more.

PHEIDIPPIDES

Peace. I will now resume the thread
   Where I broke off before.
And first I ask: when I was young,
   Did you not strike me then?

STREPSIADES

Yea: for I loved and cherished you.

PHEIDIPPIDES

Well solve me this again,
Is it not just that I your son
   Should cherish you alike,
And strike you, since, as you observe,
   To cherish means to strike?
What! Must my body needs be scourged
   And pounded black and blue,
And yours be scathless? Was not I
   As much freeborn as you?
'Children are whipped, and shall not
                sires be whipped?'
Perhaps you'll urge that children's minds
   Alone are taught by blows –
Well, age is second childhood then:
   That everybody knows.
And as by old experience age
   Should guide its steps more clearly,
So when they err, they surely should
   Be punished more severely.

STREPSIADES

But Law goes everywhere for me:
    Deny it, if you can.

PHEIDIPPIDES

Well, was not he who made the law,
    A man, a mortal man,
As you or I, who in old times
    Talked over all the crowd?
And think you that to you or me
    The same is not allowed
To change it, so that sons by blows
    Should keep their fathers steady?
Still, we'll be liberal, and blows
    Which we've received already
We will forget, we'll have no Ex-
    Post-Facto legislation.
Look at the game-cocks, look at all
    The animal creation,
Do not *they* beat their parents? Aye:
    I say then, that in fact
They are as we, except that they
    No special laws enact.

STREPSIADES

Why don't you then, if always where
    The game-cock leads you follow,
Ascend your perch to roost at night,
    And dirt and ordure swallow?

PHEIDIPPIDES

The case is different there, old man,
    As Socrates would see.

STREPSIADES

Well then you'll blame yourself at last,
    If you keep striking me.

PHEIDIPPIDES
  How so?
STREPSIADES Why, if it's right for me
    To punish you my son,
  You can, if you have got one, yours.
PHEIDIPPIDES
  Aye, but suppose I've none.
  Then having gulled me you will die,
    While I've been flogged in vain.
STREPSIADES
  Good friends! I really think he has
    Some reason to complain.
  I must concede he has put the case
    In quite a novel light:
  I really think we should be flogged
    Unless we act aright!
PHEIDIPPIDES
  Look to a fresh idea then.
STREPSIADES
  He'll be my death I vow.
PHEIDIPPIDES
  Yet then perhaps you will not grudge
    Ev'n what you suffer now.
STREPSIADES
  How! Will you make me like the blows
    Which I've received today?
PHEIDIPPIDES
  Yes, for I'll beat my mother too.
STREPSIADES
  What! What is that you say!
  Why, this is worse than all.
PHEIDIPPIDES   But what
  If, as I proved the other,

By the same Logic I can prove
    'Tis right to beat my mother?

STREPSIADES

Aye! What indeed! If this you plead,
If this you think to win,
Why then, for all I care, you may
To the accursed pit convey
Yourself with all your learning new,
Your master, and your Logic too,
And tumble headlong in.
O Clouds! O Clouds! I owe all this to you!
Why did I let you manage my affairs!

CHORUS

Nay, nay, old man, you owe it to yourself.
Why didst thou turn to wicked practices?

STREPSIADES

Ah, but ye should have asked me that before,
And not have spurred a poor old fool to evil.

CHORUS

Such is our plan. We find a man
    On evil thoughts intent,
Guide him along to shame and wrong,
    Then leave him to repent.

STREPSIADES

Hard words, alas! Yet not more hard than just.
It was not right unfairly to keep back
The money that I borrowed. Come, my darling,
Come and destroy that filthy Chaerephon
And Socrates; for they've deceived us both!

PHEIDIPPIDES

No. I will lift no hand against my tutors.

STREPSIADES

Yes, do, come, reverence Paternal Zeus.

PHEIDIPPIDES

    Look there! Paternal Zeus! What an old fool.
    Is there a Zeus?

STREPSIADES   There is.

PHEIDIPPIDES   There is no Zeus.

    Young Vortex reigns, and he has turned out Zeus.

STREPSIADES

    No Vortex reigns: that was my foolish thought
    All through this vortex here. Fool that I was,
    To think a piece of earthenware a god.

PHEIDIPPIDES

    Well rave away, talk nonsense to yourself.

STREPSIADES

    O! Fool, fool, fool, how mad I must have been
    To cast away the gods, for Socrates.
    Yet Hermes, gracious Hermes, be not angry
    Nor crush me utterly, but look with mercy
    On faults to which his idle talk hath led me.
    And lend thy counsel; tell me, had I better
    Plague them with lawsuits, or how else annoy them.
    [affects to listen]
    Good: your advice is good: I'll have no lawsuits,
    I'll go at once and set their house on fire,
    The prating rascals. Here, here, Xanthias,
    Quick, quick here, bring your ladder and
                       your pitchfork,
    Climb to the roof of their vile thinking-house,
    Dig at their tiles, dig stoutly, an' thou lovest me,
    Tumble the very house about their ears.
    And someone fetch me here a lighted torch,
    And I'll soon see if, boasters as they are,
    They won't repent of what they've done to me.

STUDENT I
  O dear! O dear!
STREPSIADES   Now, now, my torch, send out
  A lusty flame.
STUDENT I   Man! What are you at there?
STREPSIADES
  What am I at? I'll tell you.
  I'm splitting straws with your house-rafters here.
STUDENT 2
  Oh me! Who's been and set our house on fire?
STREPSIADES
  Who was it, think you, that you stole the cloak from?
STUDENT 3
  O murder! Murder!
STREPSIADES   That's the very thing,
  Unless this pick prove traitor to my hopes,
  Or I fall down, and break my blessed neck.
SOCRATES
  Hallo! What are you at, up on our roof?
STREPSIADES
  I walk on air, and contemplate the sun.
SOCRATES
  O! I shall suffocate. O dear! O dear!
CHAEREPHON
  And I, poor devil, shall be burnt to death.
STREPSIADES
  For with what aim did ye insult the gods,
  And pry around the dwellings of the moon?
  Strike, smite them, spare them not, for many reasons,
  But most because they have blasphemed the gods!
CHORUS
  Lead out of the way: for I think we may say
  We have acetd our part very fairly today.

XENOPHON
SYMPOSIUM

For myself, I hold to the opinion that not alone are the serious transactions of 'good and noble men' most memorable, but that words and deeds distinctive of their lighter moods may claim some record. In proof of which contention, I will here describe a set of incidents within the scope of my experience. The occasion was a horse-race at the great Panathenaic festival. Callias, the son of Hipponicus, being a friend and lover of the boy Autolycus, had brought the lad, himself the winner of the pankration, to see the spectacle. As soon as the horse race was over, Callias proceeded to escort Autolycus and his father, Lycon, to his house in the Piraeus, being attended also by Niceratus. But catching sight of Socrates along with certain others (Critobulus, Hermogenes, Antisthenes, and Charmides), he bade an attendant conduct the party with Autolycus, whilst he himself approached the group, exclaiming: A happy chance brings me across your path, just when I am about to entertain Autolycus and his father at a feast. The splendour of the entertainment shall be much enhanced, I need not tell you, if my hall should happily be graced by worthies like yourselves, who have attained to purity of soul, rather than by generals and cavalry commanders and a crowd of place-hunters.

Whereat Socrates: When will you have done with your gibes, Callias? Why, because you have yourself spent sums of money on Protagoras, and Gorgias, and Prodicus, and a host of others, to learn wisdom, must you pour contempt on us poor fellows, who are but self-taught tinkers in philosophy compared with you?

Hitherto, no doubt, retorted Callias, although I had plenty of wise things to say, I have kept my wisdom to myself; but if only you will honour me with your company today, I promise to present myself in quite another light; you will see I am a person of no mean consideration after all.

Socrates and the others, while thanking Callias politely for the invitation, were not disposed at first to join the dinner party; but the annoyance of the other so to be put off was so obvious that in the end the party were persuaded to accompany their host. After an interval devoted to gymnastic exercise (and subsequent anointing of the limbs) by some, whilst others of them took a bath, the guests were severally presented to the master of the house.

Autolycus was seated next his father, as was natural, while the rest reclined on couches. Noting the scene presented, the first idea to strike the mind of anyone must certainly have been that beauty has by nature something regal in it; and the more so, if it chance to be combined (as now in the person of Autolycus) with modesty and self-respect. Even as when a splendid object blazes forth at night, the eyes of men are riveted, so now the beauty of Autolycus drew on him the gaze of all; nor was there one of those onlookers but was stirred to his soul's depth by him who sat there. Some fell into unwonted silence, while the gestures of the rest were equally significant.

It seems the look betokening divine possession, no matter who the god, must ever be remarkable. Only, whilst the subject of each commoner emotion passion-whirled may be distinguished by flashings of the eye, by terror-striking tones of voice, and by the vehement fervour of the man's whole being, so he who is inspired by temperate and harmonious love will wear a look of kindlier welcome in his eyes; the words he utters fall from his lips with softer intonation; and every gesture of his bodily frame conforms to what is truly frank and liberal. Such, at any rate, the strange effects now wrought on Callias by love. He was like one transformed, the cynosure of all initiated in the mysteries of this divinity.

So they supped in silence, the whole company, as if an injunction had been laid upon them by some superior power. But presently there came a knocking on the door! Philippus the jester bade the doorkeeper announce him, with apologies for seeking a night's lodging: he had come, he said, provided with all necessaries for dining, at a friend's expense: his attendant was much galled with carrying, nothing but an empty bread-basket. To this announcement Callias, appealing to his guests, replied: It would never do to begrudge the shelter of one's roof: let him come in. And as he spoke, he glanced across to where Autolycus was seated, as if to say: I wonder how you take the jest.

Meanwhile the jester, standing at the door of the apartment where the feast was spread, addressed the company: I believe you know, sirs, that being a jester by profession, it is my business to make jokes. I am all the readier, therefore, to present myself, feeling convinced it is a better joke to come to dinner thus unbidden than by solemn invitation.

Be seated, then, replied the host. The company are fully fed on serious thoughts, you see, if somewhat starved of food for laughter.

The feast proceeded; and, if only to discharge the duty laid upon him at a dinner-party, Philippus must try at once to perpetrate a jest. Failing to stir a smile, poor fellow, he made no secret of his perturbation. Presently he tried again; and for the second time the joke fell flat. Whereat he paused abruptly in the middle of the course, and muffling up his face, fell prostrate on the couch.

Then Callias: What ails you, sirrah? Have you the cramp? The toothache? What?

To which the other, heaving a deep groan: Yes, Callias, an atrocious ache; since laughter has died out among mankind, my whole estate is bankrupt. In old days I would be asked to dinner to amuse the company with jests. Now all is changed, and who will be at pains to ask me out to dinner any more? I might as well pretend to be immortal as to be serious. Nor will any one invite me in hopes of reclining at my board in his turn. Everyone knows so serious a thing as dinner in my house was never heard of; it's against the rules – the more's the pity.

And as he spoke he blew his nose and snuffled, uttering the while so truly dolorous a moan that everybody fell to soothing him. They would all laugh again another day, they said, and so implored him to have done and eat his dinner; till Critobulus could not stand his lamentation longer, but broke into a peal of laughter. The welcome sound sufficed. The sufferer unveiled his face, and thus addressed his inner self: Be of good cheer, my soul, there are many battles yet in store for us, and so he fell to discussing the viands once again.

Now the tables were removed, and in due order they had poured out the libation, and had sung the hymn. To promote the revelry, there entered now a Syracusan, with a trio of assistants: the first a flute-girl, perfect in her art; and next a dancing-girl, skilled to perform all kinds of wonders; lastly, in the bloom of beauty, a boy who played the harp and danced with infinite grace. This Syracusan went about exhibiting his troupe, whose wonderful performance was a source of income to him. After the girl had played to them upon the flute, and then the boy in turn upon the harp, and both performers, as it would appear, had set the hearts of every one rejoicing, Socrates turned to Callias: A feast, upon my word, O princeliest entertainer! Was it not enough to set before your guests a faultless dinner, but you must feast our eyes and ears on sights and sounds the most delicious?

To which the host: And that reminds me, a supply of unguents might not be amiss; what say you? Shall we feast on perfumes also?

No, I protest, the other answered. Scents resemble clothes. One dress is beautiful on man and one on woman; and so with fragrance: what becomes the woman, ill becomes the man. Did ever man anoint himself with oil of myrrh to please his fellow? Women, and especially young women (like our two friends' brides, Niceratus' and Critobulus'), need no perfume, being but compounds themselves of fragrance. No, sweeter than any perfume else to women is good olive-oil, suggestive of the training-school: sweet if present, and when absent longed for. And why? Distinctions vanish with the use of perfumes. The freeman and the slave have forthwith both alike one odour. But the scents derived from toils – those toils which every free man loves – need customary habit first, and time's distillery, if they are to be sweet with freedom's breath, at last.

Here Lycon interposed: That may be well enough

for youths, but what shall we do whose gymnastic days are over? What fragrance is left for us?

SOCRATES: Why, that of true nobility, of course.

LYCON: And whence shall a man obtain this chrism?

SOCRATES: Not from those that sell perfumes and unguents, in good sooth.

LYCON: But whence, then?

SOCRATES: Theognis has told us: 'From the good thou shalt learn good things, but if with the evil thou holdest converse, thou shalt lose the wit that is in thee.'

LYCON [*turning to his son*]: Do you hear that, my son?

That he does, Socrates answered for the boy, and he puts the precept into practice also; to judge, at any rate, from his behaviour. When he had set his heart on carrying off the palm of victory in the pankration, he took you into his counsel; and will again take counsel to discover the fittest friend to aid him in his high endeavour, and with this friend associate.

Thereupon several of the company exclaimed at once. Where will he find a teacher to instruct him in that wisdom? one inquired. Why, it is not to be taught! exclaimed another; to which a third rejoined: Why should it not be learnt as well as other things?

Then Socrates: The question would seem at any rate to be debatable. Suppose we defer it till another time, and for the present not interrupt the programme of proceedings. I see the dancing-girl is standing ready; they are handing her some hoops.

And at the instant her fellow with the flute commenced a tune to keep her company, whilst someone posted at her side kept handing her the hoops till she had twelve in all. With these in her hands she fell to dancing, and the while she danced she flung the hoops into the air – overhead she sent them twirling – judging the height they must be thrown to catch them, as they fell, in perfect time.

Then Socrates: The girl's performance is one proof among a host of others, sirs, that woman's nature is nowise inferior to man's. All she wants is strength and judgment; and that should be an encouragement to those of you who have wives, to teach them whatever you would have them know as your associates.

Antisthenes rejoined: If that is your conclusion, Socrates, why do you not tutor your own wife, Xanthippe, instead of letting her remain, of all the wives that are, indeed that ever will be, I imagine, the most shrewish?

Well now, I will tell you, he answered. I follow the example of the rider who wishes to become an expert horseman: None of your soft-mouthed, docile animals for me, he says; the horse for me to own must show some spirit: in the belief, no doubt, if he can manage such an animal, it will be easy enough to deal with every other horse besides. And that is just my case. I wish to deal with human beings, to associate with man in general; hence my choice of wife. I know full well, if I can tolerate her spirit, I can with ease attach myself to every human being else.

A well-aimed argument, not wide of the mark by any means! the company were thinking.

Hereupon a large hoop studded with a bristling row of upright swords was introduced; and into the centre of this ring of knives and out of it again the girl threw somersaults backwards, forwards, several times, till the spectators were in terror of some accident; but with the utmost coolness and without mishap the girl completed her performance.

Here Socrates, appealing to Antisthenes: None of

the present company, I take it, who have watched this spectacle will ever again deny that courage can be taught, when the girl there, woman should she be, rushes so boldly into the midst of swords.

He, thus challenged, answered: No, and what our friend, the Syracusan here, should do is to exhibit his dancing-girl to the state. Let him tell the authorities he is prepared, for a consideration, to give the whole Athenian people courage to face the hostile lances at close quarters.

Whereat the jester: An excellent idea, upon my word; and when it happens, may I be there to see that mighty orator Peisander learning to throw somersaults into swords; since incapacity to look a row of lances in the face at present makes him shy of military service.

At this stage of the proceedings the boy danced. The dance being over, Socrates exclaimed: Pray, did you notice how the beauty of the child, so lovely in repose, became enhanced with every movement of his supple body?

To which Charmides replied: How like a flatterer you are! One would think you had set yourself to puff the dancing-master.

To be sure, he answered solemnly; and there's another point I could not help observing: how while he danced no portion of his body remained idle; neck and legs and hands together, one and all were exercised. That is how a man should dance, who wants to keep his body light and healthy. Then turning to the Syracusan, he added: I cannot say how much obliged I should be to you, O man of Syracuse, for lessons in deportment. Pray teach me my steps.

And what use will you make of them? the other asked.

God bless me! I shall dance, of course, he answered. The remark was greeted with a peal of merriment.

Then Socrates, with a most serious expression of countenance: You are pleased to laugh at me. Pray, do you find it so ridiculous my wishing to improve my health by exercise? Or to enjoy my victuals better? To sleep better? Or is it the sort of exercise I set my heart on? Not like those runners of the long race, to have my legs grow muscular and my shoulders leaner in proportion; nor like a boxer, thickening chest and shoulders at expense of legs; but by distribution of the toil throughout my limbs I seek to give an even balance to my body. Or are you laughing to think that I shall not in future have to seek a partner in the training school, whereby it will not be necessary for an old man like myself to strip in public? All I shall need will be a seven-sofa'd chamber, where I can warm to work, just like the lad here who has found this room quite ample for the purpose. And in winter I shall do gymnastics under cover, or when the weather is broiling under shade . . . But what is it you keep on laughing at – the wish on my part to reduce to moderate size a paunch a trifle too rotund? Is that the source of merriment? Perhaps you are not aware, my friends, that Charmides – yes! he there – caught me only the other morning in the act of dancing?

Yes, that I will swear to, the other answered; and at first I stood aghast. I feared me you had parted with your senses; but when I heard your explanation, pretty much what you have just now told us, I went home and – I will not say, began to dance myself (it is an accomplishment I have not been taught as yet), but I fell to sparring, an art of which I have a very pretty knowledge.

That's true, upon my life! exclaimed the jester. One needs but look at you to see there's not a dram of difference between legs and shoulders. I'll be bound, if both were weighed in the scales apart, like 'tops and bottoms', the clerks of the market would let you off scot-free.

Then Callias: O Socrates, do please invite me when you begin your dancing lessons. I will be your *vis-à-vis*, and take lessons with you.

Come on, the jester shouted. Give us a tune upon the pipe, and let me show you how to dance. So saying up he got, and mimicked the dances of the boy and girl in burlesque fashion, and inasmuch as the spectators had been pleased to think the natural beauty of the boy enhanced by every gesture of his body in the dance, so the jester must give a counter-representation, in which each twist and movement of his body was a comical exaggeration of nature. And since the girl had bent herself backwards and backwards, till she was nearly doubled into the form of a hoop, so he must try to imitate a hoop by stooping forwards and ducking down his head. And as finally, the boy had won a round of plaudits for the manner in which he kept each muscle of the body in full exercise whilst dancing, so now the jester, bidding the flute-girl quicken the time (presto! presto! prestissimo!), fell to capering madly, tossing legs and arms and head together, until he was fairly tired out, and threw himself dead beat upon the sofa, gasping: There, that's a proof that my jigs too are splendid exercise; at any rate, I am dying of thirst; let the attendant kindly fill me the mighty goblet.

Quite right, said Callias, and we will pledge you. Our throats are parched with laughing at you.

At this point Socrates: Nay, gentlemen, if drinking is

the order of the day, I heartily approve. Wine it is in very truth that moistens the soul of man, that lulls at once all cares to sleep, even as mandragora drugs our human senses, and at the same time kindles light-hearted thoughts, as oil a flame. Yet it fares with the banquets of men, if I mistake not, precisely as with plants that spring and shoot on earth. When god gives these vegetable growths too full a draught of rain, they cannot lift their heads nor feel the light air breathe through them; but if they drink in only the glad supply they need, they stand erect, they shoot apace, and reach maturity of fruitage. So we, too, if we drench our throats with over-copious draughts, ere long may find our legs begin to reel and our thoughts begin to falter; we shall scarce be able to draw breath, much less to speak a word in season. But if (to borrow language from the mint of Gorgias), if only the attendants will bedew us with a frequent mizzle of small glasses, we shall not be violently driven on by wine to drunkenness, but with sweet seduction reach the goal of sportive levity.

The proposition was unanimously carried, with a rider appended by Philippus: the cup-bearers should imitate good charioteers, and push the cups round, quickening the pace each circuit.

During this interval, whilst the cup-bearers carried out their duties, the boy played on the lyre tuned to accompany the flute, and sang. The performance won the plaudits of the company, and drew from Charmides a speech as follows: Sirs, what Socrates was claiming in behalf of wine applies in my opinion no less aptly to the present composition. So rare a blending of boyish and of girlish beauty, and of voice with instrument, is potent to lull sorrow to sleep, and to kindle Aphrodite's flame.

Then Socrates, reverting in a manner to the charge: The young people have fully proved their power to give us pleasure. Yet, charming as they are, we still regard ourselves, no doubt, as much their betters. What a shame to think that we should here be met together, and yet make no effort ourselves to heighten the festivity!

Several of the company exclaimed at once: Be our director then yourself. Explain what style of talk we should engage in to achieve that object.

Nothing, he replied, would please me better than to demand of Callias a prompt performance of his promise. He told us, you recollect, if we would dine with him, he would give us an exhibition of his wisdom.

To which challenge Callias: That I will readily, but you on your side, one and all, must propound some virtue of which you claim to have the knowledge.

Socrates replied: At any rate, not one of us will have the least objection to declaring what particular thing he claims to know as best worth having.

Agreed, proceeded Callias; and for my part I proclaim at once what I am proudest of. My firm belief is, I have got the gift to make my fellow-mortals better.

Make men better! cried Antisthenes; and pray how? By teaching them some base mechanic art? Or teaching them nobility of soul?

The latter, he replied, if justice be synonymous with that high type of virtue.

Of course it is, rejoined Antisthenes, the most indisputable specimen. Since, look you, courage and wisdom may at times be found calamitous to friends or country, but justice has no single point in common with injustice, right and wrong cannot commingle.

Well then, proceeded Callias, as soon as every one has stated his peculiar merit, I will make no bones of letting you into my secret. You shall learn the art by which I consummate my noble end. So now, Niceratus, suppose you tell us on what knowledge you most pride yourself.

He answered: My father, in his pains to make me a good man, compelled me to learn the whole of Homer's poems, and it so happens that even now I can repeat the *Iliad* and the *Odyssey* by heart.

You have not forgotten, interposed Antisthenes, perhaps, that besides yourself there is not a rhapsodist who does not know these epics?

Forgotten! Is it likely, he replied, considering I had to listen to them almost daily?

ANTISTHENES: And did you ever come across a sillier tribe of people than these same rhapsodists?

NICERATUS: Not I, indeed. Don't ask me to defend their wits.

It is plain, suggested Socrates, they do not know the underlying meaning. But you, Niceratus, have paid large sums of money to Anaximander, and Stesimbrotus, and many others, so that no single point in all that costly lore is lost upon you. But what, he added, turning to Critobulus, do you most pride yourself upon?

On beauty, answered Critobulus.

What, Socrates rejoined, shall you be able to maintain that by your beauty you can make us better?

CRITOBULUS: That will I, or prove myself a shabby sort of person.

SOCRATES: Well, and what is it you pride yourself upon, Antisthenes?

On wealth, he answered.

Whereupon Hermogenes inquired: had he then a large amount of money?

Not one sixpence: that I swear to you, he answered.

HERMOGENES: Then you possess large property in land?

ANTISTHENES: Enough, I daresay, for the youngster there, Autolycus, to dust himself withal.

Well, we will lend you our ears, when your turn comes, exclaimed the others.

SOCRATES: And do you now tell us, Charmides, on what you pride yourself.

Oh, I, for my part, pride myself on poverty, he answered.

Upon my word, a charming business! exclaimed Socrates. Poverty! Of all things the least liable to envy; seldom, if ever, an object of contention; never guarded, yet always safe; the more you starve it, the stronger it grows.

And you, Socrates, yourself, their host demanded, what is it you pride yourself upon?

Then he, with knitted brows, quite solemnly: On pandering. And when they laughed to hear him say this, he continued: Laugh to your hearts' content, my friends; but I am certain I could make a fortune, if I chose to practise this same art.

At this point Lycon, turning to Philippus: We need not ask you what you take the chiefest pride in. What can it be, you laughter-making man, except to set folk laughing?

Yes, he answered, and with better right, I fancy, than Callippides, the actor, who struts and gives himself such pompous airs, to think that he alone can set the crowds a-weeping in the theatre.

And now you, Lycon, tell us, won't you, asked Antisthenes, what it is you take the greatest pride in?

You all of you, I fancy, know already what that is, the father answered; it is in my son here.

And the lad himself, someone suggested, doubtless prides himself, beyond all else, on having won the prize of victory.

At that Autolycus (and as he spoke he blushed) answered for himself: No indeed, not I.

The company were charmed to hear him speak, and turned and looked; and someone asked: On what is it then, Autolycus?

To which he answered: On my father (and leaned closer towards him).

At which sight Callias, turning to the father: Do you know you are the richest man in the whole world, Lycon?

To which Lycon: Really, I was not aware of that before.

Then Callias: Why then, it has escaped you that you would refuse the whole of Persia's wealth, in exchange for your own son.

Most true, he answered, I plead guilty; here and now I am convicted of being the wealthiest man in all the world!

And you, Hermogenes, on what do you plume yourself most highly? asked Niceratus.

On the virtue and the power of my friends, he answered, and that being what they are, they care for me.

At this remark they turned their eyes upon the speaker, and several spoke together, asking: Will you make them known to us?

I shall be very happy, he replied.

At this point, Socrates took up the conversation: It now devolves on us to prove in turn that what we each have undertaken to defend is really valuable.

Then Callias: Be pleased to listen to me first. My

case is this, that while the rest of you go on debating what justice and uprightness are, I spend my time in making men more just and upright.

SOCRATES: And how do you do that, good sir?

CALLIAS: By giving money, to be sure.

Antisthenes sprang to his feet at once, and with the manner of a cross-examiner demanded: Do human beings seem to you to harbour justice in their souls, or in their purses, Callias?

CALLIAS: In their souls.

ANTISTHENES: And do you pretend to make their souls more righteous by putting money in their pockets?

CALLIAS: Undoubtedly.

ANTISTHENES: Pray how?

CALLIAS: In this way. When they know that they are furnished with the means, that is to say, my money, to buy necessaries, they would rather not incur the risk of evil-doing, and why should they?

ANTISTHENES: And pray, do they repay you these same moneys?

CALLIAS: I cannot say they do.

ANTISTHENES: Well then, do they requite your gifts of gold with gratitude?

CALLIAS: No, not so much as a bare 'Thank you'. In fact, some of them are even worse disposed towards me when they have got my money than before.

Now, here's a marvel! exclaimed Antisthenes, and as he spoke he eyed the witness with an air of triumph. You can render people just to all the world, but towards yourself you cannot?

Pray, where's the wonder? asked the other. Do you not see what scores of carpenters and house-builders there are who spend their time in building houses for half the world; but for themselves they simply cannot do it, and are forced to live in lodgings. And so admit that home-thrust, Master Sophist; and confess yourself confuted.

Upon my soul, he had best accept his fate, said Socrates.

Why, after all, you are only like those prophets who proverbially foretell the future for mankind, but cannot foresee what is coming upon themselves.

And so the first discussion ended.

Thereupon Niceratus: Lend me your ears, and I will tell you in what respects you shall be better for consorting with myself. I presume, without my telling you, you know that Homer, being the wisest of mankind, has touched upon nearly every human topic in his poems. Whosoever among you, therefore, would fain be skilled in economy, or oratory, or strategy; whose ambition it is to be like Achilles, or Ajax, Nestor, or Odysseus – one and all pay court to me, for I have all this knowledge at my fingers' ends.

Pray, interposed Antisthenes, do you also know the way to be a king? Since Homer praises Agamemnon, you are well aware, as being 'a goodly king and eke a spearman bold'.

NICERATUS: Full well I know it, and full well I know the duty of a skilful charioteer; how he who holds the ribbons must turn his chariot nigh the pillar's edge: 'Himself inclined upon the polished chariot-board a little to the left of the twin pair: the right hand horse touch with the prick, and shout a cheery shout, and give him rein.'

I know another thing besides, and you may put it to the test this instant, if you like. Homer somewhere has said: 'And at his side an onion, which to drink gives relish'.

So if someone will but bring an onion, you shall reap the benefit of my sage lore in less than no time, and your wine will taste the sweeter.

Here Charmides exclaimed: Good sirs, let me explain. Niceratus is anxious to go home redolent of onions, so that his fair lady may persuade herself, it never entered into anybody's head to kiss her lord.

Bless me, that isn't all, continued Socrates; if we do not take care, we shall win ourselves a comic reputation. A relish must it be, in very truth, that can sweeten cup as well as platter, this same onion; and if we are to take to munching onions for desert, see if somebody does not say of us, 'They went to dine with Callias, and got more than their deserts, the epicures.'

No fear of that, rejoined Niceratus. Always take a bite of onion before speeding forth to battle, just as your patrons of the cock-pit give their birds a feed of garlic before they put them for the fight. But for ourselves our thoughts are less intent perhaps on dealing blows than blowing kisses.

After such sort the theme of their discourse reached its conclusion.

Then Critobulus spoke: It is now my turn, I think, to state to you the grounds on which I pride myself on beauty.

A chorus of voices rejoined: Say on.

CRITOBULUS: To begin with, if I am not beautiful, as methinks I be, you will bring on your own heads the penalty of perjury; for, without waiting to have the oath administered, you are always taking the gods to witness that you find me beautiful. And I must needs believe you, for are you not all honourable men? If I then be so beautiful and affect you, even as I also am affected by him whose fair face here attracts me, I swear by all the company of heaven I would not choose the great king's empire in exchange for what I am – the beauty of the world, the paragon of animals. And at this instant I feast my eyes on Cleinias gladlier than on all other sights which men deem fair. Joyfully will I welcome blindness to all else, if but these eyes may still behold him and him only. With sleep and night I am sore vexed, which rob me of his sight; but to daylight and the sun I owe eternal thanks, for they restore him to me, my heart's joy, Cleinias.

Yes, and herein also have we, the beautiful, just claim to boast. The strong man may by dint of toil obtain good things; the brave, by danger boldly faced, and the wise by eloquence of speech; but to the beautiful alone it is given to achieve all ends in absolute quiescence. To take myself as an example. I know that riches are a sweet possession, yet sweeter far to me to give all that I have to Cleinias than to receive a fortune from another. Gladly would I become a slave – ay, forfeit freedom – if Cleinias would deign to be my lord. Toil in his service were easier for me than rest from labour: danger incurred in his behalf far sweeter than security of days. So that if you, Callias, may boast of making men more just and upright, to me belongs by juster right than yours to train mankind to every excellence. We are the true inspirers who infuse some subtle fire into amorous souls, we beauties, and thereby raise them to new heights of being; we render them more liberal in the pursuit of wealth; we give them a zest for toil that mocks at danger, and enables them where honour the fair vision leads, to follow. We fill their souls with deeper modesty, a self-constraint more staunch; about the things they care for most, there floats a halo of protecting awe. Fools and unwise are they who choose not beauteous men to be their generals. How merrily would I, at any rate, march through fire by the side of Cleinias; and so would all of you, I know full well, in company of him who now addresses you.

Cease therefore your perplexity, O Socrates, abandon fears and doubts, believe and know that this thing of which I make great boast, my beauty, has power to confer some benefit on humankind. Once more, let no man dare dishonour beauty, merely because the flower of it soon fades, since even as a child has growth in beauty, so is it with the stripling, the grown man, the reverend senior. And this the proof of my contention. Whom do we choose to bear the sacred olive-shoot in honour of Athena? Whom else save beautiful old men? Witnessing thereby that beauty walks hand in hand as a companion with every age of life, from infancy to eld. Or again, if it be sweet to win from willing hearts the things we seek for, I am persuaded that, by the eloquence of silence, I could win a kiss from yonder girl or boy more speedily than ever you could, O sage, by help of half a hundred subtle arguments.

Eh, bless my ears, what's that? Socrates broke in upon this final flourish of the speaker. So beautiful you claim to rival me, you boaster?

CRITOBULUS: Why, yes indeed, I hope so, or else I should be uglier than all the Silenuses in the Satyric drama.

Good! Socrates rejoined; the moment the programme of discussion is concluded, please remember, we must obtain a verdict on the point of beauty. Judgment shall be given – not at the bar of Alexander, son of Priam – but of these who, as you flatter yourself, have such a hankering to kiss you.

Oh, Socrates, he answered, deprecatingly, will you not leave it to the arbitrament of Cleinias?

Then Socrates: Will you never tire of repeating that one name? It is Cleinias here, there, and everywhere with you.

CRITOBULUS: And if his name died on my lips, think you my mind would less recall his memory? Know you not, I bear so clear an image of him in my soul, that had I the sculptor's or the limner's skill, I might portray his features as exactly from this image of the mind as from contemplation of his actual self.

But Socrates broke in: Pray, why then, if you bear about this lively image, why do you give me so much trouble, dragging me to this and that place, where you hope to see him?

CRITOBULUS: For this good reason, Socrates: the sight of him inspires gladness, whilst his phantom brings not joy so much as it engenders longing.

At this point Hermogenes protested: I find it most unlike you, Socrates, to treat thus negligently one so passion-crazed as Critobulus.

Socrates replied: Do you suppose the sad condition of the patient dates from the moment only of our intimacy?

HERMOGENES: Since when, then?

SOCRATES: Since when? Why, look at him: the down begins to mantle on his cheeks, and on the nape of Cleinias' neck already mounts. The fact is, when they fared to the same school together, he caught the fever. This his father was aware of, and consigned him to me, hoping I might be able to do something for him. Ay, and his plight is not so sorry now. Once he would stand agape at him like one whose gaze is fixed upon the Gorgons, his eyes one stony stare, and like a stone

461

himself turn heavily away. But nowadays I have seen the statue actually blink. And yet, may Heaven help me! My good sirs, I think, between ourselves, the culprit must have bestowed a kiss on Cleinias, than which love's flame asks no fiercer fuel. So insatiable a thing it is and so suggestive of mad fantasy (and for this reason held perhaps in higher honour, because of all external acts the close of lip with lip bears the same name as that of soul with soul in love). Wherefore, say I, let everyone who wishes to be master of himself and sound of soul abstain from kisses imprinted on fair lips.

Then Charmides: Oh! Socrates, why will you scare your friends with these hobgoblin terrors, bidding us all beware of handsome faces, whilst you yourself – yes, by Apollo, I will swear I saw you at the school master's that time when both of you were poring over one book, in which you searched for something, you and Critobulus, head to head, shoulder to shoulder bare, as if incorporate?

As yes, alack the day! he answered; and that is why, no doubt, my shoulder ached for more than five days afterwards, as if I had been bitten by some fell beast, and methought I felt a sort of scraping at the heart. Now therefore, in the presence of these witnesses, I warn you, Critobulus, never again to touch me till you wear as thick a crop of hair upon your chin as on your head.

So pell-mell they went at it, half jest half earnest, and so the medley ended. Callias here called on Charmides: Now, Charmides, it lies with you to tell us why you pride yourself on poverty.

Charmides responded: On all hands it is admitted, I believe, that confidence is better than alarm; better to be a freeman than a slave; better to be worshipped than pay court to others; better to be trusted than to be

suspected by one's country. Well now, I will tell you
how it fared with me in this same city when I was
wealthy. First, I lived in daily terror lest some burglar
should break into my house and steal my goods and do
myself some injury. I cringed before informers. I was
obliged to pay these people court, because I knew that
I could injure them far less than they could injure me.
Never-ending the claims upon my pocket which the
state enforced upon me; and as to setting foot abroad,
that was beyond the range of possibility. But now that I
have lost my property across the frontier, and derive no
income from my lands in Attica itself; now that my very
household goods have been sold up, I stretch my legs at
ease, I get a good night's rest. The distrust of my fellow-
citizens has vanished; instead of trembling at threats, it
is now my turn to threaten; at last I feel myself a
freeman, with liberty to go abroad or stay at home as
suits my fancy. The tables now are turned. It is the rich
who rise to give me their seats, who stand aside and
make way for me as I meet them in the streets. Today
I am like a despot, yesterday I was literally a slave;
formerly it was I who had to pay my tribute to the
sovereign people, now it is I who am supported by the
state by means of general taxation.

And there is another thing. So long as I was rich,
they threw in my teeth as a reproach that I was friends
with Socrates, but now that I am become a beggar no
one troubles his head two straws about the matter.
Once more, the while I rolled in plenty I had everything to lose, and, as a rule, I lost it; what the state did
not exact, some mischance stole from me. But now
that is over. I lose nothing, having nought to lose; but,
on the contrary, I have everything to gain, and live in
hope of some day getting something.

CALLIAS: And so, of course, your one prayer is that you may never more be rich, and if you are visited by a dream of luck your one thought is to offer sacrifice to heaven to avert misfortune.

CHARMIDES: No, that I do not. On the contrary, I run my head into each danger most adventurously. I endure, if haply I may see a chance of getting something from some quarter of the sky some day.

Come now, Socrates exclaimed, it lies with you, sir, you, Antisthenes, to explain to us, how it is that you, with means so scanty, make so loud a boast of wealth.

Because, he answered, I hold to the belief, sirs, that wealth and poverty do not lie in a man's estate, but in men's souls. Even in private life how many scores of people have I seen, who, although they roll in wealth, yet deem themselves so poor, there is nothing they will shrink from, neither toil nor danger, in order to add a little to their store. I have known two brothers, heirs to equal fortunes, one of whom has enough, more than enough, to cover his expenditure; the other is in absolute indigence. And so to monarchs; there are not a few, I perceive, so ravenous of wealth that they will outdo the veriest vagrants in atrocity. Want prompts a thousand crimes, you must admit. Why do men steal? Why break burglariously into houses? Why hale men and women captive and make slaves of them? Is it not from want? Nay, there are monarchs who at one fell swoop destroy whole houses, make wholesale massacre, and oftentimes reduce entire states to slavery, and all for the sake of wealth. These I must needs pity for the cruel malady which plagues them. Their condition, to my mind, resembles that poor creature's who, in spite of all he has and all he eats, can never stay the wolf that gnaws his vitals.

But as to me, my riches are so plentiful I cannot lay my hands on them myself; yet for all that I have enough to eat till my hunger is stayed, to drink till my thirst is sated; to clothe myself withal; and out of doors not Callias there, with all his riches, is more safe than I from shivering; and when I find myself indoors, what warmer shirting do I need than my bare walls? What ampler greatcoat than the tiles above my head? These seem to suit me well enough; and as to bedclothes, I am not so ill supplied but it is a business to arouse me in the morning. And as to sexual desire, my body's need is satisfied by what comes first to hand. Indeed, there is no lack of warmth in the caress which greets me, just because it is unsought by others. Well then, these several pleasures I enjoy so fully that I am much more apt to pray for less than more of them, so strongly do I feel that some of them are sweeter than what is good for one or profitable.

But of all the precious things in my possession, I reckon this the choicest, that were I robbed of my whole present stock, there is no work so mean, but it would amply serve me to furnish me with sustenance. Why, look you, whenever I desire to fare delicately, I have not to purchase precious viands in the market, which becomes expensive, but I open the storehouse of my soul, and dole them out. Indeed, as far as pleasure goes, I find it better to await desire before I suffer meat or drink to pass my lips, than to have recourse to any of your costly viands, as, for instance, now, when I have chanced on this fine Thasian wine, and sip it without thirst. But indeed, the man who makes frugality, not wealth of worldly goods, his aim, is on the face of it a much more upright person. And why? The man who is content with what he has will least of all be prone to clutch at what is his neighbour's.

And here's a point worth noting. Wealth of my sort will make you liberal of soul. Look at Socrates; from him it was I got these riches. He did not supply me with it by weight or by measure, but just as much as I could carry, he with bounteous hand consigned to me. And I, too, grudge it to no man now. To all my friends without distinction I am ready to display my opulence: come one, come all; and whosoever likes to take a share is welcome to the wealth that lies within my soul. Yes, and moreover, that most luxurious of possessions, unbroken leisure, you can see, is mine, which leaves me free to contemplate things worthy of contemplation, and to drink in with my ears all charming sounds. And what I value most, freedom to spend whole days in pure scholastic intercourse with Socrates, to whom I am devoted. And he, on his side, is not the person to admire those whose tale of gold and silver happens to be the largest, but those who are well-pleasing to him he chooses for companions, and will consort with to the end.

With these words the speaker ended, and Callias exclaimed: By Hera, I envy you your wealth, Antisthenes, firstly, because the state does not lay burthens on you and treat you like a slave; and secondly, people do not fall into a rage with you when you refuse to be their creditor.

You may stay your envy, interposed Niceratus. I shall presently present myself to borrow of him this same key of his to independence. Trained as I am to cast up figures by my master Homer – 'Seven tripods, which ne'er felt the fire, and of gold ten talents and burnished braziers twenty, and horses twelve – by weight and measure duly reckoned, I cannot stay my craving for enormous wealth.' And that's the reason certain people, I daresay, imagine I am inordinately fond of riches.

The remark drew forth a peal of laughter from the company, who thought the speaker hit the truth exactly. Then someone: It lies with you, Hermogenes, to tell us who your friends are; and next, to demonstrate the greatness of their power and their care for you, if you would prove to us your right to pride yoruself on them.

HERMOGENES: That the gods know all things, that the present and the future lie before their eyes, are tenets held by Hellenes and barbarians alike. This is obvious; or else, why do states and nations, one and all, inquire of the gods by divination what they ought to do and what they ought not? This also is apparent, that we believe them able to do us good and to do us harm; or why do all men pray to heaven to avert the evil and bestow the good? Well then, my boast is that these gods, who know and can do all things, deign to be my friends; so that, by reason of their care for me, I can never escape from their sight, neither by night nor by day, whithersoever I essay to go, whatsoever I take in hand to do. But because they know beforehand the end and issue of each event, they give me signals, sending messengers, be it some voice, or vision of the night, with omens of the solitary bird, which tell me what I should and what I should not do. When I listen to their warnings all goes well with me, I have no reason to repent; but if, as ere now has been the case, I have been disobedient, chastisement has overtaken me.

Then Socrates: All this I well believe, but there is one thing I would gladly learn of you: What service do you pay the gods, so to secure their friendship?

Truly it is not a ruinous service, Socrates, he answered – far from it. I give them thanks, which is not costly. I make return to them of all they give to me from time to time. I speak well of them, with all the strength I have. And whenever I take their sacred names to witness, I do not wittingly falsify my word.

Then god be praised, said Socrates, if being what you are, you have such friends; the gods themselves, it would appear, delight in nobleness of soul.

Thus, in solemn sort, the theme was handled, thus gravely ended. But now it was the jester's turn, and so they fell to asking him: what could he see to pride himself upon so vastly in the art of making people laugh?

Surely I have good reason, he replied. The whole world knows my business is to set them laughing, so when they are in luck's way, they eagerly invite me to a share of it; but if ill betide them, helter-skelter off they go, and never once turn back, so fearful are they I may set them laughing will he nill he.

NICERATUS: Heavens! you have good reason to be proud; with me it is just the opposite. When any of my friends are doing well, they take good care to turn their backs on me, but if ever it goes ill with them, they claim relationship by birth, and will not let their long-lost cousin out of sight.

CHARMIDES: Well, well! And you, sir (turning to the Syracusan), what do you pride yourself upon? No doubt, upon the boy?

THE SYRACUSAN: Not I, indeed; I am terribly afraid concerning him. It is plain enough to me that certain people are contriving for his ruin.

Good gracious! Socrates exclaimed, when he heard that, what crime can they conceive your boy is guilty of that they should wish to make an end of him?

THE SYRACUSAN: I do not say they want to murder him, but wheedle him away with bribes to pass his nights with them.

SOCRATES: And if that happened, you on your side, it appears, believe the boy will be corrupted?

THE SYRACUSAN: Beyond all shadow of a doubt, most villainously.

SOCRATES: And you, of course, never dream of such a thing. You don't spend nights with him?

THE SYRACUSAN: Of course I do, all night and every night.

SOCRATES: By Hera, what a mighty piece of luck for you – to be so happily compounded, of such flesh and blood. You alone can't injure those who sleep beside you. You have every right, it seems, to boast of your own flesh, if nothing else.

THE SYRACUSAN: Nay, in sooth, it is not on that I pride myself.

SOCRATES: Well, on what then?

THE SYRACUSAN: Why, on the silly fools who come and see my puppet show. I live on them.

PHILIPPUS: Ah yes! And that explains how the other day I heard you praying to the gods to grant you, wheresoe'er you chance to be, great store of corn and wine, but dearth of wits.

Pass on, said Callias; now it is your turn, Socrates. What have you to say to justify your choice? How can you boast of so discredited an art?

He answered: Let us first decide what are the duties of the good go-between; and please to answer every question without hesitating; let us know the points to which we mutually assent. Are you agreed to that?

THE COMPANY, IN CHORUS: Without a doubt (*and the formula, once started, was every time repeated by the company, full chorus*).

SOCRATES: Are you agreed it is the business of a good go-between to make him (or her) on whom he plies his art agreeable to those with them?

OMNES: Without a doubt.

SOCRATES: And, further, that towards agreeableness, one step at any rate consists in wearing a becoming fashion of the hair and dress? Are you agreed to that?

OMNES: Without a doubt.

SOCRATES: And we know for certain, that with the same eyes a man may dart a look of love or else of hate on those he sees. Are you agreed?

OMNES: Without a doubt.

SOCRATES: Well! And with the same tongue and lips and voice may speak with modesty or boastfulnes?

OMNES: Without a doubt.

SOCRATES: And there are words that bear the stamp of hate, and words that tend to friendliness?

OMNES: Without a doubt.

SOCRATES: The good go-between will therefore make his choice between them, and teach only what conduces to agreeableness?

OMNES: Without a doubt.

SOCRATES: And is he the better go-between who can make his clients pleasing to one person only, or can make them pleasing to a number?

The company was here divided; the one half answered, Yes, of course, the largest number, whilst the others still maintained, Without a doubt.

And Socrates, remarking, That proposition is agreed to also, thus proceeded: And if further he were able to make them pleasing to the whole community, should we not have found in this accomplished person an arch-go-between?

Clearly so, they answered with one voice.

SOCRATES: If then a man had power to make his clients altogether pleasing; that man, I say, might justly pride himself upon his art, and should by rights receive a large reward? And when these propositions were agreed to also, he turned about and said: Just such a man, I take it, is before you in the person of Antisthenes.

Whereupon Antisthenes exclaimed: What! Are you going to pass on the business? Will you devolve this art of yours on me as your successor, Socrates?

I will, upon my word, I will, he answered: since I see that you have practised to some purpose, nay elaborated, an art which is the handmaid to this other.

And what may that be? asked Antisthenes.

SOCRATES: The art of the procurer.

THE OTHER [*in a tone of deep vexation*]: Pray, what thing of the sort are you aware I ever perpetrated?

SOCRATES: I am aware that it was you who introduced our host here, Callias, to that wise man Prodicus; they were a match, you saw, the one enamoured of philosophy, and the other in need of money. It was you again, I am well enough aware, who introduced him once again to Hippias of Elis, from whom he learnt his 'art of memory'; since which time he has become a very ardent lover, from inability to forget each lovely thing he sets his eyes on. And quite lately, if I am not mistaken, it was you who sounded in my ears such praise of our visitor from Heraclea, that first you made me thirst for his society, and then united us. For which indeed I am your debtor, since I find him a fine handsome fellow and true gentleman. And did you not, moreover, sing the praises of Aeschylus of Phlius in my ears and mine in his? In fact, affected us so much by what you said, we fell in love and took to coursing wildly in pursuit of one another like two dogs upon a trail.

With such examples of your wonder-working skill before my eyes, I must suppose you are a first-rate matchmaker. For consider, a man with insight to discern two natures made to be of service to each other, and with power to make these same two people mutually enamoured! That is the sort of man, I take it, who should weld together states in friendship; cement alliances with gain to the contracting parties; and, in general, be found an acquisition to those several states; to friends and intimates, and partisans in war, a treasure worth possessing. But you, my friend, you got quite angry. One would suppose I had given you an evil name in calling you a first-rate matchmaker.

Yes, he answered meekly, but now I am calm. It is clear enough, if I possess these powers I shall find myself surcharged with spiritual riches.

In this fashion the cycle of the speeches was completed.

Then Callias: Our eyes are on you, Critobulus. Yours to enter the lists against the champion Socrates, who claims the prize of beauty. Do you hesitate?

SOCRATES: Likely enough he does, for possibly he sees Sir Pandarus stands high in their esteem who are the judges of the contest.

In spite of which, retorted Critobulus, I am not for drawing back. I am ready; so come on, and if you have any subtle argument to prove that you are handsomer than I am, now's your time, instruct us. But just stop one minute; have the goodness, please, to bring the lamp a little closer.

SOCRATES: Well then, I call upon you first of all, as party to this suit, to undergo the preliminary examination. Attend to what I say, and please be good enough to answer.

CRITOBULUS: Do you be good enough yourself to put your questions.

SOCRATES: Do you consider that the quality of beauty is confined to man, or is it to be found in other objects also? What is your belief on this point?

CRITOBULUS: For my part, I consider it belongs alike to animals – the horse, the ox – and to many things inanimate: that is to say, a shield, a sword, a spear are often beautiful.

SOCRATES: How is it possible that things, in no respect resembling one another, should each and all be beautiful?

CRITOBULUS: Of course it is, god bless me! If well constructed by the hand of man to suit the sort of work for which we got them, or if naturally adapted to satisfy some want, the things in either case are beautiful.

SOCRATES: Can you tell me, then, what need is satisfied by our eyes?

CRITOBULUS: Clearly, the need of vision.

SOCRATES: If so, my eyes are proved at once to be more beautiful than yours.

CRITOBULUS: How so?

SOCRATES: Because yours can only see just straight in front of them, whereas mine are prominent and so projecting, they can see aslant.

CRITOBULUS: And amongst all animals, you will tell us that the crab has loveliest eyes? Is that your statement?

SOCRATES: Decidedly, the creature has. And all the more so, since for strength and toughness its eyes by nature are the best constructed.

CRITOBULUS: Well, let that pass. To come to our two noses, which is the more handsome, yours or mine?

SOCRATES: Mine, I imagine, if, that is, the gods presented us with noses for the sake of smelling. Your nostrils point to earth; but mine are spread out wide and flat, as if to welcome scents from every quarter.

CRITOBULUS: But consider, a snubness of the nose, how is that more beautiful than straightness?

Socrates. For this good reason, that a snub nose does not discharge the office of a barrier; it allows the orbs of sight free range of vision: whilst your towering nose looks like an insulting wall of partition to shut off the two eyes.

As to the mouth, proceeded Critobulus, I give in at once; for, given mouths are made for purposes of biting, you could doubtless bite off a much larger mouthful with your mouth than I with mine.

SOCRATES: Yes, and you will admit, perhaps, that I can give a softer kiss than you can, thanks to my thick lips.

CRITOBULUS: It seems I have an uglier mouth than any ass.

SOCRATES: And here is a fact which you will have to reckon with, if further evidence be needed to prove that I am handsomer than you. The naiads, nymphs divine, have as their progeny Sileni, who are much more like myself, I take it, than like you. Is that conclusive?

Nay, I give it up, cried Critobulus, I have not a word to say in answer. I am silenced. Let them record the votes. I fain would know at once what I must suffer or must pay. Only, he added, let them vote in secret. I am afraid your wealth and his (Antisthenes') combined may overpower me.

Accordingly the boy and girl began to register the votes in secret, while Socrates directed the proceedings. He would have the lamp-stand this time brought close up to Critobulus; the judges must on no account be taken in; the victor in the suit would get from the two judges, not a wreath of ribands for a chaplet, but some kisses. When the urns were emptied, it was found that every vote, without exception, had been cast for Critobulus.

Whereat Socrates: Bless me! You don't say so? The coin you deal in, Critobulus, is not at all like that of Callias. His makes people just; whilst yours, like other filthy lucre, can corrupt both judge and jury.

Thereupon some members of the party called on Critobulus to accept the meed of victory in kisses (due from boy and girl); others urged him first to bribe their master; whilst others bandied other jests. Amidst the general hilarity Hermogenes alone kept silence. Whereat Socrates turned to the silent man, and thus accosted him: Hermogenes, what is a drunken brawl? Can you explain to us?

He answered: If you ask me what it is, I do not know, but I can tell you what it seems to me to be.
SOCRATES: That seems as good. What does it seem?
HERMOGENES: A drunken brawl, in my poor judgment, is annoyance caused to people over wine.
SOCRATES: Are you aware that you at present are annoying us by silence?
HERMOGENES: What, whilst you are talking?
SOCRATES: No, when we pause a while.
HERMOGENES: Then you have not observed that, as to

any interval between your talk, a man would find it hard to insert a hair, much more one grain of sense.

Then Socrates: O Callias, to the rescue! Help a man severely handled by his cross-examiner.

CALLIAS: With all my heart (and as he spoke he faced Hermogenes). Why, when the flute is talking, we are as silent as the grave.

HERMOGENES: What, would you have me imitate Nicostratus the actor, reciting his tetrameters to the music of the fife? Must I discourse to you in answer to the flute?

Then Socrates: By all that's holy, I wish you would, Hermogenes. How delightful it would be. Just as a song sounds sweeter in concert with the flute, so would your talk be more mellifluous attuned to its soft pipings; and particularly if you would use gesticulation like the flute-girl, to suit the tenor of your speech.

Here Callias demanded: And when our friend (Antisthenes) essays to cross-examine people at a banquet, what kind of piping should he have?

ANTISTHENES: The person in the witness-box would best be suited with a serpent-hissing theme.

Thus the stream of talk flowed on; until the Syracusan, who was painfully aware that while the company amused themselves, his 'exhibition' was neglected, turned, in a fit of jealous spleen, at last on Socrates.

THE SYRACUSAN: They call you Socrates. Are you that person commonly nicknamed the thinker?

SOCRATES: Which surely is a better fate than to be called a thoughtless person?

THE SYRACUSANN: Perhaps, if you were not thought to split your brains on things above us – transcendental stuff.

SOCRATES: And is there anything more transcendental than the gods?

THE SYRACUSAN: By heaven! no, it is not the gods above us whom you care for, but for matters void of use and valueless.

SOCRATES: It seems, then, by your showing I do care for them. How value less the gods, not more, if being above us they make the void of use to send us rain, and cause their light to shine on us? And now, sir, if you do not like this frigid argument, why do you cause me trouble? The fault is yours.

Well, let that be, the other answered; answer me one question: How many fleas' feet distance is it, pray, from you to me? They say you measure them by geometric scale.

But here Antisthenes, appealing to Philippus, interposed: You are a man full of comparisons. Does not this worthy person strike you as somewhat like a bully seeking to pick a quarrel?

Yes, replied the jester, he has a striking likeness to that person and a heap of others. He bristles with metaphors.

SOCRATES: For all that, do not you be too eager to draw comparisons at his expense, or you will find yourself the image of a scold and brawler.

PHILIPPUS: But what if I compare him to all the primest creatures of the world, to beauty's nonpareils, to nature's best – I might be justly likened to a flatterer but not a brawler.

SOCRATES: Why now, you are like a person apt to pick a quarrel, since you imply they are all his betters.

PHILIPPUS: What, would you have me then compare him to worse villains?

SOCRATES: No, not even to worse villains.

PHILIPPUS: What, then, to nothing, and to nobody?

SOCRATES: To nought in aught. Let him remain his simple self –

PHILIPPUS: Incomparable. But if my tongue is not to wag, whatever shall I do to earn my dinner?

SOCRATES: Why, that you shall quite easily, if with your wagging tongue you do not try to utter things unutterable.

Here was a pretty quarrel over wine soon kindled and soon burnt.

But on the instant those who had not assisted in the fray gave tongue, the one part urging the jester to proceed with his comparisons, and the other part dissuading. The voice of Socrates was heard above the tumult: Since we are all so eager to be heard at once, what fitter time than now to sing a song, in chorus. And suiting the action to the words, he commenced a stave.

The song was barely finished, when a potter's wheel was brought in, on which the dancing-girl was to perform more wonders. At this point Socrates addressed the man of Syracuse: It seems I am likely to deserve the title which you gave me of a thinker in good earnest. Just now I am speculating by what means your boy and girl may pass a happy time, and we spectators still derive the greatest pleasure from beholding them; and this, I take it, is precisely what you would yourself most wish. Now I maintain, that throwing somersaults in and out of swords is a display of danger uncongenial to a banquet. And as for writing and reading on a wheel that all the while keeps whirling, I do not deny the wonder of it, but what pleasure such a marvel can present, I cannot for the life of me discover. Nor do I see how it is a whit more charming to watch these fair young people twisting about their bodies and imitating wheels than to behold them peacefully reposing.

We need not fare far afield to light on marvels, if that is our object. All about us here is full of marvel; we can begin at once by wondering, why it is the candle gives a light by dint of its bright flame, while side by side with it the bright bronze vessel gives no light, but shows within itself those other objects mirrored. Or, how is it that oil, being moist and liquid, keeps that flame ablaze, but water, just because it is liquid, quenches fire. But no more do these same marvels tend to promote the object of the wine-cup.

But now, supposing your young people yonder were to tread a measure to the flute, some pantomime in dance, like those which the Graces and the Hours with the Nymphs are made to tread in pictures, I think they would spend a far more happy time themselves, and our banquet would at once assume a grace and charm unlooked for.

The Syracusan caught the notion readily. By all that's holy, Socrates, he cried, a capital suggestion, and for my part, I warrant you, I will put a piece upon the stage, which will delight you, one and all.

With these words the Syracusan made his exit, bent on organising his performance. As soon as he was gone, Socrates once more essayed a novel argument. He thus addressed them: It were but reasonable, sirs, on our part not to ignore the mighty power here present, a divinity in point of age coequal with the everlasting gods, yet in outward form the youngest, who in magnitude embraces all things, and yet his shrine is planted in the soul of man. Love is his name! And least of all should we forget him who are one and all votaries of this god. For myself I cannot name the time at which I have not been in love with someone. And Charmides here has, to my knowledge, captivated many a lover, while his own soul has gone out in longing for the love of not a few himself. So it is with Critobulus also; the beloved of yesterday is become the lover of today. Ay, and Niceratus, as I am told, adores his wife, and is by her adored. As to Hermogenes, which of us needs to be told that the soul of this fond lover is consumed with passion for a fair ideal – call it by what name you will – the spirit blent of nobleness and beauty. See you not what chaste severity dwells on his brow; how tranquil his gaze; how moderate his words; how gentle his intonation; how radiant his whole character. And if he enjoys the friendship of the most holy gods, he keeps a place in his regard for us poor mortals. But how is it that you alone, Antisthenes, you misanthrope, love nobody?

Nay, so help me heaven! he replied, but I do love most desperately yourself, O Socrates!

Whereat Socrates, still carrying on the jest, with a coy, coquettish air, replied: Yes; only please do not bother me at present. I have other things to do, you see.

Antisthenes replied: How absolutely true to your own character, arch go-between! It is always either your familiar oracle won't suffer you, that's your pretext, and so you can't converse with me; or you are bent upon something or somebody else.

Then Socrates: For heaven's sake, don't carbonado me, Antisthenes, that's all. Any other savagery on your part I can stand, and will stand, as a lover should. However (he added), the less we say about your love the better, since it is clearly an attachment not to my soul, but to my lovely person. And then, turning to

Callias: And that you, Callias, do love Autolycus, this whole city knows and half the world besides, if I am not mistaken; and the reason is that you are both sons of famous fathers, and yourselves illustrious. For my part I have ever admired your nature, but now much more so, when I see that you are in love with one who does not wanton in luxury or languish in effeminacy, but who displays to all his strength, his hardihood, his courage, and sobriety of soul. To be enamoured of such qualities as these is a proof itself of a true lover's nature.

Whether indeed Aphrodite be one or twain in personality, the heavenly and the earthly, I cannot tell, for Zeus, who is one and indivisible, bears many titles. But this thing I know, that these twain have separate altars, shrines, and sacrifices, as befits their nature – she that is earthly, of a lighter and a laxer sort; she that is heavenly, purer and holier in type. And you may well conjecture, it is the earthly goddess, the common Aphrodite, who sends forth the bodily loves; while from her that is named of heaven, Ourania, proceed those loves which feed upon the soul, on friendship and on noble deeds. It is by this latter, Callias, that you are held in bonds, if I mistake not, Love divine. This I infer as well from the fair and noble character of your friend, as from the fact that you invite his father to share your life and intercourse, since no part of these is hidden from the father by the fair and noble lover.

Hermogenes broke in: By Hera, Socrates, I much admire you for many things, and now to see how in the act of gratifying Callias you are training him in duty and true excellence.

Why, yes, he said, if only that his cup of happiness may overflow, I wish to testify to him how far the love

of soul is better than the love of body. Without
friendship, as we full well know, there is no society of
any worth. And this friendship, what is it? On the part
of those whose admiration is bestowed upon the inner
disposition, it is well named a sweet and voluntary
compulsion. But among those whose desire is for the
body, there are not a few who blame, nay hate, the ways
of their beloved ones. And even where attachment
clings to both, even so the bloom of beauty after all
does quickly reach its prime; the flower withers, and
when that fails, the affection which was based upon it
must also wither up and perish. But the soul, with
every step she makes in her onward course towards
deeper wisdom, grows ever worthier of love.

Ay, and in the enjoyment of external beauty a sort of
surfeit is engendered. Just as the eater's appetite palls
through repletion with regard to meats, so will the
feelings of a lover towards his idol. But the soul's
attachment, owing to its purity, knows no satiety. Yet
not therefore, as a man might fondly deem, has it less of
the character of loveliness. But very clearly herein is our
prayer fulfilled, in which we beg the goddess to grant us
words and deeds that bear the impress of her own true
loveliness: 'O Love Divine, how sweet thou art! When
shall I find my willing heart all taken up by thee?'

That a soul whose bloom is visible alike in beauty
of external form, free and unfettered, and an inner
disposition, bashful, generous; a spirit at once imperial
and affable, born to rule among its fellows – that such
a being will, of course, admire and fondly cling to his
beloved, is a thesis which needs no further argument
on my part. Rather I will essay to teach you, how it is
natural that this same type of lover should in turn be
loved by his soul's idol. How, in the first place, is it

possible for him to hate a lover who, he knows, regards him as both beautiful and good? And, in the next place, one who, it is clear, is far more anxious to promote the fair estate of him he loves than to indulge his selfish joys? And above all, when he has faith and trust that neither dereliction, nor loss of beauty through sickness, nor aught else, will diminish their affection.

If, then, they own a mutual devotion, how can it but be they will take delight in gazing each into the other's eyes, hold kindly converse, trust and be trusted, have forethought for each other, in success rejoice together, in misfortune share their troubles; and so long as health endures make merry cheer, day in day out; or if either of them should fall on sickness, then will their intercourse be yet more constant; and if they cared for one another face to face, much more will they care when parted. Are not all these the outward tokens of true loveliness? In the exercise of such sweet offices, at any rate, they show their passion for holy friendship's state, and prove its bliss, continuously pacing life's path from youth to eld.

But the lover who depends upon the body, what of him? First, why should love-for-love be given to such a lover? Because, forsooth, he bestows upon himself what he desires, and upon his minion things of dire reproach? Or that what he hastens to exact, infallibly must separate that other from his nearest friends? If it be pleaded that persuasion is his instrument, not violence, is that not reason rather for a deeper loathing, since he who uses violence at any rate declares himself in his true colours as a villain, while the tempter corrupts the soul of him who yields to his persuasions?

Ay, and how should he who traffics with his beauty love the purchaser, any more than he who keeps a stall in the market-place and vends to the highest bidder? Love springs not up, I trow, because the one is in his prime, and the other's bloom is withered, because fair is mated with what is not fair, and hot lips are pressed to cold. Between man and woman it is different. There the wife at any rate shares with her husband in their nuptial joys; but here conversely, the one is sober and with unimpassioned eye regards his fellow, who is drunken with the wine of passion. Wherefore it is no marvel if, beholding, there springs up in his breast the bitterest contempt and scorn for such a lover. Search and you shall find that nothing harsh was ever yet engendered by attachment based on moral qualities; whilst shameless intercourse, time out of mind, has been the source of countless hateful and unhallowed deeds.

I have next to show that the society of him whose love is of the body, not the soul, is in itself illiberal. The true educator who trains another in the path of virtue, who will teach us excellence, whether of speech or conduct, may well be honoured, even as Cheiron and Phoenix were honoured by Achilles. But what can he expect, who stretches forth an eager hand to clutch the body, save to be treated as a beggar? That is his character; for ever cringing and petitioning a kiss, or some other soft caress, this sorry suitor dogs his victims.

If my language has a touch of turbulence, do not marvel: partly the wine exalts me; partly that love which ever dwells within my heart of hearts now pricks me forward to use great boldness of speech against his base antagonist. Why, yes indeed, it seems to me that he who fixes his mind on outward beauty is like a man who has taken a farm on a short lease. He shows no anxiety to improve its value; his sole object being to take off it the largest crops he can himself. But he whose heart is set on loyal friendship resembles rather a man who has a farmstead of his own. At any rate, he scours the wide world to find what may enhance the value of his soul's delight.

Again, let us consider the effect upon the object of attachment. Let him but know his beauty is a bond sufficient to enthrall his lover, and what wonder if he be careless of all else and play the wanton. Let him discover, on the contrary, that if he would retain his dear affection he must himself be truly good and beautiful, and it is only natural he should become more studious of virtue. But the greatest blessing which descends on one beset with eager longing to convert the idol of his soul into a good man and true friend is this: necessity is laid upon himself to practise virtue; since how can he hope to make his comrade good, if he himself works wickedness? Is it conceivable that the example he himself presents of what is shameless and incontinent, will serve to make the beloved one temperate and modest?

I have a longing, Callias, by mythic argument to show you that not men only, but gods and heroes, set greater store by friendship of the soul than bodily enjoyment. Thus those fair women whom Zeus, enamoured of their outward beauty, wedded, he permitted mortal to remain; but those heroes whose souls he held in admiration, these he raised to immortality. Of whom are Heracles and the Dioscuri, and there are others also named. As I maintain, it was not for his body's sake, but for his soul's, that Ganymede was translated to Olympus, as the story goes, by Zeus. And to this his very name bears witness, for is it not written in Homer? 'And he gladdens to hear his voice.' This the poet says, meaning 'he is pleased to listen to his words.'

And again, in another passage he says: 'knowing deep devices in his mind', which is as much as to say, 'knowing wise counsels in his mind'. Ganymede, therefore, bears a name compounded of the two words, 'joy' and 'counsel,' and is honoured among the gods, not as one whose body, but whose mind, gives pleasure.

Furthermore (I appeal to you, Niceratus), Homer makes Achilles avenge Patroclus in that brilliant fashion, not as his favourite, but as his comrade. Yes, and Orestes and Pylades, Theseus and Peirithous, with many another noble pair of demigods, are celebrated as having wrought in common great and noble deeds, not because they lay inarmed, but because of the admiration they felt for one another.

Nay, take the fair deeds of today: and you shall find them wrought rather for the sake of praise by volunteers in toil and peril, than by men accustomed to choose pleasure in place of honour. And yet Pausanias, the lover of the poet Agathon, making a defence in behalf of some who wallow in incontinence, has stated that an army composed of lovers and beloved would be invincible. These, in his opinion, would, from awe of one another, have the greatest horror of destruction. A truly marvellous argument, if he means that men accustomed to turn deaf ears to censure and to behave to one another shamelessly, are more likely to feel ashamed of doing a shameful deed. He adduced as evidence the fact that the Thebans and the Eleians recognise the very principle, and added: Though they sleep inarmed, they do not scruple to range the lover side by side with the beloved one in the field of battle. An instance which I take to be no instance, or at any rate one-sided, seeing that what they look upon as lawful with us is scandalous. Indeed, it strikes me that this vaunted battle-order would seem to argue some mistrust on their part who adopt it – a suspicion that their bosom friends, once separated from them, may forget to behave as brave men should. But the men of Lacedaemon, holding that 'if a man but lay his hand upon the body and for lustful purpose, he shall thereby forfeit claim to what is beautiful and noble' – do, in the spirit of their creed, contrive to mould and fashion their 'beloved ones' to such height of virtue, that should these find themselves drawn up with foreigners, albeit no longer side by side with their own lovers, conscience will make desertion of their present friends impossible. Self-respect constrains them: since the goddess whom the men of Lacedaemon worship is not 'Shamelessness', but 'Reverence'.

I fancy we should all agree with one another on the point in question, if we thus approached it. Ask yourself to which type of the two must he accord, to whom you would entrust a sum of money, make him the guardian of your children, look to find in him a safe and sure depositary of any favour? For my part, I am certain that the very lover addicted to external beauty would himself far sooner have his precious things entrusted to the keeping of one who has the inward beauty of the soul.

Ah, yes! And you, my friend (he turned to Callias), you have good reason to be thankful to the gods who of their grace inspired you with love for your Autolycus. Covetous of honour, beyond all controversy, must he be, who could endure so many toils and pains to hear his name proclaimed victor in the 'pankration'. But what if the thought arose within him: his it is not merely to add lustre to himself and to his father, but that he has ability, through help of manly virtue, to benefit his friends and to exalt his fatherland, by trophies which he will set up against our enemies in war, whereby he will himself become the admired of all observers, nay, a name to be remembered among Hellenes and barbarians. Would he not in that case, think you, make much of one whom he regarded as his bravest fellow-worker, laying at his feet the greatest honours?

If, then, you wish to be well-pleasing in his eyes, you had best inquire by what knowledge Themistocles was able to set Hellas free. You should ask yourself, what keen wit belonged to Pericles that he was held to be the best adviser of his fatherland. You should scan the field of history to learn by what sage wisdom Solon established for our city her consummate laws. I would have you find the clue to that peculiar training by which the men of Lacedaemon have come to be regarded as the best of leaders. Is it not at your house that their noblest citizens are lodged as representatives of a foreign state?

Be sure that our state of Athens would speedily entrust herself to your direction were you willing. Everything is in your favour. You are of noble family, 'eupatrid' by descent, a priest of the divinities, and of Erechtheus' famous line, which with Iacchus marched to encounter the barbarian. And still, at the sacred festival today, it is agreed that no one among your ancestors has ever been more fitted to discharge the priestly office than yourself; yours a person the good-liest to behold in all our city, and a frame adapted to undergo great toils.

But if I seem to any of you to indulge a vein more

serious than befits the wine-cup, marvel not. It has long been my wont to share our city's passion for noble-natured souls, alert and emulous in pursuit of virtue.

He ended, and, while the others continued to discuss the theme of his discourse, Autolycus sat regarding Callias. That other, glancing the while at the beloved one, turned to Socrates.

CALLIAS: Then, Socrates, be pleased, as go-between, to introduce me to the state, that I may employ myself in state affairs and never lapse from her good graces.

Never fear, he answered, if only people see your loyalty to virtue is genuine, not of mere repute. A false renown indeed is quickly seen for what it is worth, being tested; but true courage (save only what some god hinder) perpetually amidst the storm and stress of circumstance pours forth a brighter glory.

On such a note he ended his discourse.

At that, Autolycus, whose hour for walking exercise had now come, arose. His father, Lycon, was about to leave the room along with him, but before so doing, turned to Socrates, remarking: By Hera, Socrates, if ever anyone deserved the appellation 'beautiful and good', you are that man! So the pair departed. After they were gone, a sort of throne was first erected in the inner room abutting on the supper chamber. Then the Syracusan entered, with a speech: With your good pleasure, sirs, Ariadne is about to enter the bridal chamber set apart for her and Dionysus. Anon Dionysus will appear, fresh from the table of the gods, wine-flushed, and enter to his bride. In the last scene the two will play with one another.

He had scarce concluded, when Ariadne entered, attired like a bride. She crossed the stage and sat herself upon the throne. Meanwhile, before the god himself appeared a sound of flutes was heard; the cadence of the Bacchic air proclaimed his coming. At this point the company broke forth in admiration of the ballet-master. For no sooner did the sound of music strike upon the ear of Ariadne than something in her action revealed to all the pleasure which it caused her. She did not step forward to meet her lover, she did not rise even from her seat; but the flutter of her unrest was plain to see.

When Dionysus presently caught sight of her he loved, lightly he danced towards her, and with show of tenderest passion gently reclined upon her knees; his arms entwined about her lovingly, and upon her lips he sealed a kiss; she the while with most sweet bashfulness was fain to wind responsive arms about her lover; till the banqueters, the while they gazed all eyes, clapped hands and cried 'Encore!' But when Dionysus rose upon his feet, and rising lifted Ariadne to her full height, the action of those lovers as they kissed and fondled one another was a thing to contemplate. As to the spectators, they could see that Dionysus was indeed most beautiful, and Ariadne like some lovely blossom; nor were those mocking gestures, but real kisses sealed on loving lips; and so, with hearts aflame, they gazed expectantly. They could hear the question asked by Dionysus, did she love him? And her answer, as prettily she swore she did. And withal so earnestly, not Dionysus only, but all present, had sworn an oath in common: the boy and girl were verily and indeed a pair of happy lovers. So much less did they resemble actors, trained to certain gestures, than two beings bent on doing what for many a long day they had set their hearts on.

At last when these two lovers, caught in each other's

arms, were seen to be retiring to the nuptial couch, the members of the supper party turned to withdraw themselves; and whilst those of them who were un-married swore that they would wed, those who were wedded mounted their horses and galloped off to join their wives, in quest of married joys. Only Socrates, and of the rest the few who still remained behind, anon set off with Callias, to see out Lycon and his son, and share the walk.

And so this supper party, assembled in honour of Autolycus, broke up.